Arthur
&
Stonehenge
Britain's Lost History

Emmet J Sweeney

© 2001 Emmet J Sweeney

Cover illustration Joe Mc Allister

ISBN 0-9524417-9-9

Printed by ColourBooks Ltd. Dublin

First published in November 2001 by Domra Publications

Typeset by
GUILDHALL PRESS
Unit 4, Community Service Units
Bligh's Lane, Creggan, Derry BT48 0LZ
T: (028) 7136 4413 F: (028) 7137 2949
info@ghpress.com www.ghpress.com

Foreword

The earliest history of Britain is truly a closed book, if we are to believe the earnest professors whose weighty tomes fill the great libraries of the world. Yet the darkness that hides the "megalithic" epoch of Britain is paralleled by that which obscures many of the most basic questions regarding the ancient past. Questions of both human and natural history, it is said, are enshrouded in the most impenetrable gloom.

An oft-quoted and obvious example of this, from the field of natural history, is the question of the Siberian mammoths. How is it that these creatures, frozen so completely in the permafrost that their flesh can still be eaten, nevertheless hold in their mouths and the stomachs the undigested remains of their last meal – a meal which included plants such as buttercups *in full bloom*. Another, not dissimilar question, is that of marine mammals, such as whales, seals and dolphins, as well as fish of various types, discovered perfectly preserved on the Antarctic continent many kilometres from the sea, and often many hundreds of metres above the present sea level. If such mysteries are mentioned at all in the textbooks (and usually they are not), they are dismissed in a few perfunctory sentences.

Yet a more than adequate answer to these and other "puzzles" was provided in 1950 by Immanuel Velikovsky, who suggested that the mammoth extinctions of the Pleistocene were the result of a cataclysmic upheaval of nature, of cosmic origin, which devastated the entire planet just a few thousand years ago. This explanation, presented in his *Worlds in Collision* (1950) and *Earth in Upheaval* (1955), had the uniquely satisfying advantage of being able to reconcile the scientific evidence gathered by geologists and palaeontologists with that of ancient tradition. For the cataclysms which Velikovsky discovered in the ground were also mentioned by early humans, the eyewitnesses, who recorded them in their myths and legends.

Given such agreement, the casual observer might imagine that Velikovsky's theories would have been hailed as a major advance in scientific endeavour, an important step forward in the story of man's journey along the path of knowledge. At the very least, one might expect his ideas to have been seriously examined by the scholarly community. In fact, the exact opposite happened, and the disgraceful campaign of misrepresentation and abuse which high-ranking figures in the intellectual establishment waged against him will surely be recalled as one of the darkest chapters in the history of western thought: an episode every bit as reprehensible as that of the Inquisition's attack on Galileo – though in this case the inquisitors were the high priests of the new religion of scientism. But whilst the Catholic Inquisition eventually bowed before reason, first debating and finally endorsing Galileo's cosmology, the suppressers of Velikovsky have proved much more impervious to the pleadings of the goddess of the Enlightenment. Without answering a single question raised by Velikovsky they nevertheless contrived, through their control over the most influential journals and media outlets, to put abroad the idea that their antagonist had been "debunked", and that his concepts were about as sound as those of the various Atlantean and alien theorists (with whom his name was quite deliberately linked by the learned suppressers). So successful was this tactic that in spite of Velikovsky's works being best-sellers and major talking-points in the 1950s, few of the public in the year 2000 (in Britain at least) have even heard of him

For all that the puzzles, mysteries and anomalies which Velikovsky highlighted and claimed to answer have not gone away. Indeed they have simply filled more and more space in scholarly journals, as research has discovered ever greater numbers of them. One response has been to appropriate, without acknowledgement, some of Velikovsky's less "offensive" ideas. Another has been to propose increasingly convoluted "ad hoc" theories in an attempt to rescue the prevailing paradigm. An example of the former has been the now widely accepted view that the Cretaceous dinosaurs were exterminated by a cosmic catastrophe. This concept, which would have been unthinkable in 1950, is now more or less part of accepted wisdom.

The cataclysmic destruction of the dinosaurs can be openly discussed because it occurred, supposedly, 65 million years ago, a safe distance in the past. But the Pleistocene mammals, whose end was equally sudden and catastrophic, cannot be discussed in the same way: For here we are talking about an event which even conventional scholarship places little more than a few thousand years ago. In vain will the student of palaeontology search the textbooks for an honest appraisal of these extinctions. They are either ignored or brushed aside in a few sentences. Never will he find any attempt to explain the 50 metre deep muck deposits of Alaska and Siberia, where millions upon millions of Pleistocene creatures are piled on top of each other in wildly confused, pell-mell fashion, their bones smashed, and intermixed with uprooted forests and debris of every find. Early explorers insisted that only giant flood tides, which they called "waves of translation", could account for these deposits. Yet modern palaeontologists do not venture to attempt an explanation. Instead of floods, the student of palaeontology will read of Ice Ages. Instead of sudden destruction, he will read of gradual extinction. The evidence however shows that Ice Ages are a textbook creation, whose purpose was to explain in an acceptable uniformitarian way the very clear evidence of nature's violence in every corner of the globe.

The scenario presented by Velikovsky in *Worlds in Collision* and *Earth in Upheaval* is certainly dramatic; and in retrospect the books could scarcely have been expected to cause anything but controversy. For over a century now we have been raised on the belief that the earth, as well as the other planets of the solar system, have moved undisturbed and serenely through the heavens in their respective solar orbits for hundreds of millions of years. Velikovsky speaks of a time, within the collective memory of mankind, when chaos not order reigned in the heavens, when the members of the solar system could not be relied upon to maintain their accustomed paths through the firmament. All the inner planets, he said, including Mercury, Venus, Earth and Mars, experienced near-collisions with other planets only thirty centuries ago. On the strength of this hypothesis he predicted that these bodies would display clear evidence of their violent past. All of them, he said, would be volcanically active and would be poke-marked with impact craters. He further predicted that electromagnetism would be found to play an important role in the solar system, and that most of the planets, as well as the sun, would be found to possess powerful electromagnetic fields.

If the truth of a scientific hypothesis is judged on its ability to generate accurate predictions, then Velikovsky was certainly on the right track: For the exploration of space by the Americans and Russians since the 1950s has proved him, astonishingly enough, to be right in virtually every prognostication. Yet still his name is anathema. True, no one attempts any more to prevent the publication of his ideas. Official silence has been found to be a better strategy. But why the almost pathological hostility aroused by this man's work? Why also the virtual state of denial into which some scientists place themselves when asked to consider the evidence for recent cataclysms? Certainly Velikovsky was treading upon many scholarly egos and reputations, and certainly if even a small part of what he said is true virtually every scientific and historical textbook will have to be rewritten. But not even that can explain this most effective and very real cover-up of the 20th century, the psychology of which has been the subject of numerous doctoral theses, books and articles over the past forty years.

It has been said that one of the characteristics of a truth is that it tends to meet with stern opposition; the importance of that truth being directly proportional to the violence of the opposition. If such be the case, then the truths presented by Velikovsky were indeed important. Another characteristic of a truth is its ability to illumine areas that were previously mysterious; to make sense of facts that were hitherto puzzling. As we shall see in the work to follow, the application of Velikovsky's theory to British prehistory casts dramatic new light on an epoch previously shrouded in total darkness.

Contents

"To the peoples of antiquity the isle of Britain was the very home and environment of mystery, a sacred territory, to enter which was to encroach upon a region of enchantment, the dwelling of gods, the shrine and habitation of a cult of peculiar sanctity and mystical power. Britain was, indeed, the *insula sacra* of the West, an island veiled and esoteric, the Egypt of the Occident. Legends of its strange and perilous marvels were current among the semi-civilized races who dwelt over against its ghostly white cliffs; it was regarded as the haunt and refuge of giants, demons, and spirits; by not a few, even as the paradise and resort of the dead."

"Just as in the early centuries of our era, and before them, Britain was regarded as specifically sacred, an enclosure of the gods, so throughout the Age of Romance [Middle Ages] she was thought of as peculiarly the island of faerie glamour and enchanted adventure. *This secondary phase was merely a survival of the much more venerable belief in her religious sanctity.*"

Lewis Spence *The Mysteries of Britain*

Introduction

According to the textbooks, the history of Britain before the first landing of Julius Caesar upon these shores in 55 BC. is a complete and total blank. If perchance records of the kings and heroes of the island were kept by the Druids, the mysterious priestly order which according to Caesar had its home in the country, such records were lost in the aftermath of the Roman conquest. Yet even the idea that the Druids may have preserved a history of the island is looked upon with disfavour. On the contrary, it is generally supposed that the Celtic inhabitants of the region were more or less illiterate; and that the history of the country was almost as much a closed book to them as it is to us.

But the ancient peoples of the Mediterranean had a very different view. To them, Britain was a sacred region, a holy land inhabited by a mysterious and knowledgeable race, a race of people peculiarly in communion with the gods. There seems little doubt that to some degree the country owed her venerable reputation to her location – on the very edge of the world, bordering the kingdom of Hades, which to the Greeks, Romans and Phoenicians was located where the sun set, beyond the horizon in the western ocean. Yet other reasons decreed the sacredness of the land. Britain was almost the only substantial source of tin, the essential ingredient of bronze, known to the ancients; and there were strong hints that the very art of the bronze-smith, the prototype alchemist, may have had its birth on the island. Furthermore, Britain was also the location of some of the most impressive man-made structures in the whole of ancient Europe. These of course were the "great stone" megaliths, particularly the mighty structures on Salisbury Plain and its environs, namely Avebury and Stonehenge. The ancients, we might imagine, could not have been ignorant of these monuments, and we cannot doubt that a traveller from Greece or Italy, or Phoenicia for that matter, would have been deeply impressed by them.

Could it be that a country of such importance to the ancient world has no history? That every tradition emanating from the builders of Stonehenge and Avebury, from perhaps one of the first cultures in the world to smelt bronze, are lost in the mists of time? Surely, we might imagine, the Britons themselves could not have completely abandoned such an illustrious heritage? Not without some effort at any rate being made to preserve it. Is it impossible to believe that in the legends of Wales and Cornwall there are elements of tradition and story that derive directly from those ancient astronomers, masons, and sword-smiths?

Certainly popular tradition in Britain has always had a good deal to say about both Stonehenge and the other megaliths. According to this, these structures were raised by the Druids. Indeed one Druid in particular, Merlin, the magician of king Arthur, was linked to Stonehenge, whilst various other megaliths were connected with both Merlin and other Arthurian characters. We are accustomed now to regard these traditions as totally fabulous medieval fictions, and any connection between the Arthurian age and that of the megaliths is dismissed out of hand. Yet this "debunking" of the traditional material was by no means inevitable, and the story of how it came to be denigrated and ignored is an instructive and cautionary tale.

It was only with the advent of the age of science, in the later Renaissance period, that educated men, both in England and on the Continent, began to examine the megaliths in a methodical way. At first, the Druid connection, though not the Arthurian, was reinforced, and many of the savants of the 17th and 18th centuries, most notably John Aubrey (1626-97) and William Stukeley (1687-1765) wrote lengthy treatises expounding their belief that these monuments were Druid temples.

By the end of the 19th century however the Druid connection was being openly questioned. Excavations in and around the megaliths revealed evidence which seemed to imply that they predated the Celts. This was suggested most powerfully by the fact that stone implements, such as arrowheads and axeheads, as well as bronze weapons and artefacts of various kinds, were found associated with them. At this very time a new method of historical classification, based loosely on the Greek concept of Bronze and Iron Ages, began to be adopted by scholars. A Stone Age was placed before the Age of Bronze, which in turn gave way to an Age of Iron. Since the Celts of classical times were clearly part of the Iron Age, it was soon postulated that the megaliths could not possibly have been constructed by the Celtic Druids. All of these monuments, including Stonehenge, must have been erected by some primitive forgotten race of the Stone Age.

This idea, first mooted in the latter years of the 19th century, quickly became the new orthodoxy, and by the start of the 20th century it had already been established as part of accepted wisdom. Any attempts to "reclaim" Stonehenge for the Druids (as for example that of Gordon Childe) were doomed to failure. In vain might such writers appeal to the strength of popular tradition, and in vain might they appeal even to classical sources (such as Hecataeus of Abdera) which clearly imply that Stonehenge was a sacred site well into the Celtic age. Indeed the progress of scholarship, it would appear, has removed Stonehenge even further from the Druids. Thus for example radiocarbon dating, which entered the debate in the 1950s, pushed the erection of the megaliths into the remote past, with dates of c.3,000 BC. and even 4,000 BC. reported from some sites.

Stonehenge therefore, along with the entire culture to which it had belonged, was now effectively uprooted from all known British history, culture, tradition and legend. Megalithic Britain was now a land without a history or even a context. No link, it was said, could be said to exist between the builders of Stonehenge and the ancient Britons who met and opposed Julius Caesar on the beach at Deal in 55 BC. The people who built these monuments, it was said, were unknown to the Britons of that time; and the monuments themselves as mysterious to the Druids as they are to us.

Such is the opinion now stated in textbook after textbook: And indeed it is quite possible that this view, which effectively dismisses all the native traditions about the megaliths as nonsense, would never have been effectively challenged, had not history thrown up one of those quirks of chance or fate which sometimes has the potential to change everything. It was right at the start of the 1950s, just when it seemed that all the most venerated traditions of mankind, and not just those of Britain, were one by one being discredited and debunked, that the controversial theories of Immanuel Velikovsky burst upon the scene. These theories presented in a book called *Worlds in Collision* would eventually force a dramatic reconsideration of megalithic culture and demand a reassessment of once-despised folklore and tradition.

To describe Velikovsky's ideas as radical would be almost an understatement. He proposed that much of humanity's mythology was concerned with a catastrophic upheaval of nature, or rather a series of such events, which are recalled universally in the various Deluge stories. Controversially, he held that the greatest of these disasters occurred as recently as 1,400 BC., and was the direct result of a close encounter between the earth and a great comet, a comet recalled in ancient mythology as the Cosmic Serpent, or the Dragon. This, said Velikovsky, was the monster that breathed fire and brimstone on the earth and caused a world-wide conflagration and flood. Our planet's close encounter with this body had devastating effects for all life. Giant tidal waves engulfed the continents, whilst the earth's tectonic plates buckled, producing massive vulcanism and seismic activity.

Velikovsky insisted that the survivors of this calamity were shaped by what they had witnessed in a fundamental way. Virtually all of what we recognise as primitive religion can be traced back to this event. It was then that mankind began offering blood-sacrifices to the heavenly bodies on mountain-tops or other high places. When people reoccupied the low-lying regions, they began to raise artificial hills on which to perform their fearsome rituals. In this way, high civilisation was born. Organisation was needed to erect these monuments, as were measuring and record-keeping skills.

For almost seven centuries, according to Velikovsky, the great comet threatened to pay a return visit to our planet, and mankind trembled in anticipation of such an eventuality. Enormous monuments were raised aligned precisely with the positions of the heavenly bodies, designed specifically to track and predict their movements. These "megaliths" were invariably decorated with carved stellar and serpentine images.

One problem encountered by Velikovsky was that of chronology. The textbooks said that high civilisations first developed in the Near East around 3,000 BC., with the pyramids of Giza, for example, being dated to c.2,500 BC. If the events described in *Worlds in Collision* had occurred around 1,400 BC., it was pointed out, they would surely have smashed these structures, mighty though they are. Thus at an early stage Velikovsky came to realise that there was something drastically wrong with the chronology, and he began work on a reconstruction of ancient history that proposed the subtraction of several centuries from the length of high civilisation.

As one who has examined Velikovsky's theories with a dispassionate eye (a rare occurrence, unfortunately) it has become clear to me that a dramatic reduction of ancient chronology is necessary, with the megaliths of western Europe, for example, being downdated to the 8th and 7th centuries BC. and even later. The evidence, much of it now ignored in mainstream academic publications, is in fact extensive, and suggests very clearly that what popular tradition had always insisted was true; that the megaliths, including Stonehenge, were raised by the Druids only a few centuries before the dawn of the Christian era.

That the megaliths were at least used by the Celts has, ironically enough, increasingly come to be taken seriously over the past few decades, and it is evident from the works of the classical authors that many of them were famous throughout the ancient world. None more so than Stonehenge. As late as the 4th century BC. the Greek writer Hecataeus of Abdera gives us a strong hint that the monument was of almost legendary renown, and what he said regarding Britain's great circular temple and adjacent sacred city, which can only be Stonehenge and Avebury, would suggest that the region round Salisbury Plain was an extremely important religious centre in the 4th/3rd century BC., perhaps *the* religious centre of the Celtic world. Caesar's statement that trainee Druids from Gaul usually went to Britain to complete their studies is perhaps yet another reflection of the importance of the religious metropolis that was Avebury and Stonehenge.

Such being the case, we must expect these monuments to have figured in the traditions of Britain herself. Monuments of this importance, we must assume, could not have been ignored by the natives of the very country in which they were situated. Nor were they. British tradition, we have seen, unequivocally stated that Stonehenge was built by Merlin, the magician and helper of king Arthur. Yet the problem here, of course, is that Arthur is now placed in the Romano-British period, and is regarded as a great hero in the war against the invading Anglo-Saxons during the 5th century AD. On the other hand, scholars have long been aware that most, if not all, of the essential elements in the Arthurian legend predate Christianity and the Roman occupation. Thus the search for the Grail is known to be an updated and Christianised version of the search for the Celtic magic cauldron. But the most outstanding element in the Arthur legend is of course the famous Round Table. It is highly probable that the Round Table, which makes little sense in itself, represents Stonehenge, the great Round Temple, for which Britain was famous. By late Roman times, when most of the population of Britain had become at least nominally Christian, honouring the national hero as the King of the Round Temple would perhaps no longer have been acceptable, given the monument's pagan associations. So the Round Temple could have been changed to the Round Table, an alternative symbol which had the added attraction, in Christian eyes, of emphasizing Arthur's humanity and approachability. More probably however the temple became known as the Round Table owing to the fact that the great circle of standing-stones resembled the legs of a giant table. Most of these stones are now demolished, so the resemblance is not so obvious to the modern viewer.

So, it would appear that the Arthurian tales are among the most antique of human legends, almost certainly dating from the megalithic epoch, which we shall however demonstrate was contemporary with the first Celtic settlement. This must have occurred, if Irish and Welsh tradition is anything to go by, in the wake of a final series of natural catastrophes around 800 BC. The entire Round Table myth, we will find, belongs squarely in the world of the Wessex culture, that mighty Early Bronze Age trading civilisation which raised Stonehenge and exported finished products of native bronze, especially swords and other weaponry, throughout Europe and the Mediterranean. Arthur, whose name must surely derive not from the Latin Artorius, but from the Old Celtic Art/Artos, "Bear", or Arth-gwr, "Bear-hero" (many European sources, including some of the oldest medieval references, give Arthur's name as Artus), was a British hero-figure equivalent to Hercules, and it was in his honour that Stonehenge was built. The name of Arthur's father, Uther Pendragon ("Terrible Dragon-head") underlines his divine identity as the classic dragon-slaying hero. Excalibur would originally have been the mythic weapon forged by the gods, a weapon very much like that which Perseus of Greek legend used to slay the serpent-headed monster Medusa. It was the precise equivalent of the sword of light with which the Irish hero Lugh (Celtic Lugos) used to decapitate the monster Balor. Yet the other weapon central to the tale, Sword in the Stone (not the same as Excalibur) is a peculiarly British icon; this myth relates to the skill of extracting the metal originally used in sword-making, bronze, from ore, a skill first discovered in Britain, and known only in Britain for many years.

With the fresh insights provided by our new historical perspective we may perhaps now also solve the question of the puzzling link between Wales and the dragon. William Stukeley, who dated Stonehenge to 460 BC., was obsessed with the idea that the stone circles of Britain were part of a serpent-cult: and indeed he produced a great deal of evidence to illustrate how serpent-symbols and serpent-like shapes occur in the configuration of many of the megaliths, including the great avenues of Avebury, close by Stonehenge.

Once again, Stukeley was on the right track. The monuments commemorated the destruction or "taming" of the Cosmic Serpent, the Dragon: and these great structures, which came to symbolise Britain herself, gave their emblem to the people, whose descendants are the Welsh.

In the work that follows I shall be challenging many concepts and beliefs, from many different fields of knowledge, that for a hundred years now have been taken as accepted wisdom. Some of what I have to say will appear – especially to those with a little knowledge of the subject – astonishing, even outrageous. But if the reader will bear with me and reserve judgement until reaching the end of the last chapter, I can promise the effort will not go unrewarded. What I propose to do in fact is not so outrageous as it might appear. I wish to restore to the British people their national monument from the clutches of an illiterate, nameless and ultimately non-existent people of the Stone Age; a people who only ever lived in the minds of academics and the textbooks they wrote. As a by-product I hereby also return to Arthur his Round Table. Above all, I wish to restore to Britain her antique reputation as an island of enchantment, to reveal to the reader the source of this reputation, and to reawaken a justified enthusiasm for the wonderful achievements of this land's early inhabitants.

CHAPTER 1

A Land of Legend

Two Ancient Mysteries

The island of Britain lies at the centre of two of the most enduring mysteries of antiquity; the site of ancient Europe's greatest monument and the home of her greatest hero.

At the southern end of England, on Salisbury Plain, stands the most striking pre-Roman monument in all of western Europe, indeed in the whole of Europe outside of Greece. Stonehenge has now become, along with the pyramids of Egypt, one of the photographic icons of our age. Virtually every publication dealing with a whole range of topics – from straightforward ancient history, to mysteries of the past, to the occult in all its forms, to life on other planets – will feature an image of Stonehenge. Yet in contrast to that other wonder of the ancient world, the Great Pyramid of Giza, scholars admit that they know almost nothing of Stonehenge. Its construction date, its purpose, the name of its builder – even the identity of the people who raised it – lie shrouded in the deepest mystery.

What little we know is derived entirely from the spade-work of the archaeologist. From this source we learn that Stonehenge was constructed in several stages; that it took several centuries to complete; that it was begun during the Late Stone Age (Neolithic) and completed in the Early Bronze Age. This final phase of the monument is dated to roughly 1,600 BC. Yet in the absence of written documents the mute testimony of artefacts can reveal only so much information. The most intriguing questions, it is said, must remain unanswered.

Yet, as its impressive dimensions warrant, Stonehenge was apparently a renowned monument in ancient times. Indeed its fame, it would appear, had spread to the farthest corners of the European continent. A Greek writer of the 4th and early 3rd century BC., Hecataeus of Abdera, provides us with the earliest clear reference to the structure. The relevant passage, as quoted by Diodorus of Sicily, reads thus:

"Opposite the coast of Celtic Gaul there is an island in the ocean, not smaller than Sicily, lying to the North – which is inhabited by the Hyperboreans, who are so named because they dwell beyond the North Wind. This island is of a happy temperature, rich in soil and fruitful in everything, yielding its produce twice in the year. Tradition says that Latone was born there, and for that reason, the inhabitants venerate Apollo more than any other God. They are, in a manner, his priests, for they daily celebrate him with continual songs of praise and pay him abundant honours. In this island, there is a magnificent grove (or precinct) of Apollo, and a remarkable temple, of a round form, adorned with many consecrated gifts. There is also a city, sacred to the same God, most of the inhabitants of which are harpers, who continually play upon their harps in the temple, and sing hymns to the God, extolling his actions."[1]

This remarkable passage clearly implies that Stonehenge was in use during the 4th/3rd century BC., well into the Iron Age. But this goes entirely against the grain of most modern thinking on the monument, which places it, along with the rest of the "megaliths" of Britain and Europe, firmly in the Neolithic/Early Bronze Age, ie. in the 3rd and 2nd millennia BC. Indeed the suggestion by Hecataeus that Britain, as well as its great circular temple, was well-known to the Greeks is regarded as puzzling, and it is universally assumed that the monument had long fallen into disuse by the Iron Age. It is asserted that the Iron Age Celts had no knowledge of who built Stonehenge, and that British legend, as handed down through the filter of medieval Welsh storytelling, had no tradition relating to it.

This, if true, is an extraordinary situation. The greatest monument of pre-Christian Europe, a monument known even to the Greeks of c.300

---

1 Diodorus Siculus ii, 47-50 quoting Hecataeus of Abdera's *History of the Hyperboreans*. It should be remarked here that Latone, the mother of Apollo, has a name identical to that of Lotan (Leviathan), the Phoenician dragon of the watery abyss. The national emblem of Britain, of course, is the dragon.

BC., had no native tradition attached to it! Such a structure, we might expect, could not have been ignored by the natives of the island. Even if the British Celts truly knew nothing about Stonehenge they would surely, we might imagine, have invented a story about it. Yet no such legend, it is held, exists.

Nevertheless, one tradition of Britain, mentioned by the Welsh cleric Geoffrey of Monmouth, states that Stonehenge was erected by Merlin, the magician and helper of king Arthur. Obviously influenced by the ruined appearance of the structure in his time, Geoffrey stated that Merlin had raised Stonehenge as a monument to the British nobles treacherously slain by the Jute king Hengist, during the time of the Anglo-Saxon invasions.

This claim of Geoffrey was always viewed with some suspicion, since it seemed to contradict other local traditions which held that the numerous standing-stone circles, found the length and breadth of Britain, had been raised by the Druids, the ancient pagan priestly order. With the advent of the scientific age, in the 18th and 19th centuries, scholars soon became convinced that Geoffrey's explanation of Stonehenge had to be without foundation. Early archaeologists found that the standing-stones and related monuments were of great antiquity, and were apparently raised by a people who employed implements and weapons of stone. This of course meant that Stonehenge not only predated the Romano-British epoch of Merlin and Arthur (5th/6th century AD.) but must have predated even the pagan Celts, who clearly belonged to the Iron Age.

Rather than solve the mystery of Stonehenge, the progress of scientific investigation thus seemed only to increase it. Indeed new techniques and dating-systems, such as radio-carbon analysis, have pushed Stonehenge and the other "megaliths" even further into the past, and any attempts still made to link these monuments with the Celts and Druids are now regarded as illusory. The builders of Stonehenge, it is held, must always and forever remain unknown.

As well as having ancient Europe's greatest monument, Britain was also the home of ancient Europe's greatest hero; the legendary king Arthur, whose knights and famous Round Table became the subject of many a medieval troubadour's balladeering. The legends of Arthur found their way right across the continent, with his story reaching even beyond the borders of Christendom, into the Islamic world.

In medieval legend Arthur was portrayed as the ideal Christian king, and his knights the embodiment of the chivalric principle. Yet it was also assumed that he was an actual historical character. Geoffrey of Monmouth, whose *Historia Regum Britanniae* ('History of the Kings of Britain') (1135) first popularised the legend, portrayed Arthur as a Christian king of the native British who, around the latter 5th and early 6th century AD. battled heroically against the pagan hordes of Anglo-Saxon invaders. From this time on repeated attempts were made to discover the historical Arthur – attempts which, it has to be stated, have continued till the present day. In 1190 the monks of Glastonbury claimed to have discovered the body of Arthur, along with his wife Guinevere, in the Abbey grounds. These, now accepted as a complete forgery (they also claimed to have found the bones of Patrick and a host of other worthies), were on display until the dissolution of the monastery at the Reformation, and brought great wealth to the monks.[2] A great Round Table, purporting to be that of Arthur and his knights, appeared in the middle of the 14th century in Winchester – the very place identified by the minstrels as Arthur's Camelot. The table, like the Glastonbury burial, is now known to be fake, and it is virtually certain that it was fashioned on the orders of Edward III, who, inspired by the Arthurian tradition, wished to establish his own Order of the Round Table.[3]

The more rigorous methods of the scientific age have been no more successful in discovering the historical Arthur. Indeed, the deeper we investigate the man, the more illusory and incorporeal he seems to become. It is known, for example, that not a single writer of the Dark Ages makes any mention of him. Thus for example the 6th century writer Gildas, in his *De Excidio et Conquestu Britanniae* ("On the Ruin and Conquest of Britain") gives a brief account of the various battles and campaigns of the 5th and 6th centuries, in which Arthur is supposed to have played a pivotal role, but fails completely to mention any character that could be identified with Arthur. In the same way the Anglo-Saxon chronicler Bede, writing in the 8th century and providing a fairly comprehensive account of the story of England from the arrival of the first Angles and Saxons, fails completely to warrant Arthur worthy of even a passing reference. Likewise the Anglo-

---

2 Graham Phillips and Martin Keatman *King Arthur: The True Story* (London,1992) pp.16-17
3 Ibid. p.14

Saxon Chronicle, compiled during the reign of Alfred the Great, between 871 and 899 AD. is completely silent with regard to Arthur.[4]

Even those who would like to prove a historical Arthur accept that this is pretty damning evidence.[5] How could it be that a character who left his name on monuments and natural features throughout Britain, and who is regarded as the national hero of the island, is not mentioned in any of the records contemporary with the period in which he is supposed to have lived?

The earliest writer to place Arthur in the Dark Ages is Nennius, a Welsh cleric apparently of the 9th century, who also provides what he himself admits to be a veritable hotch-potch of legends, stories and traditions about Britain. Thus, as well as placing Arthur at the Battle of Badon Hill around 518 AD. he also has the British descended from a Trojan prince named Brutus, and introduces various other mythic stories as history. Furthermore, he casually remarks that Arthur personally slew 940 Saxons at Badon Hill.

It is virtually certain that all of the later medieval traditions, which portray Arthur as a Christian king of Dark Age Britain, can be traced to this one account of Nennius. In his very brief reference to Arthur Nennius actually goes out of his way to emphasize that he was a Christian, stating that he "carried the image of Saint Mary, ever virgin, on his shoulders" into battle. Indeed almost a third of the tiny amount of information provided by Nennius is taken up with this type of redundant emphasis of his Christian identity. We might in fact almost begin to suspect Nennius of protesting too much. Was he himself sure that Arthur was a Christian?

As a matter of fact, the progress of scholarly research over the past 150 years has increasingly demonstrated that Arthur was nothing of the sort. Virtually every element of the Arthurian legend, it is now known, has its roots in the pagan Celtic past. There are clues everywhere. Thus for example Camulodunum (Colchester) is the only ancient city that could unquestionably, in terms of its name, be linked to Arthur's capital Camelot: And indeed in the years before the Roman conquest Camulodunum was the political and religious capital of a large region of southern Britain. The problem of course is that in the Dark Ages Camulodunum would have been in the very heart of Saxon territory, and could not possibly have been the headquarters of a contemporary king of

---

4 Ibid. p.48
5 Ibid.

the Britons. Again, Arthur is as much a hero of the Bretons as of the Welsh and British. Yet the main British colonisation of Armorica was over and done with by 460 AD. – well before Arthur's supposed epoch. These two circumstances alone would suggest that Arthur has been wrongly placed in the Dark Ages.

Other evidence, of an entirely different nature, and of a copious quantity, supports this conclusion. Thus Arthur's wife Guinevere and his sister Morgan le Faye are known to be Celtic goddesses, whilst the quest for the Holy Grail is now seen as an updated and Christianised version of the quest for the Celtic magic cauldron of wisdom. Likewise the mystic isle of Avalon is suspiciously similar to various mystic islands of Celtic mythology, and indeed to the land of the Hesperides, sought out by Hercules in the far west, by the Ocean stream.

By the last quarter of the 19th century scholarship had already identified and categorised the mythic elements in the Arthurian cycle. Could it be, it was asked, that Arthur, as well as his Druid Merlin, belongs lock, stock and barrel in the pre-Roman world of the Celts, and that medieval chroniclers misplaced him in the Romano-British period? By the end of the century the general consensus was that this in fact was the case. Having removed Arthur from the historical Dark Ages, the next stage should have been to reassess the link with Stonehenge and the megaliths in general, which the legend in any case insisted upon. Yet it was just at this juncture, when the truth might have been revealed, that a new element of confusion was created. For archaeologists, digging into the barrow-graves and around the stone circles, now announced that the monuments long predated the Celts and the Druids, and were raised by unknown and primitive races of the Stone and Early Bronze Ages.

The latter point shall be dealt with in due course. For the present however, I propose that we ignore the archaeology and look to the mythographers to establish a working hypothesis. Arthur, I shall argue, was not a Christian warrior, but a pre-Christian hero-deity whom the Britons nevertheless invoked in their desperate struggle for national survival in the days following the collapse of the Roman Empire. I shall further argue that the monument we now call Stonehenge was known to the early Britons as Arthur's Round Table, and that these two great mysteries of Britain are resolved simultaneously. The people of Britain, I hold, did not ignore the awesome monument in their midst. Before its destruction by the Roman legions (of which more will be said later) the structure's thirty outer standing-stones resembled the legs of a great table; and it was popularly known to the British people by this very name. The shattered monument left by the army of Claudius no longer had this appearance, and as the centuries passed the location of the Round Table faded from the popular consciousness.

Without the archaeology, if history were written solely on the basis of literary criticism, the above hypothesis is the one that would by now be found in the textbooks. But we surely cannot ignore archaeology; and in view of what it tells us, connecting the Arthurian story with Stonehenge must surely raise almost as many problems as it solves. Most obviously, accepting that Arthur was a Celtic hero-deity, how do we reconcile linking him with a megalithic monument which, we have found, was erected in the late Neolithic and Early Bronze Ages? This is surely a pertinent question, and it demands a fairly detailed response.

The Round Temples of Britain

Stonehenge is only one of literally hundreds of standing-stone monuments that dot the British Isles and the western parts of the European continent. At an early stage scholars discovered that these structures were contemporary with the great burial mounds, or barrow graves, that also dotted the continent. These megalithic ("great stone") monuments were part of a *genre* that stretched even beyond the lands of the Celts. Vast quantities of stone implements and weapons, usually axe-heads, arrowheads and spearheads, were found in association with the megaliths.

It was in the early part of the 19th century, just as Europeans began to take an active interest in the ancient monuments which surrounded them, that a new method of historical classification, based loosely on the Greek concept of Bronze and Iron Ages, began to be adopted. A Stone Age, it was surmised, was followed by an Age of Bronze, which was followed in turn by an Age of Iron. Since the Celts of classical antiquity clearly belonged to the Iron Age, it was presumed that, notwithstanding ancient tradition, the megaliths could not possibly have been raised by them. Thus the megaliths were assigned to an unknown race of the Stone Age, and were placed in the second, or even third millennium BC.

This idea quickly became the new orthodoxy, and any attempts subsequently made to "reclaim" the megaliths for the Druids were doomed to failure.

Before going one step further however it should be stated that the concept of a Stone Age, followed neatly by a Bronze Age, followed by an Iron Age, is a complete and utter fallacy. There was no point at which the Stone Age became the Bronze Age, and the Bronze Age was transformed into the Iron Age. Stone, Bronze and Iron Ages overlap. As a matter of fact, stone implements were regularly employed by the poorer classes well into the Iron Age. For centuries iron was an extremely expensive commodity, and the knowledge of how to forge it a closely guarded secret. Iron ore, as well as finished products of iron, had to be laboriously carted over vast distances through the primeval forest and bog-lands of ancient Europe. Stone of various kinds, from which peasant farmers could fashion axes, arrowheads, and tools of every kind, was readily available locally. Iron Age forts throughout the British Isles and Europe regularly reveal caches of polished stone axe-heads and arrowheads – much to the (unjustified) puzzlement of archaeologists. Heinrich Schliemann discovered large numbers of stone arrowheads and axe-heads in Late Bronze Age burials at Mycenae and Tiryns,[6] whilst George Rawlinson remarked on the occurrence of flint arrowheads in the 8th and 7th century (Iron Age) settlements of Assyria.[7] Herodotus noted that a detachment of the Persian army which invaded Greece in the early 5th century BC. was armed with stone-tipped arrows.[8] Tacitus records that the Germanic warriors of his time (first century AD.) mostly could not afford iron swords and spears, and that many were armed simply with pointed sticks.[9]

If then the discovery of stone implements in the vicinity of the megaliths cannot be regarded as proof that they predate the Celts, we may be justified in taking more seriously the native traditions about them. In Ireland, the great tombs of New Grange (*Brugh na Boinne*), which archaeology now

6 Heinrich Schliemann *Tiryns* (London,1886) p.173
7 George Rawlinson *Ancient Monarchies* Vol.1 (London, 1879) p.454n "A few stone arrow-heads have been found in the Assyrian ruins. They are pear-shaped and of fine flint, chipped into form."
8 Herodotus vii, 69
9 Tacitus *The Annals of Imperial Rome* ii,13

dates around 3,000 BC., were said to be the burial places of the island's Gaelic High Kings, who sat at nearby Tara. That this tradition was based upon some amount of genuine knowledge is confirmed by the discovery of recognisably Celtic artefacts at the site. The medieval Irish, who preserved a written history of forty generations of pre-Christian High Kings, identified virtually every megalithic monument in the country with a specific ruler or warrior-hero. The standing-stone circles, they said, were temples where the god Beal or Balor was worshipped, and to this day stone circles in Ireland are named Beltanies (ie. *Bealtaine* – "Fire of Beal"), whilst the Irish word for temple – *timpeall* – is the same as the word for circle.

It is a well-recognised fact that the burial-mound, or barrow-grave, was characteristic of the Bronze Age/Iron Age Celts and Germans. The megaliths throughout western Europe are heavily decorated with spiral designs, a motif that would later, in a slightly more developed and sophisticated form, come to be regarded as typically Celtic. In Scandinavia menhir-style standing-stones occur with great frequency, and are virtually identical to those found throughout France – particularly Brittany. Yet the menhirs of Scandinavia are decorated with runic inscriptions – usually bearing the names of those responsible for raising the stone – and Viking Age artistic motifs. Again, Scandinavian chiefs of the Viking Age were buried, often along with a ship, in barrow-graves. Sometimes these boat-burials took the shape of the vessel they entombed, and were often surrounded by standing-stones.

Yet, contrary to what is stated in textbook after textbook, it is not just in Scandinavia that megaliths are linked to Late Iron Age cultures. Thus for example the megalithic monuments of Brittany are frequently associated with Gallo-Roman remains, in spite of being separated from these remains in conventional chronology by up to 2,000 years.[10] Again, the menhir stones of southern France, which are dated to the third millennium BC. "have their counterparts in Corsica (where they are dated to the 1st millennium BC.), and in the stelae of Luni, which on account of their inscriptions are unanimously dated to early Etruscan times."[11]

Possibly some of the most spectacular evidence of all has come from one of the megalithic mounds at New Grange in Ireland, Carn H. Here

---

10 Heribert Illig "The Past Comes Down" *Society for Interdisciplinary Studies: Chronology and Catastrophism Workshop* No.1 (1991) p.10
11 Ibid. p.11

archaeologists found a whole series of artefacts of clearly Iron Age date. These included amber and glass beads, various iron objects, and bone plaques. It was the latter which caused most disquiet.

"The ornament on these bone plaques is by very general consent agreed to belong to La Tene art and probably date to the first two centuries AD. The problem presented by these objects of La Tene art together with iron objects was to explain their presence in a Passage Grave the walls of which were decorated with typical megalithic art and which was assumed by most people to have been constructed in or around 2,000 BC. It was argued by most archaeologists before Dr. Raftery's re-excavations that Carn H at Loughcrew had been used as a workshop in the Early Iron Age – perhaps the *atelier* of a Celtic artist. Professor MacAlister, for example, believed the metal-workers of the Early Iron Age produced these plaques as samples for the ornamentation of luxury items of bronze. Dr. Raftery disagreed with this view and in 1943 re-excavated Carn H.

"The 1943 Raftery excavations found no objects characteristic of the normal megalithic assemblage: what was found, however, were blue, green and yellow glass beads, small bronze rings, pieces of iron and 2,000 bone plaques of which 200 were ornamented in the late LaTene style. Raftery argued that all these finds dated to the Early Iron Age; he found some of them in what he described as an undisturbed foundation layer, while some bone plaques were actually in the stone-hole of one of the orthostats in the passage. In describing his excavations to the International Congress of Prehistoric and Posthistoric Sciences in Zurich in 1954, he thought the evidence in his excavations susceptible of only two solutions: first, that the site was a normal Passage Grave constructed , say in 2,000 BC. but entirely destroyed, removed and rebuilt in the Early Iron Age; or secondly, that it was an old style tomb or tomb still being used in the Early Iron Age. Having found no evidence for the first solution, he has put on record that Carn H was constructed in the Early Iron Age and that therefore *megaliths in Ireland survived not only to the end of the second millennium BC. but to the beginning of the first millennium AD.*" (Daniel's and O'Riordain's italics)[12]

12 Glyn Daniel and Sean P. O'Riordain *New Grange* (1964) pp.123-4

But as we have said, the excavators should not have been surprised by this discovery, in view of the fact that native Irish tradition has always insisted that the megalithic tombs of New Grange were the resting places of Ireland's Gaelic High Kings. Further proof that megalith-building continued into the post-Roman period is seen in a well-known cromlech at Ballina in the west of Ireland. This structure is reliably recorded as the burial site of four Connaught princes who had been implicated in and executed for the murder of bishop Ceallach, another royal prince of the region, who had eskewed worldly affairs and trained for the priesthood under St. Ciaran. The Irish annals record that the dolmen was raised for his killers and they were interred therein around the year 650 AD.

Clearly then the European megaliths were being erected well into the late Iron Age, and those located in the Celtic regions must indeed have been the work of the Druid priestly order. Caesar's remark that trainee Druids from Gaul went to Britain to complete their studies is perhaps a reflection of the power and prestige of the priesthood linked to Stonehenge. The Roman conquest of Dacia was followed by the destruction of a great standing-stone circle at Sarmizegetusa, which was "superficially" similar to Stonehenge, another stone circle ruined at this time.

"It is likely that the Romans were responsible [for the destruction of Stonehenge]. We know that the Romans suppressed the druids with great violence because of their opposition to the Empire and that the druids' headquarters on Anglesey were destroyed. Normally the Romans tolerated native religions, but druidism was regarded as seditious and was put down with relentless ferocity. Although it is not known whether the druids ever used Stonehenge, it looks as if the Romans thought they were using it, perhaps remembering the druidical cult centre at Sarmizegetusa in Romania, where they felt obliged to smash down the stone pillars of a superficially similar-looking stone circle ... There can be little doubting that the slighting of Stonehenge by the Romans has made it the wreck we see today."[13]

The above is a virtual admission by one of the country's most prominent academics that Stonehenge was in use at the time of the Roman

13 Rodney Castleden *The Stonehenge People* (London,1987) p.151

invasion, and represented the major shrine of Druidism in Britain.

In fact, in spite of almost endless statements by one authoritative publication after another to the contrary, it is well-known that the stone circles of Britain were used by the Druids: Indeed they were used in pagan or semi-pagan rituals throughout the Dark Ages and even into the Middle Ages. Thus in his *Liber Poenitentialis*, Archbishop Theodore of Canterbury (602-690 AD.) states, "If any may have vowed or paid a vow at trees, or at fountains, or at stones, whether at the balusters, or anywhere else, excepting at the Church of God."[14] The word "balusters" here means "encompassing rails" or stone balustrade. In Ireland Saint Patrick is said to have carved the name of Christ on three large standing-stones on the plain of Magh Slecht which were linked with pagan rituals, whilst virtually all Irish medieval traditions insisted that the Irish worshipped at menhirs before the coming of Patrick.[15] It was said that St. Samson, bishop of Dol in Brittany, when travelling in Britain surprised a group of "Bacchanalians" worshipping an idol on top of a mound within a stone circle. Whilst attempting to dissuade them from the practice, a certain youth passing in a chariot was thrown from his vehicle and broke his neck. This was taken as a sign of divine displeasure, and the pagan congregation broke up.[16]

There is abundant evidence that in Scotland courts were held in stone circles as late as the fourteenth century. Such a gathering was convened in 1349 by William, earl of Ross, at the standing stones of Rayne in Garioch, and another by Alexander Stewart, Lord of Badenoch, in the year 1380 at the standing stones of Easter Kyngucy in Badenoch.[17] This is eloquent testimony of a continuous tradition.

But there is other evidence, of an entirely different variety, pointing just as strongly to the recent origin of the megaliths.

Over the past thirty years, there has been a virtual revolution in our understanding of the so-called Megalithic civilisation. More and more the discoveries of archaeology have revealed what can only be described as the astounding mathematical and astronomical knowledge of those who raised the standing-stones and passage graves. Professor Alexander Thom was the first to put the study of megalithic architecture on a firmly scientific basis.

---

14 Lewis Spence *The Mysteries of Britain* (1994 ed.) pp.208-9
15 Ibid. p.209
16 Ibid.
17 Ibid.

In his *Megalithic Sites in Britain* (1967), a work of exhaustive research, he proved beyond all reasonable doubt that the megalith-builders knew the value of *pi*, as well as the Pythagorean theorem. The scholarly world was astounded. Richard Atkinson of Cardiff University voiced a typical reaction when he noted how "… it is almost inconceivable that mere barbarians on the remote north-west fringes of the continent should display a knowledge of mathematics and its application hardly inferior, if at all, to that of Egypt at about the same date [ie. c.2,500 BC.], or that of Mesopotamia considerably later." Yet Thom was right, and his great achievement in "decoding" the megaliths is now justly recognised. Not too long ago Sir Fred Hoyle noted that a "veritable Newton or Einstein must have been at work" in the construction of the megaliths.

In Thom's epoch-making work he referred to results from 600 sites throughout Britain, all of which were found to be aligned astronomically with great precision. Every megalith was built with an eye to the positions of the constellations and the movements of the planets. It has even been suggested, not without cause, that Stonehenge was designed as a giant astronomical clock, a clock used in the prediction of solar eclipses etc.

It is truly inconceivable that Stone Age barbarians could have raised such structures. But the problem evaporates when the chronology is put right. The esoteric order known to us as the Druids, not primitives of the Neolithic era, were the true builders of the megaliths. It is thus evident that the tradition which linked Merlin, a character accredited with mystical and esoteric knowledge, to Stonehenge, was in one sense probably derived from a clear memory of the Druid priests who raised it.[18] There can therefore be

---

18 Almost inevitably, Stonehenge is increasingly viewed, notwithstanding the opposition of conventional archaeologists, as in some way linked to the whole meaning of the Arthurian tradition. Thus John Matthews comments: "The Round Table itself came to represent far more than a meeting place for the Fellowship. Robert de Borron, tracking backward again as he had done in the story of Merlin, added a further dimension. The Table of Arthur, he declared, was made in the likeness of two earlier tables. The first, at which Christ and the Apostles sat to celebrate the Last Supper, had been copied by the Grail Kings as a suitable place for the Holy Cup itself, of which they were guardians and keepers. Finally Merlin built the third table, at which the Fellowship would meet until the Grail itself appeared and sent them forth on the greatest quest of all, for which they had long been prepared. Behind this idea lies another, subtler set of symbolic references. In the starry realms, according to many ancient traditions, met a council of mighty beings whose concern was with the execution of the divine plan of creation. They too sat at a round table, and when Merlin brought the stones of the Giant's Dance from Ireland, to create what we now know as Stonehenge, he made that circle in the likeness of the Starry Table." *The Elements of the Arthurian Tradition* (1989) p.34

no objection to linking Stonehenge with Merlin and Arthur, if indeed we can prove that these characters belong in the pre-Roman Celtic past and not to the Dark Ages, where popular tradition has placed them.

The National Myth

The national myth of Britain, the story of the island's tutelary god-king and his heroic companions, is retold in the various medieval and Welsh accounts. The final version of the story, promulgated in the Middle Ages, was essentially a medieval creation, derived nevertheless from Welsh, Cornish and most especially Breton traditions of great antiquity. The final product was an enchanting tale that has inspired knights, artists, poets and children down to the present age.

During a time of great trouble and disturbance the High King of Britain, who is named Vortigern, attempts, supposedly for defensive purposes, to erect an enormous tower. Yet the project is beset by problems; no sooner do the builders make some progress, than an earthquake razes it to the ground. The king consults his Druids in the hope of finding a solution, and is informed that if he wished to complete the tower he would need to sprinkle the blood of a spotless child, the product of a virgin birth, upon the foundation stones. The king's servants discover in the town of Carmarthen a child matching this very description, and presently both he and his mother are brought to the court. Suspecting nothing, the woman freely admits to the king that her child had no mortal father, but was begotten upon her by a mysterious golden man who appeared to her in the night. Vortigern himself finds this hard to believe, but the child Merlin intervenes, confirming his mother's story. He further reveals the true reason why the tower keeps falling: beneath the foundations, in a chamber underneath a lake, there lurk two dragons, one red and one white, who battle continuously. It is their quarrelling that causes the earth to shake. In the legend that has come down to us, Merlin tells how the white dragon symbolises the pagan enemies of Britain, and how, out of Cornwall, a hero (described as a wild boar) would emerge who would tread on the white dragon's neck and save the kingdom.

The child Merlin now develops into a wondrous youth, adept at every skill, including those of prophecy and sorcery. He becomes the oracle of the nation, and the rulers of the kingdom regularly consult his advice. In particular, he is befriended by Uther and Ambrosius, the two sons of king Constantine, who earlier, in a great battle had defeated Vortigern and claimed the sovereignty of the kingdom for themselves. It was with Uther in particular that Merlin's fate was to be entwined.

After the death of his brother Ambrosius, Uther is crowned undisputed king of the whole land, and his reign, with the help of Merlin, proves to be a happy one. The new ruler, who is as yet unmarried, chanced to set eyes upon the Duke of Cornwall's wife, the lovely Igraine, with whom he immediately falls in love. Uther reveals his desire to Igraine, but she, being a virtuous woman, rebuffs his advances and informs her husband. Quickly they steal out of the court and flee back to Cornwall; whereupon the king advances with an army and besieges the Duke, who is named Gorlois, at his two castles, Tintagel and Terrabil. Failing to make any progress in this enterprise, Uther finally seeks the assistance of Merlin, who, because he realises that the saviour of Britain is destined to be born from the union of Uther and Igraine, comes to his assistance. The wily sorcerer arranges for Gorlois to be away from the castle at Tintagel, and magically transforms Uther into his exact likeness. Under the guise of her husband, Uther then spends an adulterous night with Igraine, from which union the child Arthur is conceived.

That very night the Duke of Cornwall is killed, thus making Igraine a widow. Shortly afterwards, she agrees to marry Uther, unaware that she is already carrying his child. Later however, just before the birth, the king reveals the truth. The boy Arthur, destined to be king of Britain, is then raised, at the request of Merlin, at the residence of a knight named Sir Ector. The child grows up, unaware of his true identity.

Years go by, and Uther passes away. Once again, the kingdom is in desperate straits, with the possibility of a violent struggle for the crown imminent. At this stage, Merlin approaches the religious authority of the land to call together all the nobility of the kingdom for the purpose of choosing a new king. By Christmas, most of the great lords of Britain are assembled in London (though some traditions place the action at Caerleon in Wales). At this point, we are told, a mysterious and magical sword, embedded in a stone, or in an anvil upon a stone, appears in a holy precinct, supposedly a church-yard. Carved on the sword (or stone) is the message that the weapon could be drawn from the rock only by the true-born king of the land. Many illustrious warriors try their luck, but all fail ignominiously. Merlin then advises that a second meeting, combined with a tournament, should be called, and that every nobleman in the land should this time be present. This second meeting is to be held on New Year's day.

Fate decrees that Arthur, together with his foster-father Sir Ector, and his foster-brother Sir Kay, attend the New Year's assembly. As the knights are about to engage in a joust, Sir Kay notices he had mislaid his sword, and asks Arthur to return to their camp to retrieve it. This he agrees to do, but finds the lodgings empty, with the result that he is unable to locate the sword. Wishing not to return empty-handed, the noble youth remembers the strange sword conveniently stuck in the nearby church-yard, and resolves to bring it instead. Arriving at the spot he easily extracts the weapon from the stone. When Sir Kay and Sir Ector see the sword they are astonished, and earnestly enquire of the boy how he has come by it. Assuming he had done something wrong, Arthur admits to having taken it from the stone in the church-yard; whereupon he is accompanied by Sir Ector and Sir Kay back to the church, and is there asked to repeat, before witnesses, the feat he had earlier accomplished on his own. This he easily does, and is, after various delays, duly proclaimed the rightful and divinely-appointed king of Britain.

Arthur proves himself to be worthy of the high hopes the omens suggested. He sets about establishing justice and freedom throughout the land, a task he is assisted in by his mentor Merlin. For many years success crowns his efforts, and a great company of warrior-heroes assemble at his court. Things begin to go wrong however when Arthur chooses as his bride the beautiful Guinevere, daughter of Leodegrance of Cameliard. Merlin, foreseeing what was to transpire, opposes the match, but is unable to prevail upon the king to desist. Arthur's heart is set on Guinevere, and so, reluctantly, Merlin gives his blessing to the union. As a dowry gift Leodegrance sends Arthur the wonderful Round Table which Merlin had fashioned for Arthur's father Uther, but which had, upon Uther's death, become the property of Guinevere's father. At the wedding feast Arthur and his own knights, as well as a hundred others who had been sent by Leodegrance, sit around the wonderful Table. But the banquet is not without incident, and the flight of a white hart, pursued by a pack of hounds, as well as a mysterious damsel and a knight, through the hall, initiate some of the heroes of Camelot on three epic quests.

Arthur entrusts king Pellinore, one of his most valiant champions, to retrieve the strange damsel who had been chased through the hall; and after many adventures he succeeds in bringing her back to Camelot. The woman's name, it transpires, is Nimue, one of the Ladies of the Lake. Almost immediately Merlin falls hopelessly in love with this enchantress, an infatuation that eventually leads to his downfall. Growing tired of his persistent amorous advances, Nimue finally uses her guile to entrap him inside a stone pillar, a prison from which he could never escape. With the formidable sorcerer out of the way, Camelot's surest defence is gone, and the forces which had previously threatened to destroy the kingdom now have freer reign. Nevertheless, for a while things continue to go well. As previously, the heroic company of the Round Table is active in defending the weak, punishing wrongdoing, and promoting all the values of chivalry.

It is in this period that Arthur performs his greatest exploit, the conquest of Rome. Lucius, the Roman Emperor, had challenged the king of Britain to acknowledge him as his lord, on pain of invasion. Arthur rejects the humiliating ultimatum, takes the war into Europe, and conquers Rome itself. In the course of this campaign the man who was to be the mightiest warrior of the Round Table, Lancelot, joins the heroic company. Almost immediately however the handsome champion catches the eye of queen Guinevere, who soon falls hopelessly in love with him.

This affair would eventually have a tragic outcome, though in the meantime Arthur's knights are to become involved in their most famous quest: that of the Holy Grail.

Lancelot had introduced his son Galahad into the company of the Round Table, and he it was who was destined to take possession of the holy vessel, which, it was said, had held the blood of Jesus. We are told that after a day of jousting, in which the youthful Galahad displays his martial prowess, the court at Camelot witnesses a prodigious event. A great thundering sound is heard and a beam of brilliant light illuminates the hall. In the midst of this the Holy Grail appears, covered in a cloth of samite. There appears at the same time at the table whatever food or drink the revellers desire. Then the Grail disappears, as suddenly as it had come; at which point Sir Gawain announces his intention to retrieve it. A hundred and fifty knights in all pledge there and then to set out in search of the magical vessel.

Many adventures later, both Lancelot and Galahad at different times discover the whereabouts of the Grail, though Lancelot is unable to bear its presence. It is left to Galahad, at a later stage, to take possession of the Grail, as well as the kingdom in which he found it. After only one year however the noble Galahad dies, and, together with the Grail itself, is conveyed to heaven by the angels.

Lancelot returns from his quests only to find Camelot alive with malicious rumours about his relationship with the queen. Going then into voluntary exile, he returns as Guinevere's champion when she is falsely accused of a murder at court. Now the noble knight and the queen can no longer hide their feelings for each other, and in due course they are betrayed to the king by Sir Agravaine and Sir Modred. A trap is set by the latter two, and in the ensuing struggle Agravaine is killed and Modred wounded. Nevertheless, Guinevere is captured and sentenced to death for treason. As the sentence is about to be carried out however, Lancelot appears upon the scene and rescues her. A terrible war now begins between Lancelot's forces and those of the king. Many valiant warriors on both sides are slain, and such is the destruction wrought that a treaty is eventually concluded. Guinevere is returned to Arthur, whilst Lancelot is condemned to exile in France.

For a while, things remain calm. Presently however, at the promptings of Sir Gawain, Arthur resumes the war against Lancelot. A great host is gathered and transported across the channel. The king himself leads the expedition, but before leaving entrusts the care of the kingdom to his malevolent son Modred. Needless to say, within a very short time, Modred is plotting to seize the throne for himself. A rumour is circulated that Arthur has been killed in France, and, acting upon this Modred crowns himself and forcibly marries Guinevere. Hearing of these events, Arthur instantly returns to Britain. An inconclusive battle is fought, and this is followed by a second, more fatal engagement at a place called Camlann. Here Arthur personally slays Modred, but is himself mortally wounded. Sir Bedevere, last of the warriors of the Round Table, then casts Excalibur back to the lake whence it had come, and the dying Arthur is conveyed by Morgan le Fey and the other Ladies of the Lake across the waters to the mystical isle of Avalon.

With Arthur's departure, the world is a lesser place. But he waits, in the island of the Blessed, across the western ocean, to return to save his people in the hour of their greatest need.

CHAPTER 2

Heroe∂ an∂ Sorcerer∂

Christian Warriors or Celtic Gods?

For the better part of one hundred years scholars have been in general agreement that virtually all the essential elements in the Arthurian story derive from Celtic myth, and it is evident that Arthur's character, as we have it now, is a medieval Christianised version of a much more primeval identity.[1] Whilst it is possible that a man (or men) named Arthur played a part in the wars against the Saxons during the 5th and 6th centuries (the name was popular at the time), it has to be stated categorically that at present no evidence for the existence of such a person exists, and that the Arthur of folk tradition is never portrayed fighting the Saxons: And whilst some elements of the story, most particularly Arthur's wars,[2] as told by Geoffrey of Monmouth, are perhaps related to events surrounding the Roman conquest of Britain, it has become increasingly evident that everything else belongs squarely in the world of mythology.

   This fact would be clear enough if we only possessed the medieval version of the legend, as bequeathed to us by Wace, Chretien de Troyes,

---

1 The definitive work is that of R.S. Loomis *Celtic Myth and Arthurian Romance* (1927)

2 P.M. Hughes ("King Arthur's Battles" *Stonehenge Viewpoint* 71 (1986)) presents fairly detailed evidence to show that the Arthurian battles named by Nennius were wars waged by the armies of Claudius during the Roman conquest. Thus for example he notes that a king Claudas is actually mentioned in some of the traditions, whilst battle locations can be fairly accurately equated with known engagements of the conquest. There can be little doubt that the cataclysm of the Roman invasion would have entered into the consciousness of the British people; but it would not have given rise to a new mythology. Aside from the battles outlined by Nennius, everything else in the Arthurian legend derives from Celtic myth.

Robert de Boron, Malory and the others. But it becomes absolutely beyond question when we examine early Welsh tradition, where Arthur is routinely placed alongside characters whom we know to be Celtic deities. The *only* sources, which put Arthur in the 5th century are the fictitious histories of Nennius and Geoffrey of Monmouth – the latter almost certainly copying Nennius, whose reasons for placing Arthur in the Christian epoch will be examined elsewhere. The Arthur of tradition, along with his companions, does not belong to history, and all aspects of the story are properly placed in pre-Christian mythology. Arthur's place in the Celtic pantheon is in fact reasonably well understood.

The search for the Holy Grail, perhaps the central theme in the Arthurian epic, is known to represent a thinly-veiled version of the search for the Celtic magic cauldron of knowledge and life, a story found in the Welsh "Tale of Culhwch and Olwen". Here Arthur leads a quest on behalf of the hero Culhwch, in the course of which he rescues the god-king Mabon, hunts down a giant boar, and makes a raid upon Ireland, whence he carries off a magic cauldron. Another version of the tale, perhaps more ancient, is preserved in the poem "The Spoils of Annwn", contained in the 14th century *Book of Taliesin*. Here Arthur leads an expedition to the magical land of Annwn to steal its treasures, a fabulous cauldron and a magical sword.[3] Graham Phillips and Martin Keatman, two writers intent on proving Arthur to be a historical character of the Dark Ages, nevertheless admit that, "It could have been from this poem that Geoffrey [of Monmouth] derived Avalon and the magical sword Caliburn, and Robert de Boron took his idea of the Holy Grail; both writers making attempts to medievalise ancient, mythological concepts."[4]

The cauldron of knowledge then, a magical vessel also appearing in Irish myth as the cauldron of plenty, and belonging to the primary deity, the Dagda, clearly represents a theme widespread in early myth (eg. the Greek Horn of Plenty) and is without question the prototype of the Holy Grail.

The theme of a mystical island lying to the west inhabited by a sisterhood of enchantresses is equally primeval, and there is little doubt that Annwn of Welsh legend is Avalon. In Geoffrey of Monmouth's work the enchantress Morgan le Faye is head of a sisterhood of nine women who act as guardians of Avalon, whilst in Welsh legend Annwn is inhabited by

---

3 Graham Phillips and Martin Keatman *King Arthur: The True Story* (London, 1992) p.21
4 Ibid. p.25

nine maidens who act as custodians of the cauldron.[5] That this is a Celtic myth of great antiquity is confirmed by the fact that Pomponius Mela, a Roman author of the first century AD. speaks of a similar tradition in Armorica (Brittany), and there is little doubt that the enchanted island of the western ocean is one of the Occident's most antique traditions. Even the name of Avalon, which "seems to be of Celtic origin"[6] and derived from a word meaning "rich in apples" (Gaelic *ablach*) is of great significance, for the mystical island is thereby linked with the land of the Hesperides, the "daughters of the night" who in Greek tradition watched over an enchanted tree bearing golden apples, which grew in the western extremities of Ocean (ie. the Atlantic). The eleventh Labour of Hercules was to recover these fabulous apples.

The implied link with the Hercules myth is of fundamental importance to our investigation. Again and again our inquiry will reveal striking parallels between the story of Hercules and that of Arthur, and a thorough examination of the origin and meaning of Hercules' character will cast new and dramatic light on the Arthurian story.

It has thus become part of accepted wisdom that Arthur and his compatriots represent the Celtic pantheon or certainly some characters of the pantheon. Even in their medieval guise a number of them have held onto their ancient identities. In addition to the identifications already suggested we may note that the knights Sir Kay and Sir Bedivere represent the Mabinogion gods Cei and Bedwyr, whilst Arthur's sister Morgan le Faye and his wife Guinevere are the goddesses Morrigan and Gwenhwyfar. In the same way, his nephew Gawain (the original owner of Excalibur) is rather obviously Govannan/Gobniu, the divine smith, whilst Sir Brons is Bran, the raven god. There is less precise agreement regarding Arthur himself, though the general consensus is that he may be alter-ego of Gwydion, the son of Don, and one of the most important characters in the ancient British pantheon. Gwydion is also said to correspond to the Irish Ogma, or Ogmios, whom we know from the Greek writer Lucian the Celts of Gaul equated with Hercules.[7] In addition to some obvious parallels with Gwydion, Arthur shares much in common with Hu, the Welsh name of the old Gallic god Hesus, and with Lleu Llaw, or Lleu Llaw Gyffes "Llew

---

5 Graham Phillips and Martin Keatman loc. cit.
6 Ibid. p.44
7 Lucian *Heracles* i

of the Strong Arm", the Welsh equivalent of the Irish Lugh (pronounced Loo), who is the ancient god Lugos. This deity, as we shall see, was a fairly exact Celtic equivalent of Perseus, whose own identity was closely linked to that of Hercules.

Even the most "historical" of the Arthurian characters, the High King Vortigern – mentioned by Bede and supposed by many to be mentioned by Gildas – is shown upon examination to be nothing of the sort. His tower-building and child sacrifice, we shall see, reveal him to be a titan-god -like the biblical tower-builder Nimrod – of remote antiquity; and even his Welsh name, Gurthrigen, which the Welshman Gildas does give, is known to be not a real name, but a title, signifying roughly "High King".

An examination of the most important characters of the Arthurian epic will reveal them not only to be Celtic deities, but deities, like Vortigern, clearly identified with megaliths, megalithic culture and the very dawn of civilisation. Indeed the links between Arthur, Merlin and the rest, and the megalithic stone circles, will be shown to be very specific and all-pervasive.

Heroes of the Standing Stones

Throughout the length and breadth of Britain megalithic monuments are linked in local tradition to the Arthurian legend. Some stone circles are actually called "round tables". If these structures actually date from the Celtic period, as we say, then they further support our contention that Arthur and his heroes are Celtic deities.

British tradition makes it very clear that in origin the Round Table of Arthur was a stone circle. Thus in the story of Perceforest, which though not mentioning Arthur directly is clearly part of the Arthurian canon (Sir Bors, Morgan le Fay and the Round Table all occur), stone circles feature prominently. We read;

> "He saw through great trees a well made round table of ancient construction, covered with flat stones. The knight walked across the arena and in through the door of the temple. He found the place in its simplicity the most holy that he had ever experienced. There was an altar towards the east where he mused for a while. Turning to the

right he saw a rich throne. The sun which was then setting, directed a single ray through the door of the temple onto the throne, illuminating it brightly."

This story is said to date from the 14th century, but is clearly based on a much more ancient tradition. We note here that a round table is constructed of stones, and there are in fact a number of stone circles in Britain referred to as "round tables". In his *Traveller's Guide to Arthurian Britain* Geoffrey Ashe lists five. Among these are the Mayburgh circle near Carlisle, a circle in Clywd, one in Anglesey, and one in the grounds of Stirling Castle.

However, it is the most famous of the megaliths, Stonehenge, that is identified by us as the primary source of the Round Table myth. Its connection with the Arthur story is first recorded by Geoffrey of Monmouth; but we must not imagine for one minute that Geoffrey invented this tradition. Clearly it was of long-standing pedigree. Three facts in particular mentioned by Geoffrey have caused modern scholars to stop and think: According to him, Merlin had the stones for the temple (which had ancient magical significance) brought by ship from Killaraus in Ireland: It was raised as a monument to the British chiefs slain by Hengist; and the stones were blessed on Whitsun (ie close to May Day – Beltane).

Astonishingly enough, archaeologists have found these statements to be strangely reflected in the monument.

- The bluestones of the inner circle did indeed come from the west, and were almost certainly shipped the greater part of the way to Salisbury Plain, along the Severn Estuary, and up the Avon. They did not however come from Ireland, but from the Prescilly mountains in south-west Wales. The stones of this region, it appears, had ancient magical significance.

- The earliest monument at Stonehenge, Stonehenge I, was indeed a burial site, where the cremated remains were interred in holes around the outer circle.

- Stonehenge has at least one alignment pointing to an important connection with the May Day (Beltane) festival. (See Chapter 7).

Clearly Geoffrey had tapped into a body of genuinely ancient tradition about the monument.

Merlin is also connected in popular tradition with various sites in the region of Avebury. Marlborough, for example, the nearest large settlement to Avebury, has a long-standing link with Merlin – a link said to be displayed even in the name (originally Merlebrigia) – though this is dubious. Nevertheless, in the town there exists a large hillock, almost certainly of Late Neolithic/Early Bronze date, named Merlin's Mound.

Avebury may have yet another significant link to the myth. Arthur's order of the Round Table, we are told, was comprised of 150 knights. Yet Avebury, the most massive megalithic complex in the country, had a central series of circles which apparently originally contained 150 stones. Thus the outer circle seems to have had 96 stones, whilst the two inner structures had 28 and 26 respectively – a total of 150.

Lesser monuments throughout the country are specifically connected with Arthur and his heroes. Thus Cerrig Arthur on Sylfaen farm near Merrioneth in west Wales is a smallish stone circle. In Dyfed in south Wales there is Cerrig Marchogion, the "stones of [Arthur's] knights". The Leaze stone circle stands on King Arthur's Down, whilst nearby is King Arthur's Hall, a Bronze Age stone rectangle, thought to have been used for astronomical alignments. There is Cerrig Meibon Arthur, the "stones of the sons of Arthur" in the Prescilly mountains, and a burial mound called Maen Arthur in Herefordshire. Carreg Fyrddin on Bryn Myrddin is a large standing-stone reputedly raised in memory of Merlin.

Of great interest too are the group of stones known as the Five Kings, in Northumberland. The five kings feature prominently in Malory. In a chapter entitled "The war with the Five Kings" we read,

"As they stood talking Sir Kay saw the five kings coming on horseback by themselves alone, with their spears in their hand, even towards. 'Lo' says Sir Kay, 'Yonder be the five kings. Let us go to them and match them.'"

The Five Kings is also the name given to a row of stones in the Kielder Forest.

The nine maidens is a popular title for stone circles in Britain, and this name too is Arthurian in origin. Out of a total of sixty-eight stone circles in Britain no less than eight are called the Nine Maidens, or the Nine Stones. Strangely, most of these do not have nine stones at all. The Nine Maidens at Boscawen Un has nineteen stones, the Nine Maidens at Belstone Tor has at least eleven, and the Nine Maidens at Boskednan in Cornwall had originally twenty two stones, of which only six remain standing. In the Arthurian tradition Morgan le Fay was the leader of a sisterhood of nine priestesses who dwelt in the mystical isle of Avalon, and it is evident that these are the Nine Maidens commemorated in the stone circles. This is fully confirmed by Malory, who tells us how Morgan le Fay turns herself and her entourage into stones:

"And so they followed fast, and within a while Arthur had sight of Morgan le Fay. Then he chased as fast as he might. When she spied him following her she rode at great pace through the forest until she came unto a plain. And when she saw that she might not escape she rode unto a lake thereby and said 'Whatsoever becomes of me my brother shall not have this scabbard.' And then she threw the scabbard into the deepest part of the water. And so it sank for it was heavy with gold and precious stones.

"Then she rode into a valley where many great stones were and when she saw that she would be overtaken she shaped herself, her horses and her men into great marble stones. And anon came King Arthur and Sir Outlake but the king could not tell his sister and the knights from one another.

"And then he looked for the scabbard but it could not be found. And so he returned to the abbey where she had come from. And so when Arthur was gone they all turned their likeness to what they were before."

It was the above story that gave so many of the stone circles their peculiar name.

A large number of important megalithic monuments in southern England, including Avebury, the Cheesewring Complex, Arthur's Quoit, the Hurler's Stone Circle, and the Merry Maidens, have been found to lie along what is called the May Day line. This was an important astronomical alignment for the Beltane festival, and clearly further supports the Celtic origin of these structures. Also located along the May Day line is a series of white horses, cut into the chalk and maintained by countless generations of locals. Importantly, the white horse too has Arthurian connections. Thus in Malory Arthur's wedding is disturbed by a mystical lady on a white horse;

> "Right so came in a lady on a white palfrey [horse] and cried aloud unto king Arthur and said, 'Sir, suffer me not to have this despite, for the dog is mine that the knight led away.'"

The list of Neolithic and Bronze Age sites with Arthurian connections is so long that textbooks dealing with Arthurian sites are virtually guidebooks to Bronze Age Britain, and it would be impossible to examine all of them. The above examples however should suffice to illustrate the point that it is primarily these sites, and not Roman or Dark Age ones, that are connected to Arthur. It should be noted also that the Arthurian myth is particularly linked to the megalithic sites of south-western Britain; and indeed this area is singularly rich in Late Neolithic/Early Bronze Age structures. This is no accident, for the immensely powerful Early Bronze civilisation of Britain, which was the inspiration for the Arthurian myth, had its home in that very region.

It may, as a final resort, be argued that the megaliths only became associated with Arthur during the Middle Ages, when the story was popularised throughout England: And this in fact is the argument normally used to explain the association. However, it should be remembered that folk memory can be extremely tenuous, and we need only point to the retention even in London of traditions linking certain sites (such as Ludgate, Billingsgate and Tower Hill) to the pre-Christian Celtic past.

Merlin and Hermes

Whilst some writers have tried to suggest that Arthur is at least a partly historical character of the Dark Ages, very few have attempted to say the same about Merlin, his associate and helper, whose pre-Christian nature is all too apparent. On a very obvious level Merlin is the archetypal wizard, the shaman or Druid, who casts spells and conjures spirits. But in fact he is much more than that. When we examine him in any detail he quickly emerges as a figure of central importance in Celtic mythology, a pre-Christian god of the highest order.

The story of Merlin which can be gleaned from the various diverse traditions is that of a semi-divine child, whose father is a demigod, described as a golden man. This child is born for a high purpose, is captured and imprisoned in some way during his infancy, is very nearly offered as a sacrifice by a tyrant king who attempts to raise a great tower to the heavens and escapes this fate to become in later years a veritable oracle to his people. He becomes the supreme benefactor of mankind, bequeathing various gifts, including, almost certainly, knowledge of astronomy and the workings of the cosmos. His wisdom becomes the guiding light for the nation's High King, and for all subsequent rulers of the land.

In many of these details, Merlin displays striking parallels with Mabon, the divine-child of Celtic mythology, whose image has been found at various Romano-British sites throughout the country. According to Caitlin Matthews, Mabon/Maponus, the child imprisoned in a wall, who appears with Arthur in the "Tale of Culhwch and Olwen", was in fact the prototype of Merlin (destined to be sacrificed and buried under the foundations of Vortigern's tower).[8] But the problem here is that, in spite of his popularity in Roman times (when he was known as Apollo Maponus), we have very little knowledge of his cult. Welsh legend preserves only tantalising hints. This of course is entirely understandable if, as I will argue, Maponos/Mabon ("the son") is simply an honourary title of the child Merlin, who, we shall see, was a Celtic god of immense importance.

This notion (as of Caitlin Matthews above) that all the Arthurian characters are simply updated versions of older Celtic deities is almost universally accepted, even by those who agree fully with the mythic nature of the Arthurian heroes. Somehow it is believed that these legends represent a new mythology which only appeared in the Dark Ages. Yet Merlin, Arthur, and the rest, we shall argue, are not new gods based on old: they are in themselves pre-Christian gods, whose very names and titles are of great antiquity. Thus Merlin's two Welsh titles, Myrddin and Emrys, are,

---

8 Caitlin Matthews in *Merlin Through the Ages* (R.J. Stewart and John Matthews eds. 1995) p.299 ff.

we hope to demonstrate, titles or epithets of the Celtic god Lugos, who was identified by the Romans with Mercury/Hermes. Emrys, it is agreed by all, is the Welsh transliteration of the popular Arthurian Bors. Yet Bors, or Boras, is almost certainly to be identified with Hecataeus of Abdera's Boreas, the founder and guardian of the Hyperboreans' sacred precinct (ie. Avebury and Stonehenge), and evidently an extremely significant deity of the northern regions. By the same token Myrddin appears to mean "He of the Sea", and honours the rescuing of the child Lugos from that element

What evidence do we have for these assertions?

In the Arthurian legend Merlin is a character of possibly even greater importance than Arthur himself. Indeed Arthur is little more than the imperfect executor of Merlin's far-sighted vision. Clearly Merlin represents possibly the most important god in the Celtic pantheon. Now according to Julius Caesar the Gauls and Britons worshipped Mercury above any other deity,[9] a suggestion that sounds somewhat strange until we remember that Mercury (Hermes to the Greeks) was the god who had bequeathed the elements of civilisation, including organised religion, to mankind. The idea that Merlin is in some way the Celtic equivalent of Hermes/Mercury is not a new one, and has been argued at length by various writers.[10] I propose that this identification is correct, and that Merlin is thus linked with one of mankind's most primeval myths, a myth that refers back to the very dawn of civilisation, the dawn of our collective historical consciousness. My own researches have led me to conclude that Hermes/Mercury was the deity worshipped in the earliest years of literate culture, and is linked to the most ancient of customs, including phallus-worship and blood-sacrifice. The famous staff of Hermes (sometimes represented by the phallic *herme*) is ultimately connected with the primeval tower-legend, the tower which, in its various forms, was constructed after the Deluge in an attempt to reopen communication with the heavens. This myth is universal, but is most widely-known through the biblical story of Abraham. Abraham, whose phallic identity is expressed in his name ("father of a multitude") and his initiation of circumcision, is placed immediately subsequent to the

---

9 Caesar *Gallic Wars* i.1 Caesar states that among the Britons Hermes/Mercury was known as *Optimus et Maximus* ("Best and Greatest") and to him they erected "many images".

10 "This writer believes that Merlin is one of the names of the god Mercury, or Hermes, the European god of magic and prophecy." Jan Knappert in *Merlin Through the Ages* pp.211-2 The connection between Merlin and Mercury is examined at some length by Emma Jung and Marie-Louise von Franz in *The Grail Legend*

Tower of Babel. His wandering leads him to Canaan, where he is asked, by way of a test, to sacrifice his young son Isaac. In the end the sacrifice is not performed, and a goat caught in a nearby thicket is offered instead.

It hardly needs to be emphasised that this story corresponds very closely with that of the youthful Merlin, who is almost sacrificed by the tyrant Vortigern, who has been led to believe that such an offering would ensure the success of his tower-building project.

In case it be believed that the Merlin/Vortigern tale, with the tower, was copied from, or inspired by the biblical one, it should be emphasised that this motif is universal, and occurs in ancient cultures far removed from the Near East. Some of these will be examined at a later stage.

Now in Greek mythology Hermes plays exactly the same role occupied by Abraham in biblical and Merlin in British tradition. Thus the story of Abraham, and of Merlin, records the origin of the custom of blood sacrifice (a custom corresponding to the origins of literate civilisation), and Greek tradition was quite specific in accrediting the custom to Hermes. We are told that the child Hermes had stolen some cattle belonging to Apollo, two of which he killed and chopped into twelve parts, as an offering to the twelve gods. This, it was said, was the first flesh sacrifice ever offered.[11]

To summarise then, consider the parallels:

- Merlin's father was a god, who took the form of a golden man. Zeus, the father of Hermes, was reputed to have fathered at least one child, the hero Perseus, by coming to his mother as a shower of gold.

- Merlin is linked to a blood-sacrifice legend, and is sought out, as a young child, by a king for this purpose. Hermes, as a child, was reputed to have initiated the custom of flesh-sacrifice.

- Merlin is linked to a serpent, or dragon-cult; the battling serpents underneath Vortigern's tower become his symbol. Hermes, whose wand or staff is entwined with coiled (or battling) serpents, is likewise linked to the serpent-cult.

- Merlin initiates many civilising customs, and is a teacher of arcane knowledge. Hermes is the initiator of numerous arts and sciences, which he bequeaths to mankind.

---

11 *Homeric Hymn to Hermes* 1-543; Apollodorus iii,10,2

• Merlin acts as an intermediary or emissary between Arthur and the otherworld, the divine world. Hermes becomes the emissary of the gods, and travels between the world of the dead and living, often accompanying souls to the realm of Hades.

It is evident then that Merlin was the deity referred to by Caesar as the primary god of the Celts, and it is likewise evident why the Celts held him in such high esteem. Two questions however, both of great importance, are raised by this identification. Why is it that the myths of the ancient British correspond so closely with those of the Greeks, and even with nations further removed, like the Hebrews?[12] And secondly, what does the myth of Hermes/Merlin actually mean? What is the significance of the Tower, of the Dragon, and of blood sacrifice? The answer to both these questions will emerge as we proceed through the book, and will be shown to be quite astonishing in themselves.

Lugos, the Celtic Hermes

Julius Caesar, we have seen, stated that Mercury was esteemed above all other gods by the peoples of Gaul, and the material evidence from Gallo-Roman times demonstrates quite clearly that Caesar was not mistaken; In the words of two modern commentators,

"Far from neglecting Caesar's evidence, we ought to see in this god the chief deity of the Gauls. His cult was very widespread. Called

---

12 There is even a distinct possibility that the entire cult of Hermes was derived from the peoples of western Europe, for he was accorded the title Atlantiades as a surname, by virtue of the fact that his mother Maia was a grand-daughter of Oceanus. She herself was described as one of the Pleiades or Atlantides. Merlin's name, we recall, *Myrddin*, almost certainly means "him of the sea". The Latin Mercury (derived from *mercari* – to deal or trade) may also be connected with the sea; for the word originally seems to have implied "carried on the sea". Hermes' most basic symbol, the staff entwined with coiled serpents, the *kerykeion* or *caduceus*, is inexplicable in the Greek version of his story; yet in the British version, where the two battling serpents lurk underneath the tower of Vortigern, the icon is fully explained. As we shall see, there is strong evidence to suggest that many of the Greek mythic stories were heavily influenced by material derived directly from the Celts.

Mercury, he was adored in a dozen or more different aspects. There is a reminder of this in such place-names as Mercurey, Mercureil, Mercoeur, Mirecourt, Montemartre (Mount of Mercury). Costly statues were raised to him. One in bronze, one hundred and thirty feet high, which took Zenodore, the sculptor, ten years to complete, stood in the vast temple of Mercury Arvernus, known as Dumiatis, which was built on the summit of the Puy de Dome. There are many others throughout Gaul."[13]

But this Celtic Mercury had, as the above writers suggest, a dozen or more different aspects. Nevertheless, we are talking about the chief god of the Celts, not some obscure tribal totem. In at least one of his titles or epithets he should appear as a deity well-known and celebrated throughout the Celtic realms. Mabon/Maponus may have been one of the aspects of the child Hermes peculiarly popular in Britain, but this otherwise little-known god cannot have been the deity referred to by Caesar as the most popular god of the Celts.

It is universally agreed that the Celtic god equated by Caesar with Mercury was Lugos.[14] This is suggested by two varieties of evidence. On the one hand Lugos appears, on the evidence of place-names, to have been just about the most important of Celtic divinities. Thus for example numerous cities throughout Europe, such as Lyon (Lugdunum), Loudon, and Leiden, as well as the Gallic province of Lugdunensis and the major festival of Lugnasad were named in his honour. Such popularity would at once suggest a possible link with Caesar's Celtic Mercury, but when we look at the actual nature and deeds attributed to Lugos we find an almost precise parallel with the nature and deeds of Hermes/Mercury.

The Irish tradition, which preserves the original Celtic myth in a fairly uncorrupted state, describes Lugos, who is named Lugh, as a child-prodigy, a being excelling all the other children of Danu in knowledge of the arts and sciences. For this reason he was given the epithet *Samholdanach* – "Polytechnician". Lugh's origin and birth is a question we shall return to at a later stage. Suffice for the moment to say that he was rescued from the sea as an infant (calling to mind the name Myrddin "He of the Sea"), and was admitted as a youth into the company of the gods after a display of his

13 G. Roth and P.M. Duval in *Larousse World Mythology* (1965) pp.340-2
14 See eg. Frank Delaney *The Celts* (London,1986) p.87

wondrous talents; which of course precisely parallels Hermes/Mercury, who is admitted to the company of the Olympians as a child after a display of his numerous skills and talents.

It was in the famous war against the giants (Fomorians) however that Lugh really came into his own. The great battle between gods and giants was said to have taken place at Magh Tuireadh, the "Plain of the Tower", (or Towers) the latter name illustrating at once the connection between this story and the battles between gods and giants of Greek and Nordic mythology. In the Greek myth the giants attempted to storm Olympus by piling mountains on top of each other; but the ensuing tower was destroyed when Zeus struck it with a thunderbolt. In the Nordic myth the giants raised a huge clay tower, in the shape of a man, which they hoped would give them access to Asgard. But the tower was destroyed when Thor struck it with his mighty hammer.

This myth of a tower leading up to the heavens is one of the most primeval of human traditions, common to all races and cultures. It is also invariably placed in the immediate aftermath of a great Flood or world destruction, and is linked specifically to the story of a deity who invents the elements of civilisation, as well as initiating religious worship and sacrifice – the deity we identify with Hermes.

In the Irish story of gods versus giants the tower is not specifically mentioned as a central element, but its connection with the other tower legends is clearly preserved in the name of the battlefield. Also, another Irish myth, clearly related to the contest between gods and giants, speaks of a great tower erected by the titan-god Conan, a Fomorian giant of the same clan as Balor. As in the Greek story, where Hermes plays a major part in the victory of the gods, Lugh's role in the victory of the children of Danu is decisive. He it is who organises the latter for war. Some of the gods, including Nuada ("of the Silver Hand") and Ogma/Ogmios are actually killed by the giants (though they are resuscitated by Lugh), and it is left to Lugh to destroy the most fearsome of them, the wicked Balor – Lugh's own grandfather – whose glance alone could kill. This Lugh accomplishes with a missile hurled from his magical sling, or, according to other accounts, with his magical shining spear.

The battle between gods and giants, whose cosmogenic origins will be elucidated at a later stage, was to become the archetypal battle between good and evil, the original war between the good angels and the followers of Satan.

It is also, as we shall see, the prototype of the battle of Camlann, fought between Arthur and his knights and the followers of the evil Modred. Arthur, who will be revealed to be an incarnation of Lugh himself, was killed at this battle, though he lived on in the Celtic Paradise in the western Ocean.

Magic Wands and Magic Circles

The esoteric ("hermetic") knowledge accredited to Hermes/Mercury became the basis of the entire idea of the Magus, the magician or wizard, the man of power who could divine the past and the future, who could heal and who could kill.

Yet the myth of the Magus was closely interwoven with that of the megaliths. Thus in the Hellenic world the cult of Hermes was typically centred round a single standing-stone, or menhir, known to the Greeks as a *herme*, which was identified by them both with the sacred phallus, and with the staff, or caduceus, of Hermes. It is this staff that is the origin of the magician's magic wand, Merlin's indispensable tool of enchantment.

It is scarcely to be doubted that the isolated standing-stones of western Europe were sacred to the god held in highest esteem by the Celts, Merlin/Mercury/Lugos, and British tradition states very clearly that it became the custom of Arthur's knights to gather round a standing-stone, within which Merlin was believed to be imprisoned, before setting out on a quest.[15] We shall presently see how the entire custom of menhir-building is intimately linked with the tower-legend, which we have connected with events directly preceding the rise of civilisation.

The other symbol of the Magus was of course the magic circle, within which he safely performed his sacred rituals. Orthodox scholarship is in no doubt as to the origin of this concept. Thus in his *Stonehenge People*, Rodney Castleden describes the megalithic circles as the first magic circles, "the beginning", he says "of a long European tradition that persists down to the present day."[16] We are told by Geoffrey of Monmouth that Merlin

---

15 John Matthews *The Elements of the Arthurian Tradition* (Element Books,1989) p.23 Merlin's entrapment by Nimue bears striking comparison with the way Lleu Llaw Gyffes (the Welsh Lugos) was trapped and killed by Blodeuedd.
16 Rodney Castleden *The Stonehenge People* (London, 1987) p.50

Handle of flint knife, from Egypt
(Early Dynastic) showing
interlocking serpents.

The prototype magic wand. Mercury / Hermes' staff the caduceus.

Vortigern and Merlin with the battling dragons
(after Miranda Grey *The Book of Merlin*).

was responsible not only for the building of Stonehenge, but also for the fashioning of the Round Table, which was later presented to Arthur and Guinevere as a wedding-gift.[17] I would suggest that this myth be interpreted as suggesting that the skills and knowledge (especially of astronomy/astrology) bequeathed to mankind by Merlin/Hermes were used by the people of the time to erect Stonehenge in honour of Arthur, a god whose identity shall be examined presently.

The entire concept of the Magus is also intimately connected with that of the Alchemist, whose primary concern – the search for the Philosopher's Stone – is intended to confer the power to transmute base metals into gold. This part of the Magus' identity can also be traced to the epoch of Stonehenge III, whose builders were among the first people (perhaps the very first) to perfect the art of bronze-working. This secret knowledge, we shall see, was particularly linked to Britain, and explains both the wealth of the Stonehenge III people, as well as the other mystical icon of the country, the Sword in the Stone. It was Merlin, we remember, who called attention to the Sword by organising a festival, which coincided with its appearance in the churchyard.

We must stress at this point that the secret science of alchemy was inseparably linked with the cult of Hermes/Mercury. This was the case both in antiquity and during the Middle Ages and Renaissance. As the epitomy of arcane, secret knowledge, alchemy was very obviously linked to Hermes. Yet the connection becomes even more understandable when we realise that with alchemy we are taken back to the dawn of civilisation, to the epoch of the megaliths and the Early Bronze swordsmiths.

The Magus, however, is primarily an astrologer, and this is expressed both in his star-covered robes, and also in the magic-symbol *par excellence*, the five-pointed star, the pentacle: And Merlin too conforms to this archetype, an aspect of his personality illustrated most clearly perhaps in "The Prophecies of Merlin", a little discussed section of Geoffrey of Monmouth's *History*. Here the sage presents a panoramic view of Britain's future, predicting a time of decadence which would be followed by strange signs in the heavens, leading to a cataclysmic destruction of humanity;

---

17 The Round Table was made, according to the legend, at the bidding of Arthur's father Uther Pendragon, and was later given to Arthur by Guinevere's father, who presented it as a dowry. John Matthews *The Elements of the Arthurian Tradition* (1989) p.28

"A man shall embrace a lion in wine, and the dazzling brightness of gold shall blind the eyes of beholders. Silver shall whiten in the circumference, and torment several wine presses. Men shall be drunk with wine, and regardless of heaven, shall be intent upon the earth.

"From them shall the Stars turn away their faces and confound their usual course. Corn will wither at their malign aspects, and there shall fall no dew from Heaven.

"A root and branch shall change places, and the newness of the thing shall pass as a miracle. The brightness of the Sun shall fade at the amber of Mercury, and horror shall seize the beholders. Stilbon of Arcadia shall change his shield; the Helmet of Mars shall call Venus.

"The Helmet of Mars shall make a shadow; and the rage of Mercury shall exceed its orbit. Iron Orion shall unsheathe his sword; the marine Phoebus shall torment the clouds. Jupiter shall go out of his lawful paths; and Venus forsake her appointed circuits.

"The malignity of the star Saturn shall fall down in rain, and slay mankind with a crooked sickle. The Twelve Houses of the Stars shall lament the irregular excursions of their inmates.

"The Gemini shall omit their usual embrace, and will call the Urn (Aquarius) to the fountains. The Scales of Libra shall hang awry, till Aries puts his crooked horns under them. The tail of Scorpio shall produce lightning, and Cancer quarrel with the Sun. Virgo shall mount upon the back of Sagittarius, and darken her Virgin flowers.

"The Chariot of the Moon shall disorder the Zodiac, and the Pleiades break forth into weeping. No offices of Janus shall return hereafter, but his gate being shut shall lie hid in the chinks of Ariadne.

"The seas shall rise up in the twinkling of an eye, and the dust of the Ancients be restored. The winds shall fight together with a dreadful blast, and their sound shall reach to the Stars."

All these symbols and concerns are traced directly back to the megaliths, which are now known to be temples of a sky-religion, a religion worshipping the heavenly bodies. This of course was the very religion, complete with its blood-sacrifices, bequeathed to mankind by Hermes, and the origins of this sky and catastrophe-obsessed cult will be elucidated further as we proceed. Hermes/Mercury was linked to the planet of the same name, and the Celtic deities were likewise gods of the constellations. Thus to the Irish the Milky Way was known as "Lug's Chain", and the Welsh gods, the children of Don, were equally celestial figures; "For the Welsh the constellation of Cassiopeia was called Llys Don, 'Court of Don'; and Caer Gwydion, 'Castle of Gwydion' referred to the Milky Way. It seems highly probable that Arianrod herself was the moon."[18] The origin of this planetary religion, observed in every corner of the globe, is a topic of immense importance.

We find then that Merlin is linked in virtually every detail not only with the god Hermes/Mercury, but also with the megaliths, and that the ancient religion founded by him was, to some degree, alive and well long into the Christian epoch.

---

18 G. Roth and P.M. Duval in *Larousse World Mythology* (1965) p.348

CHAPTER 3

Britain's Hercules

The Wheel of Heaven

Arthur's mythic identity is well understood. He is a warrior-king who is also the guardian of the land, the source indeed of all royal authority. In the words of John Matthews;

> "... Arthur conforms in every detail to the mythic archetype. Strangely born, his end is mysterious. His relationship with the Goddess of the land and her avatars is established early. He summons a great fellowship of heroes to sit at his circular table which echoes, as Merlin says, 'the roundness of the world', and also the circle of the heavens. He is placed in polarised balance by the presence of Morgan, who acts always against him until the end, then appears as his guardian and protectress. He possesses magical weapons – in particular, of course, Excalibur, which must be returned to the lake when he no longer requires it. With his going the world is a lesser place; though his dream, of a unified, perfected earthly kingdom, remains, to be taken up and renewed throughout time to our own days, and doubtless beyond."[1]

Yet a major point of the present work is that Arthur is not merely a Dark Age hero who has taken on the mantle of a mythical deity, but an actual mythical deity himself, a Celtic god who has been misplaced in the Dark Ages. We have already identified Merlin as the Celtic Mercury, the

1 John Matthews *The Elements of the Arthurian* Tradition (1989) p.10

Taranis with his wheel, as portrayed on the Gundestrup Bowl.

most venerated god of the Gauls and Britons. Arthur too must represent a pre-Christian god, his name being an epithet for an extremely important Celtic deity. Thus we have seen how ancient Roman-age inscriptions refer to 'Apollo Maponus' ("Apollo the Son") and, as we shall see, 'Mercurius Artaius' ("Mercury the Bear"). If the name Arthur really were derived from the Celtic *artos* "bear", this would suggest that he is in some way an alter-ego of Mercury/Hermes, the Celtic Lugos. Yet we have already discovered in Merlin/Myrddin the true counterpart of Hermes/Lugos. Who then is Arthur the counterpart of? As a warrior-king, we might expect him to represent a warrior-god, probably the Celts' greatest warrior-god.

It so happens that one of the most popular Celtic gods, Taranis, the god of thunder (the name is identical to Thor's, and he appears as Taran, father of Gluneu, in Welsh legend), was linked, like Arthur, to a wheel or circle-symbol. In all portrayals, as for example on the famous Gundestrup Bowl, Taranis is portrayed with his peculiar spoked wheel. There can be little doubt that this wheel has a cosmic significance, representing no doubt the sun, the circle of the heavens, or some other cosmic body. As John Matthews rightly states, Arthur's Round Table has precisely the same meaning, and we may reasonably suppose that being so closely linked to the circle symbol Arthur is in some way connected to Taranis.

It is interesting to note that the famous Round Table in Winchester Castle bears an uncanny resemblance to the wheel of Taranis. Although of medieval date, it may be that the makers of this Table were aware of some tradition which stated that the original table of Arthur was wheel-like. It is virtually certain that the wheel of Taranis had twelve spokes, just like the Table of Winchester, to represent the months of the year.

In fact, the symbol of the circle or wheel is of fundamental importance in British megalithic culture – whose stone circles we have already identified as the prototype of the magician's circle – as well as in Welsh mythological tradition. Thus Aranrhod, one of the children of the primary god Don, has a name that means "Silver Wheel", whilst the whole philosophy of Bardism, as described in medieval Welsh literature, is concerned with describing different states or planes of existence in terms of circles or cycles. This latter was a topic examined at great length by Lewis Spence, who describes three quite separate cycles of existence postulated by the Bards. These were, starting at the bottom, Annwn, the nether world; Abred, the physical world; and Gwynvyd, the plane of perfected beings.

Above the latter, however, the Bards also spoke of Ceugant, the impenetrable circle of deity, a sphere that no created being could ever enter. Evidently the Bards, and their Druid predecessors, regarded existence as a cyclical process, much like the Buddhist wheel of life, with birth followed by death, followed by rebirth.[2]

None of this is to say that the original Wheel of Taranis was in any way connected to this highly sophisticated philosophy. Taranis' wheel with its twelve spokes was without question initially a symbol of a stellar religion concerned primarily with the worship of the heavenly bodies, combined with close attention to their movements. Nevertheless, it seems that the Druids used this basic imagery of cosmic and stellar cycles to illustrate the much more subtle and altogether philosophical idea of spiritual cycles, which they came to develop in the years following the erection of the first stone circles.[3]

Taranis' name derives from the Celtic word for "thunder", and as a thunder-god he undoubtedly shares much in common with the Greek Zeus, as well as the Roman Jupiter. Yet he was not the major warrior-deity of the Celts; and his tiny role in the Welsh literature (he is mentioned only once), would suggest that he is not, in most respects anyway, the deity we should identify with Arthur.

Gwydion and the Heroes of the Mabinogion

It is an oft-repeated idea that Arthur and his companions bear close comparison with many of the characters encountered in the medieval Welsh collection of tales that has come to be known as the Mabinogion. In particular, it is said that in many of its essentials Arthur's story is similar to that of Gwydion, a central character in the Mabinogion and one of the most important offspring of the god/dess Don. The family of Don (equivalent to the Irish Danu), it is generally agreed, represent nothing

---

2 Lewis Spence *The Mysteries of Britain* (1994 ed.) pp.98ff
3 It cannot be doubted that the stone circles represented to their builders a microcosm or representation on earth of the great circles of the heavens. Sure enough, as Spence notes, the number twelve (ie. the phases of the moon) is twice repeated at Avebury, in the Scottish circle of Clessernish, and in certain Cornish monuments. Ibid. p.211

more or less than the Celtic pantheon. Thus it is claimed that Gwydion, a patron of learning and the arts, as well as a benefactor of mankind, is in many respects similar to Ogmios (Irish Ogma), the Celtic Hercules, though it is admitted that he also shares many features in common with Lugos/Lugh, the Celtic Hermes, as well as with various other gods. The name Gwydion seems to be related to Woden, and apart from the name he displays many parallels with this Teutonic deity. Whether some Celtic deity was given the name Gwydion/Woden during the period of the Anglo-Saxon invasions, or whether the title goes back to the semi-Teutonic nature of the Belgic inhabitants of southern Britain is a question that has not yet been satisfactorily answered.

But it is Gwydion's relationship to Arthur (and also Merlin) that has caused most comment. In the words of one authority, Arthur "is surrounded by characters who are strikingly similar to those in Gwydion's entourage in the fourth branch of the Mabinogion. His wife Gwenhwyer (Guinevere) is the daughter of the giant Ogyrvan, protector and inventor of bardism; in the early texts she was Arthur's sister before she became his wife."[4] This of course is a precise parallel of the union of Gwydion and his sister Arianrhod. The writer quoted above continues, "Their two sons (or nephews?) Gwalchmai and Medrawt (one good the other bad), correspond to the two deities of light (Lleu) and darkness (Dylan) [the two sons of Gwydion]."[5]

Yet the resemblance between Gwydion and Arthur, or indeed Merlin, has I would suggest been somewhat exaggerated. Aside from the above parallels, the Gwydion tale bears little obvious relationship to the Arthurian: And it needs to be stressed here that Arthur himself, as well as Merlin (Myrddin), and other recognisable heroes of the Round Table, also occur in various medieval Welsh sources, (though not in the four Mabinogi), where they are placed alongside divine figures who are equally prominent in the Mabinogi tales; or, more accurately, alongside the children of characters who are prominent in the Mabinogion.

The idea that Arthur's character must somehow be based upon Gwydion is, I would suggest, one result of the mistaken notion that Arthur is essentially a historical character of the 6th century – whereas it is

---

4 G.Roth and P.Duval "The Celtic Lands: Myth in History" in *Larousse World Mythology* (Paris,1963) p.351
5 Ibid.

accepted that Gwydion and the other Mabinogion heroes are Celtic gods. They are indeed Celtic gods; but so is Arthur. Although Arthur does not occur in the Mabinogion, his companions, or usually the fathers of these, do: Thus in the "Dream of Rhonabwy" (found, like the four Mabinogi stories, in *The Red Book of Hergest*) various sons of the Mabinogi gods Nudd, Llyr, Bran, Gofannon, and Aranrhod, are mentioned as servants of Arthur. In the "Tale of Culhwch and Olwen" (also from *The Red Book of Hergest*) Amaethon and Don serve Arthur, whilst two sons of Beli, who have been turned into oxen, plough for him. In the same story Manawydan son of Llyr, Gwyn son of Nudd, and Pryderi son of Pwyll, rally round at Arthur's call to seek the treasures of Britain.

From the above we see that, in general, Arthur and his companions belong mythologically to the next generation of gods. This at a stroke explains Arthur's non-appearance in the Mabinogi tales and Gwydion's non-appearance in the Arthur cycle. As the texts themselves make abundantly clear, the Mabinogi stories deal with events prior to the birth of Arthur. By the time of Arthur's appearance, Gwydion has already gone to his fate, which, as Taliesin informs us in "The Spoils of Annwn" was an apparently perpetual imprisonment in Annwn itself. Indeed, in "The Spoils of Annwn" Gwydion appears to be present when Arthur and his entourage arrive in the Underworld to plunder the mystical cauldron.

The stories of Arthur were widely known and told in medieval Wales, where his status was every bit as prominent as in other regions of Britain and north-west France. The four Mabinogi tales do not retell these stories because their purpose is to preserve an account of what happened prior to Arthur, an account that was probably in danger of being lost. The absence of Arthur from this collection should not therefore delude us into believing that he does not belong with the gods mentioned in the collection, most of whom the other medieval Welsh sources regard as Arthur's subjects, vassals and helpers.

If we wish to discover Gwydion's true mythic identity, we must consider his personality. He is essentially a shape-shifter and promoter of vegetative regeneration who appears as a stag and a wild boar, and who fathers Lleu Llaw Gyffes (Lleu of the Strong Arm – the Welsh Lugos). His appearance as a stag would in particular suggest a link with Cernunnos, the "Horned One" of Celtic myth, who figures prominently in ancient cultic art. There is evidence that Cernunnos was specifically linked to Annwn/Hades, and we recall here that Gwydion was chained forever in the same place. As such, he strongly resembles vegetation and rejuvinative gods such as Osiris, Tammuz and Dionysus. As the father of Lleu/Lugos (whom he conceals in a chest), he has close parallels with the Irish Balor (British Beli/Belinos), the Celtic Gorgon-deity whose identity will be elucidated at a later stage.

The suggestion therefore that Gwydion or any other Mabinogion character is the "source" of the Arthurian legend must be abandoned. Arthur, we shall argue, was worshipped under his own name (ie. Artos), in pre-Christian times, and was a British equivalent of Hercules, who shared many features in common with Ogmios, a deity appearing in Irish tradition as Ogma, and named in a Romano-British inscription as Ogmia. Yet though Arthur, as the heroic champion-god of the land, shares many of Ogmios' attributes, he is not the same being. For Ogmios was not the greatest champion of the gods: That honour went to Lugos, who played by far the major part in the destruction of the fearsome army of the giants, when they threatened to plunge the whole of creation into chaos. The next greatest hero, after Lugos, was not Ogmios but a reincarnation of Lugos himself; a character named Lugos Artaios, or, in a Roman-age *ex voto* inscription, Mercurius Artaius. And here we must stress another point. The stories found in Welsh legend are unquestionably much altered from the original mythology of pre-Roman Britain, and are not necessarily in every respect of greater antiquity than the (usually Breton) sources upon which the popularised Arthurian stories of the Middle Ages were based. Indeed, in a number of details, the Breton Arthurian traditions (where Arthur is routinely named Artus) seem more authentically ancient. Where the Welsh and Franco-Breton sources disagree, we may occasionally be justified in seeing the latter as more true to the original myth.

In the Mabinogion much space is devoted to the story of Bran, child of the sea-god Llyr and lord of Britain, a deity who also figures prominently in the Arthurian epic, and was, originally (we shall argue), one and the same as Arthur's father Uther Pendragon.

We are informed that in an age long past the king of Ireland asked for the hand of Branwen, sister of king Bran. The match is duly agreed and the marriage takes place in Anglesey. During the wedding there is some trouble, and it becomes necessary to placate the Irish king. For this purpose Bran presents him with his most treasured possession – a wondrous cauldron that can bring the dead back to life.

Branwen then takes up residence in Ireland, but her marriage is far from happy. Secretly she dispatches a message to her brother, pleading for help. Immediately Bran gathers an army and sets off for Ireland. We are told that in those days the channel was not so wide (a reference probably to the inundation of the kingdoms of Llys Helig and Cantref Gwaelod), and Bran himself (evidently of gigantic size) wades across. In the ensuing war the Irish make use of the mystic cauldron which Bran was foolish enough to present them with, and rejuvenate all their dead (just as in the Irish battle of Magh Tuireadh, where the side led by Lugh rejuvenate their dead in a magical well). After great slaughter on both sides, Bran is mortally wounded in the foot by a poisoned spear, and, dying, commands that his head be cut off and taken to the "White Mount" in London, where it is to be buried as a protective talisman for the kingdom.

The seven British survivors – among whom are the well-known Arthurian figures Taliesin and Pryderi – set out for London, and, after many other adventures duly accomplish the task set for them. Branwen herself dies of grief and is buried in Anglesey.

It would appear that in medieval Welsh tradition the major task performed by Arthur is the recovery from Ireland of Bran's mystical cauldron. Thus in the *Red Book of Hergest* "Tale of Culhwch and Olwen" Arthur travels to Ireland specifically to recover a cauldron, whilst in the "Spoils of Annwn" Arthur journeys to the nether regions – here replacing Ireland – in an attempt to retrieve its cauldron. Of great importance is the fact that only seven men return alive from this venture (as in Bran's expedition to Ireland), and two of these are Taliesin and Pryderi, who also are among the seven to survive Bran's war in Ireland. The close relationship between the Bran story and the Arthurian can in fact be illustrated in a whole host of ways. Thus Pwyll, the ally of Bran and Lord of Annwn, is identical to Pelles or Peleur, who in the Normanised Grail romances is the keeper of the Holy Grail (the relationship between the cauldron and the Grail will be explored further in due course), whilst another tradition stated that the Holy Grail was actually brought to Britain by the Fisher King Bron – ie. Bran himself. Like the Fisher King Bran is wounded by a spear, and as Bran is decapitated so is a character appearing in the Welsh Grail legend of Peredur – where a spear tipped with blood is carried in front of a severed head on a platter.

From this, it begins to look as if the entire story of Bran, as found in the Mabinogion, is little more than a "prequel" to the story of Arthur; the Bran legend explaining how Britain's greatest national treasure, the cauldron, which it is Arthur's task to retrieve, came to be located in the mystic isle in the west in the first place. When in the Mabinogion myth Bran is mortally wounded by a poisoned arrow, he instructs his followers to cut off his head and bury it in London as a protective talisman for the island. British tradition however stated that the head was later dug up by Arthur, on the pretext that he alone should be responsible for the kingdom's defence. This also suggests a continuity between the two legends. But there is an even more direct link. The severed head of Bran was popularly known in medieval Wales as *Uther Ben* ("Terrible Head"). Yet this is virtually identical to the name of perhaps the most central character in the Arthurian legend, none other than Arthur's own father Uther Pendragon ("Terrible Dragon Head"). Such an interpretation has been accepted by various authorities, among them G. Roth and P. Duval.[6]

At a later stage we shall have occasion to examine the origins of both Bran and Uther Pendragon, and shall see that the head of Bran was indeed anciently regarded as a "terrible dragon head". In the same place we shall observe how the entire cult of the dragon, as well as the universal decapitation legend associated with it, has its origins in actual events occurring in the heavens in the early part of the first millennium BC.

The Magical Cauldron

The central theme of the medieval Arthurian epic was of course the search for the Holy Grail, popularly believed to be the cup used by Christ at the Last Supper. Scholars have long been aware that the Grail is a Christianised version of a much more ancient vessel, the magical cauldron of Celtic lore. In the Welsh poem "The Spoils of Annwn", this cauldron is the prime

---

6 G. Roth and P. Duval op. cit.. The decapitation legend of course is also the origin of the Celtic custom of head-hunting, and the idea that a decapitated head possessed magical protective powers is also found in a myth from the far side of Europe, that of Perseus and the Gorgon. We shall see however that this story was actually located by the Greeks in the lands of the Celts, and was evidently of Celtic origin.

target of Arthur's mission to Annwn, ie. Hades.[7]

Over the past hundred years or so it has become increasingly evident just how important the cauldron was in the mythology of the Celts. Thus we know now that the sacred cauldron is commemorated in numerous place-names the length and breadth of Britain, as well as Ireland. In his *Druidism Exhumed* (1871) the Rev. James Rust refers to a great number of Scottish localities connected by name to the cauldron-cult, the two most notable being Bennachie "Mountain of the Cauldron" and Maidsemaaighe "The Knoll of the very great Cauldron". Rust also suggested that places with names containing the component Aden, Eden, or Edin, of which there are countless examples, were also connected with the cult of the cauldron, through the Gaelic *aidheann* "a cauldron, kettle, or goblet".[8]

The mystical cauldron is of central importance in the traditions of Ireland. Gobniu the magical smith, brewed beer conferring immortality in a great cauldron for the otherworld feast, whilst the Dagda's inexhaustible cauldron could bring the dead back to life. The mighty hero Cuchulainn, of whom more will be said presently, plundered the divine cauldron from the mystical land of the dead, Dun Scaith.

It would appear that we possess an illustration of this Irish vessel in the famous Gundestrup Bowl, where a deity is shown dipping a man head-first into a great cauldron. The divine cauldron, as with so much else we have examined, seems to trace its origin to the megalith-building epoch; "is the vessel in which the dead are rejuvenated," asks Michael Senior, "remotely related to the hollow dish-like troughs in which they were placed in the chambers of the burial mounds – one may still be seen in place at New Grange – or to those urns in which the succeeding age, the Bronze Age, placed the cremated remains of their dead, buried in their cysts or round barrows?"[9] In addition, the ubiquitous bronze cauldrons which from the very outset of the metal-using age the peoples of Europe prepared their life-giving meals on the sacred family hearth, offer a rather obvious prototype for the divine cauldrons of the deities these peoples worshipped.

---

7 Lewis Spence loc. cit. p.240 "The literature of the Grail also contains certain evidences of the survival and continuance of this [Druidic] tradition in Britain for centuries. Its dramatis personae are merely those of Keltic myth in another shape, the Cauldron of *Annwn* is, indeed, the Grail itself."

8 Ibid. p.163

9 Michael Senior *Myths of Britain* (1979) p.212

In Welsh tradition there were at least two separate cauldron myths; that of Bran, which we have already mentioned, and that of Ceridwen, a vessel of supreme importance in the Bardic tradition of Wales. The origin of the latter cauldron was explained thus.

The goddess Ceridwen, it was said, gave birth to a hideously ugly son named Avagddu, whose deformity she resolved to compensate for by giving him the gift of supernatural knowledge. She then prepares a cauldron of inspiration, whose arcane ingredients must be brewed for a year, after which three drops of divine fluid will be produced. Ceridwen entrusts the mixing of the cauldron to a servant named Gwion, who eventually consumes the three magical drops when they had fallen upon his finger. In her rage, Ceridwen pursues Gwion, who assumes various forms, a hare, a fish and a grain of wheat in his attempts to escape. For her part, she takes on the shape of a greyhound, an otter, and at last a hen, in which guise she swallows the grain, later bearing Gwion as a child, whom she abandons to the sea in a coracle. But the child survives, maturing into the magical bard Taliesin – a contemporary and colleague of Merlin.

Later, the cauldron is found in Annwn, where, like the Holy Grail, it is protected by a group of nine enchantresses. According to Taliesin, nine maidens who dwelt in the "island of the strong door" warmed the cauldron with their breath.[10]

The importance of both Ceridwen and her magical cauldron in ancient British tradition cannot be overestimated. In the words of Lewis Spence,

"The Druidic bards who lived and sang under the Welsh princes unanimously represent Keridwen as presiding over the hidden mysteries of their ancient cult. Cynddelw, who flourished about the middle of the twelfth century, sings: 'How mysterious were the ways of the songs of Keridwen! How necessary to understand them in their true sense!' Llywarch ap Llywelyn, who wrote between 1160 and 1220, asks for 'inspiration as if it were from the Cauldron of Keridwen', and says that he will address his lord 'with the dowry of Keridwen, the Ruler of Bardism'. It was essential for those bards who aspired to the Chair of Song to have tasted the waters of inspiration from her cauldron, to have been initiated into her mysteries."[11]

---

10 Lewis Spence loc. cit. pp.82-3
11 Ibid. p.79

The cauldron of Ceridwen then, in British tradition, represented little other than divine wisdom and knowledge, the fountain of all inspiration. The deeper or mystical meaning of both the cauldron and the journey Annwn/Hades has been a subject exercising the minds of many writers over the past century; and it is evident that the wisdom contained in the cauldron is to be found only by those who have entered the other universe, the world of the dead, the kingdom of Annwn. "It is those fatal drops from her cauldron" writes Michael Senior, "which lie behind the ravings of the Taliesin of early literature, and hence, through his colleague the prophet Myrddin, indirectly behind Merlin's pronouncements too."[12] But Ceridwen and her cauldron lived on in an altogether more sinister sense into the Middle Ages. The same writer continues; "Ceridwen's cauldron has survived in the stereotyped image of the witch throughout the ages, those cauldron-stirring, prophesying, spell-binding old hags. They are seen as evil now, dominated by their horned god [Cernunnos], himself perhaps exiled into this outlawry from our established religion."[13]

In yet another sense then we see that the whole concept of witchcraft and sorcery, with its magic wands, circles, astrology and cauldrons, is but a survival of the old religion of Europe, which itself however has a pedigree that can be traced directly to the megalith-builders.

The Harrowing of Hell, which forms a central theme in the cauldron myth, is equally attributed to the divine heroes of ancient religion and to Arthur. This concept of plundering the sacred treasures of Hades is an achievement by no means confined to the heroes of the west. It is also encountered in the cults of the Near and Middle East. But before looking at these, we need to examine the story of some other great heroes of the west, who also took a cauldron from Hades, and whose legends offer very precise parallels with that of Arthur.

---

12 Michael Senior loc. cit. p.207
13 Ibid.

Arthur's Irish Incarnations

Ever since the pioneering work of R.S. Loomis, it has been demonstrated repeatedly, beyond all reasonable doubt, that Arthur of Britain represents, in almost equal measure, a precise counterpart, or, more accurately, a synthesis of ancient Ireland's greatest heroes, Cuchulainn and Fionn MacCumhaill. Before looking at some of the fairly stunning parallels between these characters, one point needs to be clarified. Beginning with the medieval Irish chroniclers themselves, there has been a fairly persistent attempt to suggest that the cycle of legends relating to Cuchulainn (popularly known as the Ulster Cycle), as well as those relating to Fionn (known as the Fenian Cycle), are in some way historical, and thus separate from the great mythic cycle relating to the Fomorii giants and the children of the goddess Danu. Indeed, both Cuchulainn and Fionn were very precisely dated to early in the Christian era by the clerical chroniclers of the Middle Ages.

Yet the tales relating to Cuchulainn and Fionn Mac Cumhaill are as mythical as those of the better-known Celtic gods, of Danu's children Lugh, Ogma and the rest: And it is evident that they are in all essentials denizens of the mythic world: gods and demigods who belong in the remote antiquity of the Heroic Age every bit as much as their relatives, the children of Danu. This is a point that needs to be stressed. Cuchulainn and Fionn are closely related to the children of Danu, with whom incidentally they interact on an everyday basis. And all their deeds are superhuman in a very obvious way: They cut off mountaintops with a single sword-stroke, and excavate lakes with no greater effort. We are told that,

"… compared with the modest exploits of the heroes of the Iliad … [those of Cuchulainn and his associates] were those of giants. Where Greek warriors slew their tens, these men of Ulster dispatched their hundreds. They came home after such exploits so heated that their cold baths boiled over. When they sat down to eat, they devoured whole oxen and drank their mead from vats. The gods themselves hardly did less, and it is easy to understand that in those old days not only might the sons of gods look upon the daughters of men and find them fair, but immortal women also need not be too proud to form passing alliances with mortal men"[14]

14 Geddes and Grosset *Celtic Mythology* (1999) p.131

Yet Cuchulainn was hardly a mortal man. The same writer proceeds,

"If Achilles and Heracles were, as some think, personifications of the sun, Cuchulainn is not less so. Most of his attributes, as the old stories record them, are obviously solar symbols. He seemed generally small and insignificant, yet when he was at his full strength, no one could look him in the face without blinking, while the heat of his constitution melted snow for thirty feet all round him. He turned red and hissed as he dipped his body into its bath – the sea. Terrible was his transformation when solely oppressed by his enemies, as the sun is by mist, storm or eclipse. At such times, according to the *Tain Bo Cuailgne*, 'among the aerial clouds over his head were visible the virulent pouring sparks of ruddy fire which the seething of his savage wrath caused to mount up above him. His hair became tangled about his head, as it had been branches of a red thorn bush stuffed into a strongly fenced gap .... Taller, thicker, more rigid, longer than the mast of a great ship was the perpendicular jet of dusky blood which out of his scalp's very central point shot upwards and then was scattered to the four cardinal points; whereby was formed a magic mist of gloom resembling the smoky pall that drapes a regal dwelling, what time a king at nightfall of a winter's day draws near to it.'"[15]

This passage from the epic *Tain* makes the cosmogonic nature of Cuchulainn very obvious indeed. The real origin of the ancient gods, and their relationship with the cosmos, is a question of immense importance, a question to be addressed at a later stage.

For the moment however it should be sufficient to note that Cuchulainn and Fionn are very definitely not historical characters of the first centuries AD., but rather Celtic gods indistinguishable from the others; Celtic gods peculiarly linked to Lugh/Lugos. Yet they are also virtually indistinguishable from Arthur, particularly the Arthur of Welsh tradition. The two mythic cycles which concern Cuchulainn and Fionn fill in, as it were, various details of the British Arthurian story. Let's first consider the story of Cuchulainn.

Cuchulainn's conception and birth was mysterious. His mother, the

---

15 Ibid. pp.132-3

princess Deichtire, is about to be married at the great fort of Emain Macha in Ulster to a chieftain named Sualtam. Whilst seated at the wedding feast a mayfly flies into her cup, and she swallows it. Soon afterwards she falls into a deep sleep, in the course of which the god Lugh appears, informing her that it was he whom she had swallowed and now bears within her. Lugh then orders the princess, along with fifty attendant maidens, to quit the palace. To ease their departure the god temporarily transforms them into a flock of birds. Nothing is heard of the maidens until one day, many months later, the warriors of Emain Macha are led by another flock of birds to Brugh na Boinne, where the great gods have their homes. Suddenly the men behold a splendid palace, into which they are led by a tall and handsome man. Within the hall they find Deichtire and her fifty maidens, with whom they feast and rest the night. Sometime before morning, the warriors' sleep is disturbed by the cry of a new-born child. At daybreak, the tall, handsome man reveals himself as Lugh, and orders the warriors to take the child whose cry they had heard and bring him up amongst the men of Ulster.

The mysterious conception and birth of Cuchulainn thus offers rather obvious parallels with that of Arthur, whose true father Uther Pendragon was magically given the appearance of Igraine's husband by the sorcery of Merlin, whom we have revealed to be an alter-ego of Lugh/Mercury.

At a very early stage the child Cuchulainn, initially named Setanta, displays his prodigious abilities, and whilst still a boy slays the ferocious hound of the smith Culann, whose anger at the loss of such a valuable beast is assuaged when the young Setanta promises to search for a dog of equal worth, offering himself as a replacement until such an animal can be found. Culann accepts this compromise, and from that time onwards the youth is known as *cuchulainn*, "the hound of Culann".

After this, Cuchulainn's fame spreads, and he finds favour with all the maidens of Ulster. But the heroic youth is hard to please, and swears that he will have only one. This is Emer, daughter of Forgall the Wily, reputedly the most beautiful woman in Ireland. In order to win Emer's favour, Cuchulainn sets out to learn the craft of the warrior from the Amazon Scathach, who resides in Alba (Scotland). It is during the course of his stay in Alba that Cuchulainn learns the use of the Gae Bholg (the "shining spear", the mystical weapon with which Lugh slew Balor) from Scathach, and fathers a son named Connlai on Aoife, another Amazon whom he defeats in combat.

Cuchulainn then returns to Ireland, where he slays Forgall and all his men, and rides off with Emer as his bride.

We next hear of Cuchulainn's greatest exploit, the single-handed defence of Ulster against all the hosts of Ireland, an exploit recounted in the *Tain Bo Cuailgne*, popularly regarded as Ireland's *Iliad*. Aside from the heroic feats of arms displayed by Cuchulainn during this campaign, three incidents in particular are of interest. Firstly, in the midst of the campaign, the goddess of battle Morrigan falls in love with him, and, appearing to the hero, offers herself to him. When her advances are rejected she tries to destroy him; and when this too fails contents herself with offering assistance. This of course precisely parallels Morgan le Faye's love-hate relationship with Arthur. Secondly, whilst Cuchulainn is at his lowest ebb, his father Lugh appears, heals his wounds, and gives him three days' sleep. Again, this precisely parallels the help given to Arthur by Merlin/Lugos. Thirdly, during the invasion Fergus Mac Roth (Fergus, son of the Wheel) an old friend and ally of Cuchulainn, who had however joined the forces opposed to Ulster, meets Cuchulainn in single combat on the battle-field. But rather than really fight, they agree a compromise, and Fergus, refusing to use his invincible sword *Calad Bholg* ("Shining Sword") against Cuchulainn, pretends to run away. Now this same Calad Bholg appears as Arthur's sword Caledfwylch in "The Tale of Culhwch and Olwen", and is agreed by all to be the direct prototype of Excalibur.

Yet in all senses, and not just in these, the story of Cuchulainn is more or less identical to Arthur's. After he saves his native land from invasion (and it should be noted here that he is not a king but a war-leader, just as Arthur initially is a war-leader, *dux bellorum*), Cuchulainn then accomplishes his greatest exploit: The retrieval of the magical cauldron of the gods from the kingdom of Hades, here named the island of Dun Scaith ("Shadow Town"). The parallel here with Arthur needs no emphasis.

Next comes the great tragedy of Cuchulainn's life, the killing of his own son Connlai, whom he had earlier fathered in Scotland by the goddess Aoife. The parallels with Arthur's slaying of Modred, whom he had earlier fathered, apparently also in Scotland, by his sister Morgan le Fay (for she was married to King Lot of Orkney), hardly needs to be stressed. Shortly after this, we are told, the vengeful Queen Medb (Maeve) of Connaught stirs up Cuchulainn's enemies against him, and, after a great battle, he is finally mortally wounded. At this stage, rather than die on his back, he ties himself to a post, and expires strapped to it.

The myth of the dying god strapped to the Tree of Life, or the Pillar or Tower, is one that is encountered universally, and shall be discussed further presently.

It is clear then that in most respects Cuchulainn is one and the same god as the deity known in Britain as Arthur. This divine hero had intimate links with Lugh/Lugos, the Celtic Mercury, who in British myth appears as Myrddin. The same god, it now seems certain, is also referred to in the Gaulish inscription of the first or second century dedicated to 'Mercurius Artaius'. But this "Artaius", it will be objected, was surely just an epithet of Mercury/Lugos. Not quite. The Celts, we know, believed implicitly in the concept or transmigration, or reincarnation, an idea reflected in numerous stories from the Celtic lands. We cannot doubt that the Celtic concept shared many features with the Hindu: And one of the fundamental Hindu beliefs in this regard is the idea that gods too can be reborn, or reincarnated. In Hinduism, the reincarnation of a god is called an *avatar*. Thus in Hindu tradition Krishna is an avatar of Vishnu. From the story of Cuchulainn it is quite evident that in him the god Lugh had become flesh; that Cuchulainn was in fact a reincarnation of Lugh/Mercury. Thus the god 'Mercurius Artaius' was not the original Mercury (though this Mercury was his continual guide and helper), but an avatar of Mercury named "Artus" – our own Arthur: (It needs to be stressed here that in some of the earliest medieval references to Arthur on the Continent he is known as "Artus" – not Arthur). This new Mercury/Lugos sought out the divine wisdom of his earlier incarnation by entering Hades and taking from it the vessel of all knowledge, wisdom and life, the Holy Grail and cauldron of the gods.

Whilst it may be that Arthur has his closest counterpart in Cuchulainn, it should be noted that he shares almost as many features with that other great hero-deity of ancient Ireland, Fionn MacCumhaill. But in the Fionn legends Lugh not only appears as a reincarnated avatar, he also appears under precisely the same name as in Britain; Art, the Bear. For the royal master of Fionn was named Cormac MacArt.

Cormac's grandfather was Conn "the Hundred Fighter", and a fifteenth century manuscript named "the Champion's Prophecy" tells us how the god Lugh, appearing to Conn in a mystical fortress on a hilltop, revealed to him the number of his descendants, the length of their reigns, and the manner of their deaths. Conn's most illustrious son was to be Art, whose name reveals him to be an incarnation of Lugh himself, and it is Art who becomes High King of the island. Here then is a precise match for the British tale, with Lugh (one and the same as Merlin) revealing to Conn (identical to Uther) the birth of his son Art (Arthur). King Art's brother Connlai, we are told, was borne away, like Arthur, in a boat of glass to the Earthly Paradise beyond the sea. There are abundant other parallels; though the order of events differs from that of the British tale. For the Irish story has Fionn, the greatest hero of the cycle, live not during the time of Art himself, but during the time of Art's son, Cormac MacArt. If however we can accept that variations in details are in any case to be expected in tales handed down by word of mouth, the parallels between the British and Irish legends strike us as astonishing rather than anything else.

To begin with, Fionn's company of champions, the Fianna, has long been recognised as a close equivalent of Arthur's knights, whilst Fionn himself, who gains supernatural wisdom by sucking his finger during the preparation of a mystical meal, is identical in name to the Arthurian Gwion who also gains supernatural wisdom by precisely the same means. Strikingly similar too are the deeds performed by Fionn's champions, which include the hunting of some other-worldly wild boars, the slaying of dragons and giants, the conquest of Europe, and journeys to the Otherworld. Fionn's betrayal by his chosen bride Grainne, who runs off with the handsome Diarmuid, is also strikingly reminiscent of Guinevere's betrayal of Arthur with Lancelot. On a number of occasions the same characters appear in the Fenian and Arthurian tales. Thus Niamh of the Golden Hair, daughter of the sea god Manannan MacLir, entices Fionn's son Oisin into the mystical Land of Eternal Youth (Tir na nOg), whilst in the Arthurian tale the same goddess (here named Nimue) entices Merlin into the same place.

Well aware of the connections between Arthur and Fionn, the medieval Irish chroniclers have the two actually meeting, with Arthur becoming a vassal of the Irish hero.

It would therefore appear that the character known to the British as Artos, the avatar and incarnation of Lugos, has two mythic manifestations in Ireland, where he is also known by his name Artos, the Bear, but also by the name Cunos, the Hound: And it is under this title, Cuchulainn, that Arthur finds his closest Irish counterpart in one very important respect. It is he, not Fionn, who undertakes the supreme task of the hero: the plunder of Hades. Yet the semi-human semi-divine demigod, who seeks out the wisdom of the Netherworld, is a character also encountered far away from the lands of the Celts – at the very opposite end of the European continent. Indeed, the quest for the treasures of Hades is the most important deed of one of the ancient world's most beloved characters, the archetypal hero himself, from whose name the very word "hero" is said to be derived: Hercules.

Arthur and Hercules

As a semi-divine dragon (or hydra) slaying hero whose various quests or labours lead him to retrieve treasures from far-off lands, Hercules offers a rather obvious parallel with Arthur. Yet the closer we investigate the two characters the more precise the parallels become. Indeed they begin to appear almost uncanny.

- Arthur was conceived when Uther Pendragon magically assumed the form of Igraine's husband, the Duke of Cornwall. In the same way, Hercules was conceived when Zeus magically assumed the form of Alcmene's husband Amphitryon.

- Arthur, it was said had twelve knights. Hercules performed twelve labours.

- Arthur's journey to the island of Avalon, the island of apples, is very similar to Hercules' journey to the Garden of the Hesperides, to retrieve the Golden Apples which grow there. Avalon is a mystical land in the far west, guarded by nine enchantresses, whilst the Garden of the Hesperides, who are also mystical enchantresses, was placed by the Greeks in the far west, by the Ocean stream.

- Arthur took spoils from Annwn, the otherworld, or land of the dead. Hercules likewise, in his Twelfth Labour, plundered the kingdom of Hades.

- Arthur was betrayed by his wife Guinevere, a betrayal which ultimately (though inadvertently) leads to his death; and in Malory Arthur is sent a poisoned cloak by his sister/wife Morgan le Faye. Hercules was

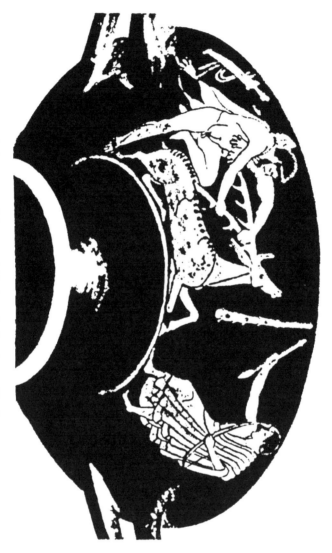

Hercules' capture of the sacred hind, as depicted on a Greek vase.

The sacred apple-tree of the Hesperides, guarded by the dragon Ladon
and by the Hesperides themselves, the 'Daughters of the Night'.

inadvertently killed by his wife, who unknowingly sent him the poisoned shirt of Nessus to wear.

- Arthur takes part in a great boar-hunt (as in the Tale of Culhwch and Olwen), and the wild boar was a sacred animal to the Celts, whilst Hercules' Fourth Labour is to slay the fearsome Erymanthean Boar. Hercules also takes part in the famous Calydon boar-hunt, a feat which is of immense significance for us; for this story seems to offer a link between mythical Greece and early Celtic Britain, in the form of the name Calydon, or Caledon, the ancient title of Scotland.

We might be tempted to dismiss this latter parallel as mere coincidence, as indeed scholars have done from time immemorial, were it not for the fact that the Greeks themselves placed many of the exploits of Hercules in the far west, in the regions of the Celts, whom incidentally he was supposed to have sired.[16] Thus a number of Hercules' Labours, perhaps even the majority of them, took place by the Atlantic seaboard of Europe. This is specifically stated in the case of the Tenth, Eleventh and Twelfth Labours, and is implied in the case of the Third Labour, the hunt for the Ceryneian Hind, which Hercules pursued into the land of the Hyperboreans, a land clearly identified by the earlier Greek writers as Britain.

Indeed virtually every element in the story of the Ceryneian Hind is intimately tied to the Celtic world, and to northern Europe in general. This creature, it was said, was one of a group of five, the others of which the goddess Artemis had captured and yoked to her chariot. These does all had antlers. Robert Graves comments; "In Europe, only reindeer does have horns, and reports of these may have come down from the Baltic by the Amber Route; reindeer, unlike other deer, can of course be harnessed."[17] According to Graves the hunt for the Ceryneian Hind,

"seems to concern Heracles the Dactyl, identified by the Gauls with Ogmius, who invented the Ogham alphabet and all bardic

---

16 Diodorus Siculus iv,19 and 24. According to Diodorus, Hercules established the city of Alesia in central Gaul, where he married a princess named Galata, by whom he became the father of the Gauls. These events took place on his return journey with the cattle of Geryon, his Tenth Labour
17 Ibid. p.112

lore. The chase of the hind, or roe, symbolized the pursuit of Wisdom, and she is found, according to the Irish mystical tradition, harboured under a wild-apple tree. This would explain why Heracles is not said by anyone, except the ill-informed Euripides, to have done the roe any harm: instead he pursued her indefatigably without cease, for an entire year, to the Land of the Hyperboreans, experts in these very mysteries. According to Pollux, Heracles was called Melon ("of apples"), because apples were offered to him, presumably in recognition of his wisdom; but such wisdom came only with death, and his pursuit of the hind, like his visit to the Garden of the Hesperides, was really a journey to the Celtic Paradise."[18]

It is not without significance that Arthur only travels to Avalon, the island of apples, at his death, whilst his search for the Holy Grail is above all a search for wisdom.

But other elements of this tale link it much more specifically with the Celtic world. The hero's hunt for a mythical roebuck forms a central theme of much Irish and Welsh legend. In Britain, famously, this magical deer is known as the White Hart, a beast immortalised in numerous English place and public house names, and specifically connected with Arthur. Arthur's wedding-feast, we are told, was disturbed when a white hart ran into the hall, pursued by a pack of hounds. One of Arthur's knights was knocked over by the hart as it leapt in the air, and this man seized the leading dog and departed. A mysterious lady then rode into the hall, pursued by a knight who seized her and carried her off. Merlin announced that these events could not be viewed frivolously, and so Arthur sent two of his knights, Sir Gawain and Sir Tor out after the white hart and the dog respectively. Sir Pellinore, a tried and trusted warrior, was

---

18 Robert Graves *The Greek Myths* Vol.2 (1955) p.112. Graves also suggests a specifically Celtic origin for the Tenth Labour, the Cattle of Geryon. Geryon, who was said to have lived on the isle of Erytheia, by the Ocean stream, had three heads along with three separate torsos, which were joined together at the waist. According to Graves, this myth is related to the Gallic *Tarvos Trigaranos* ("the bull of three cranes"), and he sees the name Geryon "a meaningless word in Greek" as derived from the Celtic *garanos*, "crane". Ibid. p.143 Supporting Graves' theory is a statement of Diodorus, who notes "in the course of his campaign against Geryones, Heracles visited Celtica." v,24,1

sent to retrieve the lady.[19]

It would appear that the Greeks, the greatest of eclectics, derived much of their traditions about Hercules from the Celts, specifically from the British Celts. I suggest that the Calydon Boar Hunt does refer to Scotland, and the name of the principal heroine of the story, Atalanta, could certainly be interpreted as placing the action in the far west. I further suggest that much of Greek mythology was heavily influenced by the myths of the British Celts, and that the Greeks were in direct and frequent contact with Britain from around 700 BC. onwards, just at the most formative period of their cultural history. I propose that the character of Hercules is largely based on two hero-deities of the Celts, one known as Ogmios,[20] and the other, whose character we have already examined in some detail, known as Lugos the Bear ("Lugos Artaios").

The battle of gods and giants, in which both the Greek Hercules and the Celtic gods Lugos and Ogmios played a pivotal role, is, as I have suggested, the prototype of Arthur's final showdown against the forces of evil, the battle of Camlann. In the Greek myth it is Hercules who saves the gods: only he has the power to kill the fearsome monsters who threaten to overturn the whole of creation and plunge the universe into primeval chaos. The son of Zeus has to personally despatch each one of them. In the Celtic myth Ogmios is an important warrior for the gods, though the greatest champion by far is Lugos, who brings slain gods back to life and personally despatches Balor, the most fearsome of the giants.

It is of interest to note here that one tradition from Ireland names Arthur (here spelled Artur) as the leader of the gods in their struggle against the giants. This myth describes Artur as a son of the primeval god Nemed (ie. "the Holy" cf. Gaulish Nemetona) who leads his people against the Fomorian giants at Cramh Ros. This Irish Arthur is may *possibly* be influenced by the British, yet should this be the case, it is evident that when the Irish received the story the Britons still understood Arthur to be a pre-Christian deity.

---

19 John Matthews op. cit. p.28
20 According to Graves, Ogmios of the Celts was "a mixture of the gods Cronos, Hercules and Apollo." *The White Goddess* (1961) p.132

Hercules, Lord of the Round Temple

Having identified Arthur as the national deity of pre-Roman Britain, the British Hercules, and having shown beyond reasonable doubt that his cult was linked to the various cromlechs, barrow-graves and stone circles that dotted the British landscape, it would be of interest to look at whether the Hellenic Hercules was also associated with megalithic structures in that part of the world. That question in itself is answered easily enough; for Hercules gave his very name (the Age of Heroes) to the great age of megalith-building in Greece and the Aegean, an age we have come to know as the Mycenaean. But if we could establish that the Greek Hercules was particularly linked to stone circles, or to a cult involving the use of such circles, our case for linking Arthur to Stonehenge would be greatly strengthened.

In his encyclopaedic *White Goddess*, Robert Graves presents a fairly detailed analysis of Hercules' character, and he accurately notes that the hero known to the Greeks as Hercules was a composite figure containing elements from a wide variety of sources. "...'Hercules' is a word of very many meanings. Cicero distinguishes six different legendary figures named Hercules; Varro, forty-four."[21] Graves himself goes on to describe what he regards as the root legend, Hercules as a pastoral sacred king. I make no apology for quoting him at length, for what he says is most instructive:

"Hercules first appears in legend as a pastoral sacred king and, perhaps because shepherds welcome the birth of twin lambs, is a twin himself. His characteristics and history can be deduced from a mass of legends, folk-customs and megalithic monuments. He is the rain-maker of his tribe and a sort of human thunder-storm ... He carries an oak-club, because the oak provides his beasts and his people with mast and because it attracts lightning more than any other tree. His symbols are the acorn; the rock-dove, which nests in oaks as well as in clefts of rock; the mistletoe, or *loranthus*; and the serpent. All these are sexual emblems ... This Hercules is male leader of all orgiastic rites and has twelve archer companions, including his spear-armed twin, who is his *tanist* or deputy. He performs an annual green-wood marriage with a queen of the woods, a sort of

---

21 Ibid. p.124

Maid Marian. He is a mighty hunter and makes rain, when it is needed, by rattling an oak-club thunderously in a hollow oak and stirring a pool with an oak branch – alternatively, by rattling pebbles inside a sacred colocinth-gourd or, later, by rolling black meteoric stones inside a wooden chest – and so attracting thunderstorms by sympathetic magic.

"The manner of his death can be reconstructed from a variety of legends, folk customs and other religious survivals. At mid-summer, at the end of a half-year reign, Hercules is made drunk with mead and led into the middle of a circle of twelve stones arranged around an oak, in front of which stands an altar-stone; the oak has been lopped until it is T-shaped. He is bound to it with willow thongs in the 'five-fold bond' which joins wrists, neck and ankles together, beaten by his comrades till he faints, then flayed, blinded, castrated, impaled with a mistletoe stake, and finally hacked into joints on the altar-stone. His blood is caught in a basin and used for sprinkling the whole tribe to make them vigorous and fruitful. The joints are roasted at twin fires of oak-loppings, kindled with sacred fire preserved from a lightning-blasted oak or made by twirling an alder- or cornel-wood fire-drill in an oak log. The trunk is then uprooted and split into faggots which are added to the flames. The twelve merry-men rush in a wild figure-of-eight dance around the fires, singing ecstatically and tearing at the flesh with their teeth. The bloody remains are burnt in the fire, all except the genitals and the head. These are put into an alder-wood boat and floated down a river to an islet; though the head is sometimes cured with smoke and preserved for oracular use. His tanist succeeds him and reigns for the remainder of the year, when he is sacrificially killed by a new Hercules."[22]

Graves mentions a number of mythological characters whom he identifies with this pastoral Hercules, yet curiously omits Arthur. But the parallels are clear. Arthur has twelve knights. Hercules has twelve merry-men. Indeed, as Graves puts it, "This Hercules is the leader of his people in war and hunting and his twelve chieftains are pledged to respect his

---

22 Ibid. pp.125-6

authority."[23] At his death, Arthur's body is taken by boat to the island of Avalon; whilst Graves' pastoral Hercules is put into an alder-wood boat and floated down-river to an islet. According to Graves, this Hercules is completely identified with his people; "The health of the people is bound up with his and he is burdened with numerous royal taboos."[24] It is important to remember also that Hercules, as Graves remarks, was in various places a god of lightning, or the thunderbolt, which of course ties him very clearly with Taranis, the thunder-god with the celestial wheel. Graves continues;

> "In the Classical myth which authorizes his sovereignty he is a miraculous child born in a shower of gold; strangles a serpent in his cradle, which is also a boat, and is credited (like Zeus) with causing the spurt of milk that made the Milky Way; as a young man he is the undefeated monster-slayer of his age; kills and dismembers a monstrous boar; begets countless sons but no daughters ... willingly undertakes the world-burden of the giant Atlas; does wonderful feats with his oak-club and his arrows; masters the wild horse Arion and brings up the dog Cerberus from the Underworld; is betrayed by his lovely bride; flays himself by tearing off his poisoned shirt; climbs in agony to the top of mount Oeta; fells and splits an oak for his own pyre; is consumed; flies up to heaven on the smoke of the pyre in the form of an eagle, and is introduced by the Goddess of Wisdom into the company of the Immortals."[25]

From our own point of view, the parallels listed above further confirm the link already identified between Arthur and Hercules. Yet the most crucial piece of evidence has yet to be explored. We have stated that the entire myth of Arthur was connected to the round standing-stone temples, particularly Stonehenge. Graves states that Hercules, or the sacred king who annually played the role of Hercules, was sacrificed inside a circle of standing-stones. As a matter of fact, standing-stone circles were found throughout Europe, including Italy and Greece, and they were always associated with Hercules. In the words of Graves, "The sacrifice of the

---

23 Ibid. p.126
24 Ibid.
25 Ibid.

agricultural Hercules, or the victim offered in his stead, continued to take place within a stone-circle dedicated to the Barley Mother. At Hermione, near Corinth, the stone-circle was in ritual use until Christian times."[26]

So the final piece of the jigsaw now fits into place. Having presented detailed parallels between Arthur and Hercules, we now also find that the latter deity was the god worshipped in the circular standing-stone temples of Europe. This phallic Hercules, known in Greece as the 'green Zeus', is without question one and the same as the character depicted on the chalk hillside at Dorchester known to us as the Giant or the Rude Man of Cerne Abbas, whose lightning-conducting oak club also links him to Taranis. We might also be tempted to see in him an alter-ego of the Green Man of British legend, a figure immortalised in countless public house names throughout England. Yet this character, though he does share much in common with Hercules, is more accurately seen as an alter-ego of the vegetation god Cernunnos (Herne the Hunter), who appears in the traditions of Wales as Gwydion.

Arthur's pagan nature and identity with Hercules is strikingly confirmed by one of the most ancient of all references to him, in Otranto cathedral, where he appears riding on a goat and wielding, in the words of Tiller, "the unmistakable phallic club of the Sun-hero Hercules," and is encircled by the twelve signs of the zodiac.

We have therefore reached a stage where we can say with a fair degree of confidence that not a single element of the Arthurian tradition relates to an historical king of Dark Age Britain. Every motif, without exception, is primeval and pre-Roman; very often directly related to what we call megalithic culture, yet equally well related to the myth of a god named Hercules by the Greeks and Romans. Thus we have the following:

Arthur – Artos/Hercules. A god of civilisation who battles to establish order and is the victor in a great conflict with the giants.

Merlin – Lugos/Mercury. A god of arcane mystical knowledge, a wand-carrying emissary between the gods and mankind.

Morgan le Fay – Morrigan. A goddess of death and the Underworld.

Camelot – Camulodunum. Capital and major religious centre of pre-Roman Britain.

---

26 Ibid. p.132

Round Table – Stonehenge. A temple of the Early Bronze Age apparently dedicated to Lugos/Artos/Hercules.

Holy Grail – The cauldron of Wisdom and Life, taken by Lugos/Hercules from Hades.

Avalon – The Garden of the Hesperides/Tir na nOg, the Otherworld which lay beyond the western Ocean.

The above list, we must emphasize, merely scratches the surface; it could be increased almost as much as we wish, simply by adding as many Arthurian characters and elements as exist.

Yet one or two puzzles remain. If Hercules was the god worshipped in the prehistoric round temples, how is it that Hecataeus describes Stonehenge as a temple of Apollo: And how is it that Irish tradition, as well as British, seems to imply that the stone circles were temples of the god Balor/Beli (the Irish name for a stone circle we remember was actually 'beltany')? Was it not Lugos' incarnation as the Bear, Artos, rather than Belinos, that we identified as the Celtic equivalent of Hercules?

The Apple-God

Robert Graves makes it very plain that the deity known to the Greeks as Herakles (Hercules) was actually a composite figure containing characteristics and attributes normally associated with other gods. Thus Hercules is the greatest of all warriors, and is linked to Ares/Mars, the war-god. He is the slayer of dragons and monsters, which links him to Zeus: he is a patron of wisdom and learning, which implies an association with Apollo; he is a god of fertility, which in turn offers a parallel with Hermes/Mercury.

We encounter precisely the same thing in the belief-system of the Celts. In this way, for example, Ogmios, who with his club and lion-skin is perhaps in some ways closest to the Greek Hercules, is nevertheless portrayed as an old man and honoured as a patron of wisdom and letters. This implies that the Celtic Hercules incorporated many of the characteristics normally associated by the Greeks with Apollo: And this

The mosaic of Arthur riding on a goat and holding the club of Hercules
from Otranto Cathedral.

impression is strengthened when we consider that the Irish version of Ogmios, Ogma, was titled 'Sun-Face'.[27] The Greek Hercules was also linked to the sun-god. "The mythographers record that he [Hercules] borrowed the golden cup of the Sun, shaped like a water lily or lotus, for the homeward journey from one of his Labours. This was the cup in which the Sun, after sinking in the West, nightly floated round again to the East along the world-girdling Ocean stream."[28] So close indeed became his link with the sun that "'Hercules' in Classical Greece became in fact another name for the Sun."[29]

The link between Arthur's Holy Grail, ie. the cauldron of wisdom taken from the land of the dead, and the golden cup of the sun borrowed by Hercules should not of course be ignored. Nor should the fact that the golden cup offers a precise parallel with the glass vessel *caer wydr*, employed by Arthur in his journey through the waters of the Underworld to Annwn/Avalon.

But the parallels between Hercules, in his Celtic and Greek forms, with the sun-god Apollo, go far beyond one or two points. They are in fact detailed and far-reaching.

Like Hercules, Apollo was armed with a bow, and like Hercules, he is credited with slaying various serpent-monsters. However, the most important link comes in the association of both gods with the sacred apple. Hercules, we remember, was known to the Greeks as *Melon* 'of apples', a name applied to him in virtue of his Eleventh Labour, fetching the Golden Apples from the Garden of the Hesperides. Now this sacred apple-tree was identical to the biblical Tree of Life and there is a strong suggestion that the dragon Ladon, which guarded the tree, was one and the same as Apollo's mother Latona. Indeed it may well be that Apollo, whose symbol was the apple, derived his name from the Celtic word for 'apple' (Old Irish *abal*); whilst the mystical land of Avalon, the Otherworld, was the land of apples. We recall here that as early as 300 BC. Hecataeus had specifically linked Latona with Hyperborea/Britain. Why the island of Britain should be so closely linked to the Tree of Life, or World Tree, is a question we shall return to presently.

So, if the Greeks had the identities of Hercules and Apollo so

---

27 R. Graves loc cit. p.133
28 Ibid.
29 Ibid. p.134

thoroughly confused, we should not be surprised to find the Celts doing much the same thing with their gods; and in fact it would appear that Beli, or Belinos, normally identified as the Celtic equivalent of Apollo, appears to be virtually identical in many respects to Ogmios. Indeed, I would venture to suggest that Ogmios is simply an honourary title of Belinos, probably meaning something like 'youthful hero'. According to Graves, "in Britain, Amathaon was Hercules as Dionysus; his father Beli was Hercules as Apollo."[30] But Graves states quite emphatically that "All the available evidence points to Stonehenge as Beli's seat."[31] Since Ogmios is a title of Beli, it is clear that our linking Stonehenge to Hercules/Arthur is not mistaken.

But this British Hercules was not just another member of a polytheistic pantheon. Julius Caesar noted that in his time the Celts of Gaul had already evolved the concept of a Supreme Being, a divine intelligence behind all creation whose identity was nevertheless manifested in various deities, who in fact reveal different aspects of the Supreme Being's personality.[32] Such a concept is of course very close to pantheism, a system of belief often associated with the concept of reincarnation, and hinted at in Irish and Welsh poetry. This system finds its best-known modern expression in the religious philosophy of India, where the concept of reincarnating avatars of the Supreme Being is of central importance. We have seen how Lugos, the divine source of all knowledge and wisdom, reincarnated himself in the form of Cuchulainn, and therefore almost certainly also in the form of Arthur. According to Caesar, the name of the Gallic Supreme Being was *Dis Pater* ("Father of the night").

A great part of Robert Graves' *White Goddess* is concerned with proving that much of medieval Welsh and Irish literature had as its theme the hidden name of the Supreme God worshipped by the Druids. This supreme god was the High King of Heaven, the protector of the island, in whose honour Stonehenge was raised.

---

30 Ibid. p.58

31 Ibid. The name Beli/Belinos has of course long been connected with the Phoenician Baal. The present writer supports this view, and the Phoenician connection is examined in some detail in Chapter 4.

32 Caesar *Gallic Wars* i,1

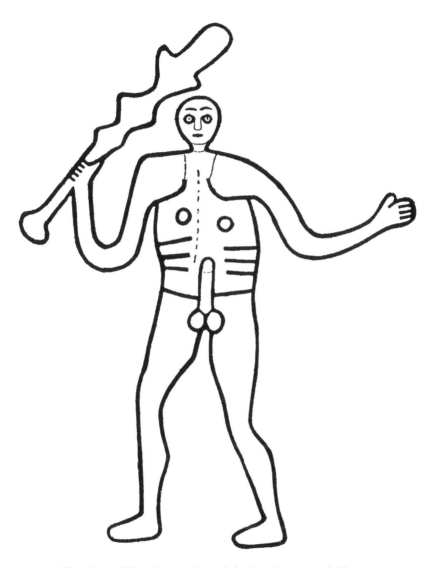

The Cerne Abbas Giant, whose club shaped very much like an
oak-leaf and erect phallus (symbol of potency) identify him as
Artos / Hercules, the tutelary deity of Britain.

Hercules on coin of Cunobelinos.

Glastonbury

Robert Graves makes it very clear that in the years during which the Christian religion spread throughout the Roman Empire, the mantle of the god Hercules was placed upon Jesus of Nazareth. It may very well be that the ease with which Greeks and Romans could identify the figure of Jesus with Hercules was a major factor in facilitating the acceptance of the new creed throughout the Mediterranean world.

The parallels between Hercules and Jesus were rather obvious, and, it should be stated, almost certainly not just coincidental. Both Hercules and Christ were the products of virgin births, semi-divine beings destined to be world-saviours. Thus Zeus begat Hercules with a view to creating a hero capable of saving both gods and men from destruction.[33] The name Jesus of course means "saviour". Both Hercules and Christ were enemies of the serpent-deity. We are told how Hercules strangled two snakes sent to destroy him in his cradle.[34] Both were linked to the number twelve. The Greek Hercules performed twelve labours, whilst the Hercules of the western Mediterranean had twelve followers or merry men.[35] Jesus of course had twelve apostles. The deaths of both were similar. Some versions of the Hercules myth had the hero crucified upon a sacred tree. Graves points out that crucifixion was in origin a form of human sacrifice,[36] and we must not forget here that Arthur's Irish alter-ego Cuchulainn dies after voluntarily tying himself to a post (Odin, a related character of Scandinavian myth does the same thing upon the World Tree Yggdrasil). In becoming a victim of human sacrifice Hercules abolishes this very custom, whilst Christ abolishes once and for all the entire custom of blood sacrifice. Both Hercules and Christ entered Hades, the realm of the dead, and returned from it. Both ascended bodily to heaven.

We have of course already identified Hercules with Arthur, so we should not be surprised to find him also, at a later stage, being identified with Christ. That this identification did occur is obvious enough from the

---

33 Hesiod *Shield of Heracles* 4ff.

34 Apollodorus ii,4,8

35 R. Graves loc. cit. p.124

36 Ibid. In Norse mythology Odin (very much a Hercules figure) hangs himself upon the World Tree Yggdrasil, with the intention of visiting the Underworld and gaining the wisdom that only such a visit could confer.

Hercules journeys through the waters of the Underworld in the Golden Bowl of the Sun. This is the precise equilavent of the Glass Vessel used by Arthur in his voyage to the Underworld.

well-known elements of the Arthurian myth. Thus the Grail, originally the cauldron of wisdom, becomes the cup used by Jesus at the Last Supper. In the medieval legend the Grail is "said to have been brought to Britain by Joseph of Arimathea, who collected the blood of Christ in the vessel and conveyed it to the West, or gave it to one Bron or Brons to convey thither."[37] The writer of these words immediately adds "Brons, it is clear, is merely Bran the Blessed of Welsh literature." But Bran was an early Celtic god, a god whose cult, as we have seen, was closely connected with that of Arthur.

Strikingly, just as Christ, having ascended to heaven like Hercules, to sit at the right hand of his father, will return to save mankind in its darkest hour, so Arthur, in the Isle of the Blessed, awaits the call of his people in their hour of need.

Perhaps the most holy place in Britain is Glastonbury, the destination, incidentally, of Joseph of Arimathea. The sacred thorn tree at Glastonbury was popularly believed to have sprouted from Joseph's staff. Another legend said that the boy Jesus had actually accompanied Joseph to Britain, and that he had constructed a small wooden building at the site, the latter destined to become the first church in the country. It was this story that inspired William Blake to write his great poem 'Jerusalem'.

But if Glastonbury is inseparably linked to Jesus it is equally powerfully linked to Arthur. In the poem "The Spoils of Annwn" Arthur enters Hades in a vessel of glass, named Caer Wydr. This is on one level a Welsh version of Charon's boat which ferried the dead across the Styx, or, more likely, of the golden bowl of the sun employed by Hercules to journey across the waters of the underworld. That Arthur's entry into the underworld in the glass vessel was believed to have taken place at Glastonbury is confirmed both by tradition and by the name of the town (Welsh *Ynis Gutrin* ie. "Isle of Glass"); a name applied to the locality at least as early as the seventh century. The village was associated with Arthur and his heroes in many a medieval and Welsh treatise, and was said to be the site of the legendary isle of Avalon, a tradition which inspired the monks of the Abbey to claim that an ancient skeleton found there was Arthur himself. Its close proximity to Stonehenge and Avebury leaves little doubt that Glastonbury must have been a religious centre of the highest importance in Druid times; almost

---

37 Lewis Spence loc. cit. p.138

certainly a centre devoted to the Cult of the Dead.[38]

The ancient importance of Glastonbury has been further confirmed by the discovery that the site was originally encircled by a vast system of landscape gardening that represented the twelve signs of the zodiac (Hercules' Labours),[39] and there is an abundance of other evidence suggesting the area's religious significance during the megalithic-Early Bronze Age.

Why, it might be asked, should a grassy island in what was anciently a tidal inlet, dominated by a steep conical hill, be called Glass Island? The answer may well have been supplied by Michael Senior, who notes that in the Irish burial mounds,

> "... particularly at New Grange, one can see that the huge tomb was, originally, covered over with lumps of white quartz. These, perhaps with the chipped faces set on the outside to reveal the sparkle of their crystals, must have glittered like the substance to which the name glass was given. Around the edges of the similar but small mounds of the burial chambers in Wales large numbers of white quartz pebbles have been found; and it seems perverse of archaeology to attribute to the quartz of these mounds some sort of ritual significance, rather than to conclude that they were intended to decorate the tomb's outer face. If I am right, the Glass Castle was a good description for the place you went when you died. And Glass Island would well describe a collection of such sites."[40]

It should be noted here that, in the tradition popular throughout Britain, it is within a cave underneath a hill that Arthur sleeps – by all accounts a very good description of a megalithic Passage Grave.

The entire myth and cult of Glastonbury thus provides powerful additional support, if any was needed, for the belief that the Arthurian

---

38 In the words of Comyns Beaumont, "Avalon lay at the very heart of the Underworld cult, the 'Blessed Isle', the actual and original Paradise ... These ancient legends are in no sense related to the Arthur who lived in the sixth century AD." The *Riddle of Prehistoric Britain* (1946) p.153

39 See eg. Brian Stone *Sir Gawain and the Green Knight* (Penguin, 1974) p.153 The various zodiacal animal symbols at Glastonbury have also been suggested as the source of the Arthurian legend of the Questing Beast.

40 Michael Senior *Myths of Britain* (London, 1979) p.180

legend is the native British version of the Hercules legend, and that the traditions and motifs linking the Arthurian myth with Christ and Christianity in fact merely emphasise the antiquity of the myth. Above all, it was the confused identification of Arthur with Christ that led medieval writers, beginning with Nennius, to place him in the Christian era. We recall that Nennius again and again emphasises Arthur's Christian identity, as if vaguely aware that he was speaking of some divine or semi-divine being. If we are correct, he was just that: The Celtic Hercules, the divine prototype upon whom most of the Christ idea was based.

CHAPTER 4

Greeks and Celts

The Myth of Perseus

We have stated that many of the Greek myths were derived directly from the peoples of northern and western Europe, particularly the Celts, or were at least heavily influenced by them. This is particularly so with regard to a series of hero-deities who were dragon-slayers with certain affinities with the Solar God. Of all the Greek myths with a Celtic element, the story of Perseus displays by far the clearest parallels with Celtic tradition. The Greeks themselves were very clear that the major action in this tale, the death of the Gorgon Medusa, took place in an island in the western Ocean, and many of them specifically identified Britain as the location. Thus for example in his *Tenth Pythian Ode* the Greek writer Pindar links Perseus with the land of the Hyperboreans:

> "Neither by ships nor by land can you find the wonderful road of the trysting-place of the Hyperboreans. Yet in times past, Perseus the leader of his people partook of their banquet when he entered their homes and found them sacrificing glorious hecatombs of asses in honour of the God. In the banquets and hymns of that people Apollo chiefly rejoices and laughs as he looks upon the brute beasts in their romping lewdness. Yet such are their ways that the Muse is not banished, but on every side the dances of the girls, the twanging of lyres and the sound of flutes are continually circling, and with their hair crowned with golden bay-leaves they make merry ... yet avoid divine jealousy by living aloof from labour and war. To that home of happy folk, then, went Danae's son [Perseus] of old,

breathing courage, with Athena as his guide. And he slew the Gorgon and returned with her head."[1]

The actual story of Perseus is of the greatest interest. In many respects he is the archetypal dragon-slaying hero, even to the extent of rescuing the damsel in distress (Andromeda) from the sea serpent. As such, we can scarcely doubt that Perseus is closely related to Hercules, and indeed the Greeks identified him as the grandfather of the latter. But his story finds its closest parallel in that of Lugh, the Celtic Hermes.

It was prophesied that Acrisius, the king of Argos, would have a grandson who would slay him. Having only one child by whom the prophecy could be fulfilled, his daughter Danae, the king determined that she should never have the chance to conceive by imprisoning her in a dungeon beneath the ground. Yet Zeus came to the girl as a shower of gold, and she shortly gave birth to a baby boy, Perseus. Acrisius had the girl and her child sealed in a chest, which he cast into the sea.[2] But the chest was washed ashore on the island of Seriphos, and the two were taken in by king Polydectes. Perseus grew to be a handsome prince and a powerful warrior. The champions of the land were asked by king Polydectes to bring him one of their best horses each, as a dowry-gift for his intended bride Hippodameia. Perseus had no horses, but volunteered instead to bring back the head of the Gorgon Medusa. To achieve this Perseus was given a magical sickle, or sword, by Hermes, and a brightly-polished shield by Athena. The goddess further advised the hero to seek out the land of the Stygian nymphs, where he would obtain winged sandals, a wallet for the head of the Gorgon, and a magical helmet of invisibility. Having secured these treasures, Perseus flew to the wind and rain-swept island of the Hyperboreans wherein the Gorgons dwelt.[3] The hero entered the domain of the three fearsome sisters whilst they slept. Anyone looking straight at Medusa was turned to stone, and to avoid this fate Perseus guided himself by gazing at her reflection in his shield. Then with the sword given to him by Hermes he decapitated the hideous monster. He performed numerous

---

1 Pindar *Pythian Odes* x,50-55 Gerald Hawkins (*Stonehenge Decoded* (1965) p.86) is one of numerous writers who think that the "wondrous road to the trysting place of the Hyperboreans" may well be another classical reference to Stonehenge or Avebury, or both.
2 Pausanias ii,25,7; Strabo viii,6,11
3 Ovid *Metamorphoses* iv,780; Apollodorus ii,4,3

other feats of heroism on his way home, most notably rescuing the maiden Andromeda at Joppa on the Palestinian coast. The prophecy that he would slay his grandfather was eventually fulfilled when he accidentally hit the old man with a discus during an athletics contest.

The story of Perseus is precisely paralleled by that of Lugh (Lugos), a character whom we have already identified as one of the most important of the Celtic gods. Lugh appears in Welsh legend as Lleu, but it is only Irish tradition that has preserved his story in its original form. We are told that Balor, the hideous king of the Fomorian giants, was told by a Druid that his grandson would slay him, whereupon he imprisoned his only child, his daughter Eithne, in a crystal tower on an island off the north coast of Ireland. The girl was guarded by a group of women, with instructions never to let her set eyes upon a man, or even to know of their existence. Yet one day a hero named Cian succeeded in reaching the girl, and shortly afterwards she gave birth to a boy, whom she named Lugh. Infuriated by this discovery, Balor ordered that the girl and her child be concealed in a chest and cast into the sea. But mother and child were rescued, and the boy grew to be a great hero. He was admitted to the company of the children of Danu (we recall at this point that Perseus was a son of the goddess Danae) by showing he could perform any task or skill with as much dexterity as the best craftsman in the land, and later joined the Tuatha in their great battle against the Fomorians, who were of course led by Balor. It was said that Balor could kill anyone who looked upon his hideous evil eye, and Lugh slew him by running his shining spear through the eye.[4] Other versions of the story say that Lugh decapitated Balor with a magical sword of light, and that some of Balor's toxic blood fell upon the Poisoned Glen, in the Derryveigh hills in Donegal, rendering it barren.

To say that the stories of Perseus and Lugh display certain similarities would be understatement. They are in most respects identical. Who then copied who? The answer is clear. The Greeks themselves placed the action in the far west, on the Atlantic seaboard; the home of the Gorgons was a wind-swept island just off the land of the Hyperboreans. On his way to their island home, Perseus we are told had to pass through a countryside littered with the figures of men and beasts who had been turned to stone

---

4 *Larousse World Mythology* "Celtic Lands: Myth in History" p.352 The British story of Culhwch and Olwen parallels that of Lugh. The giant Ysbaddaden is fated to die if his daughter marries Olwen; and it is through the efforts of Arthur that the marriage takes place.

by Medusa.[5] These "stone" men, it is universally agreed, sound like an imaginative description of the vast numbers of megalithic standing-stones that still cover the whole of north-western Europe, but which were even more in evidence in antiquity. It begins to look fairly evident that it must have been the Greeks who got the story from the Celts, almost certainly the British Celts.

Yet we have already identified Lugos with the Greek Hermes, whom we have also shown to be the prototype Merlin. How is he then also to be linked with Perseus? This does not present as great a difficulty as may be imagined. The parallels between classical and Celtic mythologies are, as we have already stressed, not precise but approximate. Thus not every detail of the Lugos myth can be expected to match that of Hermes. Lugos, it is evident, is more accurately seen as a combination of Hermes and Perseus. Yet even the Greeks viewed the latter two as closely linked; for the magical weapons with which Perseus destroyed Medusa were given to him by Hermes; and indeed the Classical portrayals of Perseus, which show him flying through the air on his winged sandals, present the image of a character strikingly similar to that of Hermes himself.

Here then is yet more detailed evidence of close contact between Greece and Britain at an extremely early date, evidence which also supplies, as we shall see, an interesting link with the Arthurian tale.

Medusa, Bran and the Terrible Dragon Head

There are numerous connections between the myth of Lugh and Balor and the Arthurian legend. To begin with, the magical sword of light with which Lugh (the name Lugos, apparently related to Latin *lux*, implies "Light") decapitated Balor (and with which Perseus decapitated the Gorgon) is almost certainly one and the same as Excalibur, the magical sword of Arthur – who incidentally also employs his sword for the destruction of monsters. The word Excalibur first appears in the medieval balladeer Wace, and is an adaptation of Geoffrey of Monmouth's Caliburn. In the "Tale of Culhwch and Olwen" Arthur's sword is called *Caledfwlch*, which is evidently related to the Old Irish *Caladbolg*, the "flashing sword" carried by Fergus MacRoth,

---

5 See eg. Ovid *Metamorphoses* iv,780-88

Male Medusa on gold coin of Tincommius.

Medusa Head from temple of Sulis-Minerva, Bath.

the friend and companion of Cuchulainn.[6] If Lugh, as we have suggested, is the same as Merlin, then the connection becomes even more poignant: For it was the sorcery of Merlin that delivered Excalibur to Arthur.

The whole concept of the magical sword has an extremely ancient pedigree. In various Near Eastern and Mediterranean mythologies the god of war is depicted with an enchanted sword. "The Roman god Mars was pictured with a sword ... The Chaldaean god Nergal is called 'Sword-god'."[7] The Scythians, like the Celts and the Romans honoured the war-god. Solinus informs us, "The god of this people is Mars; instead of images they worship swords."[8] Herodotus claimed that the Scythians worshipped Ares (Mars), and that an iron sword served as an image of him.[9]

Robert Graves held that pulling a sacred sword from a stone was part of a Near Eastern coronation ritual of the Bronze Age, and there is certainly evidence that it formed an essential element of Hittite ritual.[10] The British tradition of the Sword in the Stone also dates from the Bronze Age, as we shall see, and as a myth it is directly related to the origins of Bronze Age civilisation. It is thus one of the most antique of human legends, and of an age equal to the oldest of Greek myths. Malory claimed that the Sword in the Stone had appeared in the churchyard of "the greatest church in London,"[11] a circumstance which further links the Arthurian myth to that of Lugos/Perseus. We know that the sacred bird of the god Lugh/Lugos was the raven, and London was also the site of a legend linked to that bird. The god Bran, whose name means raven, asked that his head be buried in Tower Hill in London, where it would act as a charm to protect the kingdom. From that time onwards a group of ravens roosted at the site, and are there to this day. But the crow of course was also a symbol of Arthur, and, according to Lewis Spence no Englishman in olden times would kill a crow lest it held the hero's spirit.[12] It was said that Arthur

---

6 Graham Phillips and Martin Keatman *King Arthur: The True Story* (London,1992) p.39

7 I. Velikovsky *Worlds in Collision* (1950) p.252

8 Solinus *Polyhistor* Ch.xxiii

9 Herodotus iv, 62

10 R. Graves *The Greek Myths* Vol.1 (1955) p.327 "The drawing of a sword from a rock seems to have formed part of the Bronze Age coronation ritual." Joseph Campbell (*The Masks of God: Occidental Mythology*) linked the sword in the stone to the almost magical ability of the Bronze Age smiths to turn stone into metal swords.

11 Graham Phillips and Martin Keatman loc. cit. p.40

12 Lewis Spence *The Mysteries of Britain* (1994 ed.) p.128

actually dug up the magical head, and so he is specifically linked to the myth. Yet the story of Bran's head also offers striking parallels with that of Perseus, who uses the head of the Gorgon as a protective weapon in precisely the same way as Bran's head is used.

More than one commentator has suggested a link between the Irish Balor and the British Bran. But if Bran is indeed to be identified with Balor/Medusa, we might expect him to figure prominently in the mythology and iconography of Roman and pre-Roman Britain. Is this the case?

As a matter of fact, the cult of the Gorgon, or the Medusa-head, or simply the sacred head, is one of the most important characteristics of British (indeed Celtic) religious belief. So entrenched was this icon in the British psyche that it survived well into the Middle Ages; and to this day countless old churches all over the country display strategically-placed defensive severed heads. J.M.C. Toynbee, whose encyclopaedic *Art in Britain Under the Romans* (Oxford,1964) provides an exhaustive overview of religious iconography in the early Roman epoch, remarks on the fact that Medusa pendants were common personal adornments in Roman Britain, worn to ward off evil from the wearer.[13] This of course is entirely in accordance with Graeco-Roman belief, where Perseus used the head of Medusa as a weapon against various opponents. Yet the Medusa head of Britain had an outstanding characteristic that differentiated it from that of Greece and Rome; it was male. In the words of Toynbee, "we seem to have a British male Medusa."[14] Icons of the male Gorgon are found throughout Britain, though perhaps the most famous example is the impressive carved head from the temple of Sulis Minerva in Bath.

Yet this very British Gorgon predated the arrival of the Romans, for his head is found on a gold coin of the native king Tincommius (20 BC.-5 AD.)[15]

The male Gorgon portrayed on these monuments and artefacts is unfortunately never named, and is identified solely from his appearance – typically with coiled serpents and wings sprouting from the head. Yet it is virtually certain that he is one and the same as Bran. In particular, we should certainly be justified in seeing the wings sprouting from the skull as the mark of Bran, the raven. The Graeco-Roman Gorgon is never

13 J.M.C. Toynbee *Art in Britain Under the Romans* (Oxford,1964) p.367
14 Ibid. p.431
15 Ibid. p.32

portrayed in such a way.

But if the antiquity of the Bran legend, and its connection with the Gorgon myth of Greece is now beyond question, we are simultaneously presented with yet more proof of the antiquity of the Arthurian tradition. We have seen how Arthur is mythically connected to Bran/Balor in a variety of ways. He it was, in the guise of Bron, who brought the Holy Grail to Britain, whilst Bran's whole legend, which tells how he was decapitated and thus became the protective emblem of the kingdom, is little more than a precursor to the tale of how Arthur in his turn became the nation's protector. We have seen how G. Roth and P.M. Duval identified Bran, or *Uther Ben* ("Terrible Head") with Arthur's father Uther Pendragon ("Terrible Dragon Head").[16] Knowing, as we now do, that Bran's head was identical to that of the Gorgon, whose hair was composed of writhing, coiling serpents, the term dragon-head becomes all the more comprehensible.

If Arthur is therefore actually the son of Bran/Balor, his removal of the protective head makes perfect sense. As the rightful heir to the throne, and son of the now dead Bran/Uther Pendragon, Arthur (in digging up the sacred head) simply assumes his kingly responsibility.

Thus in numerous ways the Arthurian legend is shown to be linked to that of Bran, whose own identification with the Gorgon Medusa takes us back into the remotest antiquity.

---

16 G.Roth and P.M. Duval in *Larousse World Mythology* (1965) p.351 There is some evidence to suggest that the Britons themselves regarded the Orkneys as the home of Bran/Medusa. These islands (Orcades) were apparently earlier known as Phorcydes, or Gorgades. Statius Sebosus, a Roman writer of the first century BC. stated that it took 40 days to sail from the isles of Gorgades, or Gorgons, to the Hesperides. Comyns Beaumont also felt the islands were linked to the Gorgons, "for their begetter was Phorcys – the same as Orcus, the first name of an underworld deity – one of the Titans, who was in addition parent of the dragon Ladon, fiery guardian of the Apples of the Hesperides." Beaumont *The Riddle of Prehistoric Britain* (1946) p.111 In view of this statement of Beaumont it is intriguing to find a hint in the Arthurian legend suggesting the Orkneys as the home of the dragon Lotan/Latona. In these stories the islands were the domain of king Lot (who gave his name to the Lothian region). This latter character, who appears in Welsh tradition as Lud/Lludd, and is there associated with the dragon-myth, was slain in battle against Arthur; and we have here a clear parallel with Hercules' defeat of the dragon Ladon during his quest for the apples of the Hesperides.

Links Across a Continent

For centuries scholars accepted as given fact that close contacts had existed between the early inhabitants of Britain and the ancient peoples of the Near East, particularly the Greeks. From the beginning of the present century archaeological discoveries appeared to be providing strong support for such ideas, though the tendency over the past forty years has been to move in the opposite direction, and to play down what is now viewed as a far too reckless cultural diffusionism.

Nevertheless, evidence of primeval contacts between Atlantic Europe and Greece has always been abundant, and throughout the past century the debate has been rekindled, sometimes to the annoyance of the academic establishment, by more than one writer. In his *White Goddess* for example Robert Graves identified literally hundreds of detailed parallels between Greek and Celtic mythology, and made it very plain that he saw most of these as the result of close contact between the Aegean and Celtic worlds at a very early date. Whilst not all the claims made by Graves and others of his school can be regarded as proved, they nevertheless tend to highlight many intriguing facts and anomalies that are now either ignored or glossed over by mainstream scholarship. Indeed many of the parallels are so specific that even sceptics have been forced to concede some form of mutual influence. In this way Michael Senior for example has remarked on the striking similarities between various British and Greek legends: one example of which he quotes being that of Tristan and Hippolytus;

"An example of ... correspondence occurs in a striking form in the case of Tristan, whose situation and career bear remarkable similarities to those of the Greek hero Hippolytus. They both had stepmothers who tried to kill them. They both liked hunting. Hippolytus fell in love with his stepmother, and Tristan with his uncle's wife, or, if Mark was originally his father, with his stepmother. Both heroes then become the object of attempted destruction by the wronged husband. They both, in the end, die near the sea. Certainly the connection with horses, emphasized by the names Hippolytus and March [King Mark] and by the hunting habit of the heroes, and the association of horses with the sea (epitomized by the horse- and sea-god Poseidon) seem to indicate that both myths refer to the memory of a horse cult."[17]

Ancient writers spoke of the links between Greeks and Celts at some length, and insisted that many of the adventures of Greek heroes and demigods took place in or around Britain. We have already seen this with regard to the various myths relating to Hercules and Perseus, yet such was the importance of Britain, the island of the Hyperboreans, in the national psyche of the Hellenes, that many other heroes and gods were linked to the same place. Indeed there is evidence to suggest that amongst the Mediterranean peoples Britain was viewed with awe, a land of enchantment, and the gateway to Hades itself. In the words of A.W. Whatmore,

"It is clear that in very primitive age the cultured nations of the Mediterranean regarded our island with peculiar reverence and fear. The entrance to Hades lay in these seas, and here apparently Charon ferried the departed souls across the River of Death. The curious basaltic columns of Ulster and the Western Isles, and the awe-inspiring portals of Fingal's Cave, probably had something to do with these extraordinary notions, but it is certain that such stories were common gossip in the time of Homer, and that they were sufficiently credited after the Christian era to daunt the well-trained soldiers of Agricola."[18]

More than one writer has suggested that Fingal's Cave, on the island of Staffa, was the inspiration for the Scylla and Charybdis episode in the *Odyssey*, whilst the mystical island of the seafaring Phaecians, to whom generosity is a sacred duty, has often been identified as Britain. But it was with the Perseus legend in particular that Britain was above all connected. We have already suggested that the decapitated head of Bran, which protected the island, was the source of the Gorgon story. Yet further proof of this comes from the Greek writer Plutarch (1st century AD.), who records very definitely the idea that Britain was the location of much of the action recounted in Hellenic mythology:

---

17 Michael Senior *Myths of Britain* (London, 1979) p.170 The connection between Hippolytus and Tristan and Poseidon, the god of earthquakes and tidal waves, is significant, as we shall see at a later stage.
18 Cited from Beaumont loc. cit. p.135

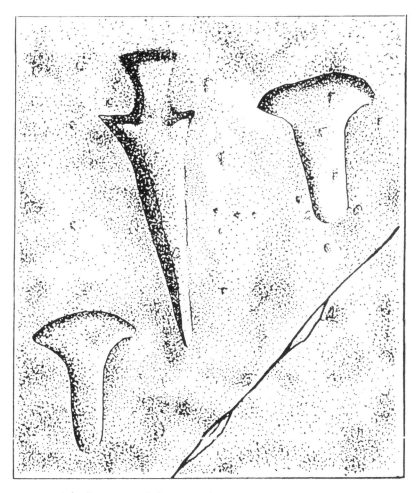

The "Mycenaean" dagger, with two Early Bronze axeheads,
at Stonehenge (after Atkinson, 1978).

"A little time before Callistratus celebrated the Pythian games, two holy men from the opposite parts of the habitable earth came to us at Delphi – Demetrius the grammarian from Britain returning home to Tarsus, and Cleombrotus the Lacedaemonian. But Demetrius said that there are many desert islands scattered around Britain, some of which have the name of being islands of genii and heroes; that he had been sent by the emperor, for the sake of describing and viewing them, to that which lay nearest to the desert isles, and which had but few inhabitants; all of whom were esteemed by the Britons sacred and inviolable. Very soon after his arrival there was great turbulence in the air, and many portentous storms; the winds became tempestuous, and fiery whirlwinds rushed forth. When these ceased, the islanders said that the departure of some one of the superior genii had taken place. For as a light when burning, say they, has nothing disagreeable, but when extinguished is offensive to many; so likewise lofty spirits afford an illumination benignant and mild, but their extinction and destruction, frequently, as at the present moment excite winds and storms, and often infect the atmosphere with pestilential evils. Moreover, that there was one island there wherein Saturn was confined by Briareus in sleep; for that sleep had been devised for his bonds; and that around him were many genii as his companions and attendants."[19]

It is of interest to note here that in Plutarch's original Greek the sleeping god, here given the Latin name of Saturn, is none other than Cronos (known to the Greeks as the "Horned One", very much like his apparent Celtic counterpart, Cernunnos), a titan-deity identified both by Greeks and Celts as Lord of the Underworld. Strangely enough, it seems that we may be able to identify Plutarch's sleeping titan, as well as the island in which he was said to be imprisoned, in medieval Welsh tradition. Gwydion, whom we have already suggested as an alter-ego Cernunnos, is said to have been imprisoned in Annwn, the Welsh Hades, which was always portrayed as an island lying to the west. Yet a very particular place, Lundy Island, off the coast of Devon, was identified as the resting-place of Gwydion; For which reason it is still known in Welsh as Ynis Wair, the Isle of Gwair (Gwair being a recognised variant of Gwydion). Could it be that

---

19 Plutarch *Why Oracles are Silent* v

The Rillaton Cup, a Mycenaean Greek import, discovered in a Wessex grave.

Demetrius of Tarsus, whom Plutarch quotes, was directed to Lundy Island as the resting place of Cronos/Cernunnos? But Myrddin too, or as he would then have been known, Lugos or Boras, was also reputed to be imprisoned on an island, Bardsey, situated just off the north coast of Wales. So it could have been to here that the Britons directed Demetrius.

But if the Mediterranean peoples in general viewed Britain as a land of mystery inhabited by genii and the denizens of the Underworld, some were better informed. Indeed it is apparent that Greek travellers were so familiar with Britain from at least the sixth century BC. that friendly relations were established with individual states, particularly Athens and Delos. After his initial description of the Hyperboreans' island, Hecataeus refers to these links:

> "The Hyperboreans use a peculiar dialect, and have a remarkable attachment to the Greeks, especially to the Athenians and the Delians, deducing their friendship from remote periods. It is related that some Greeks formerly visited the Hyperboreans, with whom they left consecrated gifts of great value, and also that in ancient times Abaris, coming from the Hyperboreans into Greece, renewed their family intercourse with the Delians."[20]

Another tradition states that this Abaris instructed Pythagoras in philosophy,[21] a tradition which calls to mind the astonishing mathematical ability of the builders of Stonehenge, as well as the Druid teaching on reincarnation – a teaching that was to become a central plank of Pythagoreanism.

British tradition too, although with less authority, also speaks of primeval links with Greece.

Until the 1960s the discoveries of archaeology appeared to be on the way towards providing definitive endorsement to the ancient traditions. Close links between Britain and the ancient Near East were attested, it seemed, by the simple fact that numerous artefacts of apparently eastern Mediterranean origin had been discovered in Britain – particularly around the region of Stonehenge. It was Sir Arthur Evans, the excavator of Knossos, who first suggested the Mycenaean connection as a tool for dating

---

20 Diodorus Siculus ii,50
21 Ibid.

the British megaliths. By far the great majority of the most impressive of the seemingly Mycenaean and Middle Eastern artefacts were discovered in tombs of the Wessex culture, the culture responsible for raising Stonehenge. Thus for example Egyptian beads dating from the time of Akhnaton were discovered on Salisbury Plain,[22] whilst the famous Pelynt dagger and Rillaton cup, discovered in the same region, were almost certainly of Mycenaean manufacture: And the contact was two-way; gold earrings of Irish manufacture were discovered in an Egyptian tomb of Hyksos (contemporary with early Mycenaean) date.[23] One of the stones at Stonehenge has the image of what appears to be a Mycenaean dagger or short sword clearly engraved upon it. Could this be, it was asked, a symbol of the ancient links between Britain and Greece referred to by Hecataeus? In the words of Lord William Taylour;

"... echoes of their [Mycenaean Greek] influence reached as far as Britain. The Rillaton gold cup, if not a Mycenaean import, resembles the horizontally fluted cup from Shaft Grave IV [at Mycenae]. It need not of course have been brought in a Mycenaean ship. But the so-called Mycenaean dagger incised on one of the trilithons of Stonehenge is doubtful evidence. The hilt is unlike that of a Mycenaean dagger. There is perhaps some resemblance to the weapon engraved on one of the shaft grave stelae, which is certainly not a dagger and is probably a crude portrayal of the Type B sword ... a surer indication of trade relations between Britain and Mycenae is provided by the amber spacer-beads found at Mycenae, Kakovatos, and Pylos, all of the fifteenth century, and these could well have borne the trade-mark 'Made in England'. The Mycenaeans may even have prospected for tin in Cornwall, for, apart from the Rillaton cup, the fragment of a L.H.III sword (the 'Pelynt dagger') was found there in the tomb of a Wessex chieftain."[24]

In addition to these very concrete examples of contact between Britain

22 Stanley Thomas *Pre-Roman Britain* (London, 1965) p.25

23 Flinders Petrie *The Making of Egypt* (London,1939) p.150 In the words of Stanley Thomas "From the Mediterranean civilizations, most especially Mycenaean Greece, to Ireland, from Spain to Scandinavia, the trade routes carried not only metal goods and trinkets but also the secrets of metallurgical techniques and doubtless many other ideas." *Pre-Roman Britain* (London,1965) p.25

24 Lord William Taylour *The Mycenaeans* (London,1964) p.152

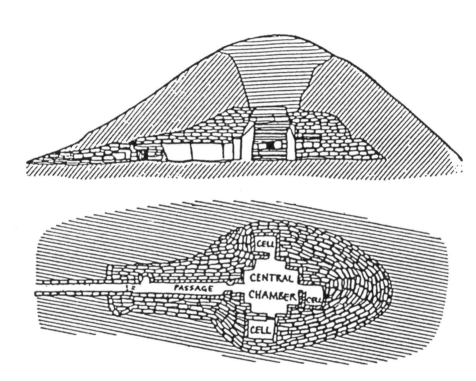

Plan of Maes Howe passage grave, Orkney.

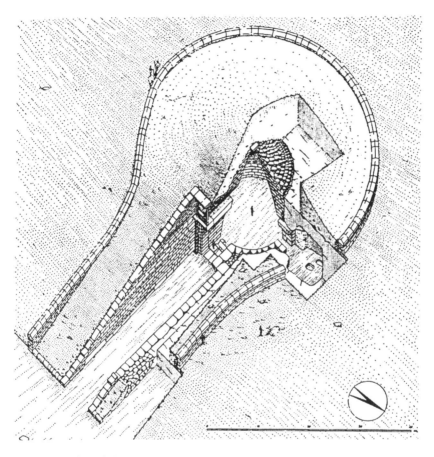

Isometric plan of the Treasury of Atreus, Mycenaean tholos tomb, showing clear parallels with megalithic passage graves of western Europe. (after Taylor)

and the Aegean, there was evidence, it seemed, of striking cultural parallels that could only be explained as a result of a certain degree of familiarity. The megalithic passage-graves of Britain and Ireland, for example, closely resemble the great tholos tombs of Mycenaean Greece. Both types of tomb have a central burial chamber approached by a long passageway, or *dromos*. The burial chamber itself is flanked, in both varieties of tomb, with two adjacent cells, one on either side. The ceilings of these monuments are corbelled. Corbelling was a technique by which a fairly large space could be roofed without the use of the arch proper or large lintels. Both megalithic passage graves and tholos tombs display fine examples of corbelling. Again, the artistic motifs employed by the megalith-builders, particularly in relation to the all-pervasive spiral-designs, strongly resemble those of Greece in the Mycenaean epoch.

Inspired by a statement of Homer that builders, along with poets, were welcomed by kings everywhere, British archaeologists began to consider the possibility that Stonehenge itself could have been designed by a wandering Achaean architect. R.J.C. Atkinson, as hard-headed an archaeologist as it is possible to find, wrote,

> "We have seen that through trade the necessary contacts with the Mediterranean had been established. The Stonehenge dagger too may be seen, if one wishes, to point more directly at Mycenae itself. We know from Homer that architects, like the poets of whom he himself was one, were homeless men, wandering from city to city. Is it then any more incredible that the architect of Stonehenge should himself have been a Mycenaean, than that the monument should have been designed and erected, with all its unique and sophisticated detail, by a mere barbarian?
>
> "Let us suppose for a moment that this is more than mere conjecture. Under what circumstances, then, could a man versed in the traditions and skills of Mediterranean architecture find himself working among barbarians in the far cold north? Only, surely, as the skilled servant of some far-voyaging Mycenaean prince, *fortis ante Agamemnona*; or at the behest of a barbarian British king, whose voice and gifts spoke loudly enough to be heard even in the cities of the Mediterranean …
>
> "I believe … that Stonehenge itself is evidence for the

concentration of political power, for a time at least, in the hands of a single man, who alone could create and maintain the conditions necessary for this great undertaking. Who he was, whether native-born or foreign, we shall never know; he remains a figure as shadowy and unsubstantial as King Brutus of the medieval British history. Yet who but he should sleep, like Arthur or Barbarossa, in the quiet darkness of a sarsen vault beneath the mountainous pile of Silbury Hill? And is not Stonehenge itself his memorial?"[25]

If only Atkinson could have realised how close he was to the truth!

Yet in spite of such statements by leading academics, by the end of the 1970s the Mycenaean connection was being written out of the textbooks; and the traditions of the ancients, which spoke of the close British-Hellenic links, were being decreed as having no basis in fact. Ironically, it was the advent of the supposedly most full-proof of dating methods, that of radiocarbon analysis, which undermined what until then had seemed the increasingly irrefutable proof of Greek influence. Astonishingly, radio-carbon data seemed to suggest that the Wessex culture was hundreds of years older than Mycenaean civilisation, with the result that over the past thirty years scholars have engaged in an embarrassed and futile search for alternative places of origin for the "Mycenaean" artefacts in the Wessex tombs.

Yet such measures are unnecessary. Radiocarbon dating, as we shall see, is probably the greatest red herring ever to enter the archaeological debate, and it needs to be entirely ignored in any attempts at chronological reconstruction. Using the Mycenaean artefacts, Evans down-dated the Wessex culture (and therefore Stonehenge III) to circa 1350 BC., which, although in our opinion still too early, was at least in the right direction. (Interestingly, the great Mycenaean monuments, conventionally dated from the 16th to 13th centuries, were believed for many years to be the work of a "pre-Greek" people – just as the contemporary megaliths of western Europe are now held to be the work of a "pre-Celtic" folk. But the builders of the Mycenaean structures were proved to be Greeks when in 1956 Michael Ventris deciphered their Linear B script. Is it too much to hope that some future discovery will put beyond question the Druid origin of the western megaliths?)

It should by now be apparent that I do not accept the conventional

25 R.J.C. Atkinson *Stonehenge* (Pelican Books, 1960) pp.165-67

chronology provided for Egyptian and Greek history, and an abundance of evidence clearly points to the 8th and 7th centuries BC. as the correct date for both the Mycenaean epoch of Greece and the Hyksos and 18th Dynasty epoch of Egypt (as well as the megalith-epoch of western Europe).[26] Now it was just around 800 BC. that some incredibly important events in the history of trade and technology occurred, events to be discussed more fully as we proceed.

The Hyperborean Cult

We have seen how Hecataeus of Abdera spoke of a strong link between the Athenians and Delians and the Hyperboreans. Herodotus, writing around a hundred and forty years earlier, also referred to this link, but added the detail that an actual cult dedicated to the Hyperboreans existed at Delos. The Delians, he says, told how certain "sacred things, wrapped in wheat-straw" had anciently been brought to Delos from the land of the Hyperboreans.[27]

Curiously, Herodotus seemed to imagine that the Hyperboreans were a nation of north-eastern Europe, contiguous to Scythia, and he tells how the sacred gifts of the Hyperboreans were conveyed southwards to Greece, by way of Thrace and Macedonia.[28] With these sacred objects, he says, came two virgins, named Hyperoche and Laodice, as well as five male attendants. All these died at Delos, where they were honoured in the temple of Artemis.[29]

As well as being a centre of the Hyperborean cult, Delos was also closely linked to the worship of Apollo, and the connections between the two are so strong as to make us wonder whether the latter deity was in fact a British/Hyperborean god. Hecataeus, we saw, claimed that Apollo's mother Latone had been born in the land of the Hyperboreans, for which reason he was worshipped there more than any other god: And it is worth

---

26 For the true chronology of these nations I refer the reader to Gunnar Heinsohn's *Die Sumerer gab es nicht* (1988) and *Wann lebten die Pharaonen?* (1990)

27 Herodotus iv, 23

28 Ibid.

29 Ibid. iv,34

reminding the reader here that the very name Apollo may be Celtic in origin, derived, thought Robert Graves, from the Celtic *abol*, "apple".[30] We recall also that the sacred apple-tree (identical to the Tree of Life in the Garden of Eden) of the Hesperides was guarded by the dragon Ladon – a name that sounds suspiciously similar to that of Apollo's mother Latona.

According to Robert Graves, there is evidence to suggest that a Hyperborean cult, linked to the worship of Apollo and Latona extended even to the east of Greece, into the coastal regions of Palestine/Phoenicia:

"Delos was the centre of this Hyperborean cult which, it seems, extended south-eastwards to Nabataea and Palestine, north-westward to Britain, and included Athens. Visits were constantly exchanged between the states united in this cult."[31]

Graves surmised a Palestinian connection from the fact that Latona was almost certainly in origin a Palestinian goddess known as Lat.[32] Yet the full name of the (actually Canaanite/Phoenician) goddess is Lotan (biblical Leviathan), the seven-headed dragon-serpent who dwelt with Yamm, the god of the ocean abyss. Thus there is scarcely any question that the dragon of Greek legend, Ladon, is identical to Apollo's mother Latona (born in Britain/Hyperborea, according to Hecataeus), who is also identical to the dragon of Phoenician legend, Lotan and, as I shall argue, to king Lot or Lludd of British legend. In the popularised Anglo-French legends Lot is named simply as King of Orkney; yet in his Welsh guise of Lud, or Lludd, he is indeed associated with dragons. The Mabinogion tale of "Lludd and Llefelys" informs us how in the days of Lludd Britain was beset by three plagues, the second of which was "a shriek that came on every May eve over every hearth in the island of Britain, and went through people's hearts and so scared them that the men lost their hue and their strength." Communicating the problem to his divine brother Llefelys, through the agency of a long bronze tube (down which insults were passed by a malevolent race of sorcerers named the Coranaid)), Lludd was informed that the scream was raised by a red dragon, because it was being attacked

---

30 R. Graves *The Greek Myths* Vol.1 p.57 "the word *Apollo* may be derived from the [Celtic] root *abol*, – 'apple', rather than from *apollunai*, 'destroy', which is the usual view."
31 Ibid. p.80
32 Ibid.

by a white dragon. Lludd was instructed to find the exact centre of Britain (the axis of the country), to dig there a pit, into which should be placed a vessel contained the best mead. The dragons would appear and fight in the air until exhausted, after which they would fall into the mead, which they would then drink. After this they would, naturally, fall asleep. As soon as Lludd was sure they were helpless, he was to place both of them in a stone coffin and bury it in the strongest place in Britain. All this was accomplished, and no more was heard of the shriek.

In its original pre-Christian version, Lludd/Lot would himself have been one of the battling dragons, and his brother Llefelys the other. Nor, we shall see, was the identification of Lot/Lludd with the northern regions, particularly Orkney, without significance. For that region was anciently regarded as the actual location of the World Tree, or Pillar, or Axis, round which the battling dragons entwined themselves. The ancient custom of dancing round the May Pole, where creeper-like decorations were entwined round the sacred tree, is evidently related to this legend: And a glance at any illustration of the May Pole should leave us in no doubt about the connection (more on this in Chapter 5).

But what, we might, ask, could possibly have connected the peoples of Palestine/Phoenicia, Greece and Britain? How is it that an ancient dragon-deity of Phoenicia (and Greece) was also known and worshipped in Britain? And what are we to make of this Hellenic fascination with all things Hyperborean? Clearly as well as being an exotic race from the ends of the earth they were also seen as being highly cultured and knowledgeable. The story of Abaris, the Hyperborean tutor of Pythagoras, who was said to have conveyed (flown on?) an arrow round the earth, seems to refer in some way to the cult of Apollo, though in view of Abaris' reputed wisdom, we may wonder whether the tale alludes to some cosmological or astronomical theory linked to his name.[33]

Fascinatingly, it may well be that Abaris is also recalled in British tradition. In his *History of the Kings of Britain*, Geoffrey of Monmouth devotes considerable space to a primeval monarch named Bladud. From this account it is clear that Bladud was an Icarus-type figure, an inventor and innovator. Like Icarus, he had the ability to fly, and we are told that, ascending above the "temple of Apollo" at "New Troy" (ie. London), he flew too close to the sun and crashed to his death. We recall at this point that Abaris too was associated with the cult of Apollo, and indeed the two

---

33 Herodotus iv, 34

names may be identical, given the interchangeability of "l" and "r". Modern scholarship has identified Bladud with a Celtic god of Hermes-like characteristics named Vlatos, and it is by no means improbable that the latter could be identical to both Abaris and Apollo as well as Belinos.[34]

We may then imagine, as a possible source of the Abaris legend, a group of travellers from Britain instructing Pythagoras in the teachings of the god-king Bladud/Vlatos (possibly then spelled Bratos or Abratos).

Further suggestions of direct links between Greek and British traditions are by no means in short supply. It should be noted that even the title Boreas (the personified North Wind, after whom the Hyperboreans were named), has a clear echo in Arthurian legend. After his description of the sacred precinct of Apollo in the land of the Hyperboreans, Hecataeus continues;

> "And the kings of this city and the supervisors of the sacred precinct are called the Boreades, since they are the descendants of Boreas, and the succession to these positions is always kept in the family."[35]

It so happens that the name Boreas, or Bors, is prominent in the Arthurian saga. We are told that Sir Bors, alone of Arthur's knights, was the only one to return from completing the Grail quest. All the others die. So just as Boreas was the custodian of the Hyperboreans' sacred precinct, Sir Bors was, in a sense, the custodian of the Grail secret. In the Arthurian saga then Bors was a figure of immense significance; and this is reflected in a variety of ways. In the Glastonbury area the local name for the Glastonbury Tor is Boras Hill, an indication that the name Bors/Boras was particularly linked to the Glastonbury/Avebury region. Of great importance too is the fact that in the legend the father of Sir Bors is also called Bors, implying that the name was a hereditary title.

Could it be then that Bors/Boras of British tradition (in Welsh, Emrys, after whom Stonehenge was named Gwaith Emrys), whose name is certainly identified with the region immediately to the west of Stonehenge, was one and the same as Boreas of Greek tradition, whose family was

---

34 The first writer I know of to identify Abaris with Bladud was John Wood, an architect from Bath, whose *Choir Gaure, Vulgarly called Stonehenge, on Salisbury Plain, Described, Restored, and Explained* (1747) contains some very colourful ideas.
35 Diodorus Siculus ii, 52

entrusted with the stewardship of the sacred precinct, which we have already identified with Stonehenge and Avebury? The idea seems astonishing, but it is clearly far from impossible.

It begins to look then as if all the mythical characters identified by Hecataeus with Britain – Apollo, Latona and Boreas – also occupy important positions in the Arthurian legends. Thus Apollo (Greek Apollon) appears as Beli/Sir Belin, Boreas as Emrys/Sir Bors, and Latona as Ludd/King Lot. If these identifications are correct it means that the popularised medieval (ie. "Vulgate") legend of Arthur was based upon material of great antiquity, much of it possibly even predating the native Welsh traditions as found say in the Four Ancient Books of Wales. The names surviving in the Vulgate tales are apparently less changed from their antique originals than those in the Welsh literature. It is important to remember that it is the medieval material, promulgated by Wace, de Boron and co., (and not the Welsh) that tells us of the Round Table (which we know to be Stonehenge) and of the Sword in the Stone (which we shall argue recalls the skills of the Early Bronze swordsmiths of Cornwall). Could it be that these French writers had access to ancient material unavailable to the Welsh? I believe that they could. Brittany, it appears, acted for centuries as a safe haven not only for refugees fleeing the depredations of Saxons, Picts and Scots, but for British scholarship fleeing the same dangers. In this way there may have been preserved, in fairly pristine condition, the national mythology of the land as it would have been known to the pre-Roman Celts. The traditions of Wales, I will argue, are derived from the same material, but often in a debased and folklorised form, having survived for centuries in many areas only by word of mouth.

In this context it should be recalled how the story of the youthful Merlin, which we know from Geoffrey of Monmouth (whose source is almost certainly Breton), is a myth of extreme antiquity, recalling the Tower Legend and the origins of human sacrifice. Yet the Mabinogion story of Lludd and Llefelys (whilst accurately linking Ludd/Lot to a dragon myth) nevertheless purports to explain how the dragons discovered in the pool under Vortigern's tower originally got there. Since we know that these dragons are the primeval creatures (Ladon/Lotan) which entwined themselves around the World Tree, it is evident that any attempt to explain how they got into a pool under the ground is almost certainly contrived.

Sure enough, in the words of one prominent writer, this tale "dates from the fourteenth century and might therefore be nothing more than a conscious addition to the Geoffrey of Monmouth story."[36] This should be a salutary warning against unquestioningly presuming the superior antiquity of the Welsh material.

Returning to our main topic, Hecataeus of course identifies Britain as the land of the Hyperboreans, and indeed it is clear that many of the Greek writers, including Homer and Hesiod, also appear to have had a very good understanding of its geographical location. All these placed it squarely in the north Atlantic. Various other Greek traditions suggested that the mystical land lay in the direction of the source of the Ister (Danube); in other words, in the direction of the Alps. Yet in the pages of Herodotus its true location has become obscured. All he knows is that it lies to the north. Why should this be so? A clue may lie in Herodotus' statement that the sacred gifts of the Hyperboreans had come to Greece by way of Dodona. Dodona was an important shrine of Zeus, situated on the borders of Illyria, the modern land of Albania. But Albania was also one of the ancient names of Britain (Latin *Albion*; Gaelic *Alba*).[37] Did Herodotus' uncertainty with regard to the Hyperboreans result from this confusion of Illyria with Britain? Certainly this would appear to be a plausible explanation.

A further answer may lie in the fact that by the time of Herodotus (mid fifth century BC.) Britain was already so familiar to the Greeks that it was then known by its own name, the earlier mythical title of Hyperborea having, in some quarters, fallen out of use, with the original location of Hyperborea becoming increasingly obscure.

Tin and Bronze

Why, the reader might ask, should the early Greeks have displayed such a keen interest in Britain? Why establish friendly relations with a people thousands of miles away, outside the Mediterranean, who could only be

36 Michael Senior *Myths of Britain* (1976) p.74
37 We know that Britain was known as Albion from at least the fourth century BC.

reached by a dangerous voyage in the treacherous seas of the north Atlantic? The answer is no mystery. Britain, or rather Cornwall and the south-west, was a primary source of tin, that indispensable ingredient of bronze, for the civilizations of the ancient Near East: And indeed, as we shall see, Britain itself played a pivotal role in the metallurgical revolution that launched the Bronze Age. According to Professor Rawlinson, "From the time that the Phoenicians discovered the Scilly Isles [the collection-point for Cornish tin]... it is probable that the tin of the civilised world was almost wholly derived from this quarter."[38] The exploitation of Britain's tin, it is generally agreed, commenced in the 8th century BC., by which time the Phoenicians had established a series of colonies throughout the western Mediterranean which acted as depots or supply bases in the journey to and from Britain. One of these settlements, the city of Gades (modern Cadiz) was on an island off the Atlantic coast of southern Spain; and indeed the Phoenicians established control over a remarkably large area of the region, which became known as Tartessus.

It is highly likely that the appearance of tin bronze in the eastern Mediterranean was a direct result of these trading links. Yet no one has ever suggested that the Phoenicians opened this trade route before c.800 BC. The establishment of the western Mediterranean colonies around that time is almost certainly to be linked to the Atlantic tin-trade. Indeed, it seems likely that Carthage and Cadiz were established specifically to service the tin-trade. Put simply, then, this would mean that the Bronze Age only commenced around 800 BC., though for a century and a half now scholars have dated the beginning of the Bronze Age, in both Europe and the Near East, in the early second and even third millennia. This is a problem which, as we shall see, has arisen quite unnecessarily, and has caused no end of confusion.

The exploits of the early Phoenician entrepreneurs were recalled by one of their number, Himilco, who is reckoned to have lived sometime in the 6th century BC. Himilco apparently left a detailed record of a voyage to the north-western seaboard of Europe, which was unfortunately lost in antiquity. Nevertheless, the gist of what he said is preserved in a fragment from Rufus Festus Avienus, a 4th century AD Roman administrator, who composed poetry using material from Himilco and other ancient writers:

---

38 George Rawlinson *A History of Phoenicia* (London,1889) p.301

PHOENICIAN AND GREEK PENETRATION OF THE WESTERN MEDITERRANEAN, 8TH CENTURY BC.

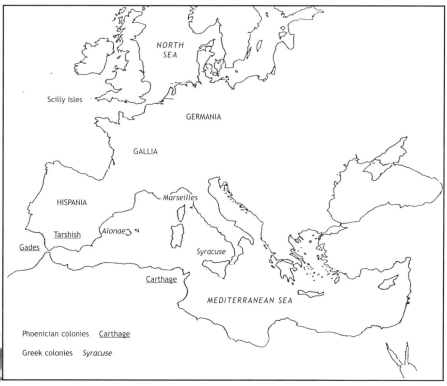

Phoenician trade-routes to Britain were established shortly after the founding of the western colonies of Carthage and Gades in the 8th century BC. It was only then that tin-bronze became available to the Levantine civilisations. Yet scholars date the onset of the Bronze Age over a thousand years earlier, without any attempt to explain where the bronze came from.

"Here is the city of Gadir, formerly called Tartessus; here are the Pillars of stubborn Hercules, Abila and Calpe ... they groan under the hard north wind, but stand fixed in their place. And here rises the head of the mountain chain (an older age called it Oestrymnis) whose whole lofty and rocky mass runs chiefly towards the warm south wind. Under the head of this range the Oestrymnic gulf opens before the inhabitants, in which stand the Oestrymnic islands, wide scattered, and rich materials, tin and lead. Here is a vigorous people, proud in spirit, skilful at their work. Zeal for business displays itself on all the hills, and in their famous skiffs they sail widely over the turbid gulf, and the abyss of the monster-infested ocean. These people have no knowledge of building ships of pine ... but – a thing to marvel at – they always construct their ships of skins sewn together ... From thence it is a two days' voyage to the Sacred Island (so the ancients called it). This lies amid the waves, abounding in verdure, and the race of the Hierni dwell there, wide spread. Next after it extends the island of the Albiones. The Tartesii were accustomed to trade as far as the limits of the Oestrymnides, as were the Carthaginian colonists, and a multitude, sailing between the Pillars of Hercules, used to visit these waters."[39]

This remarkable passage illustrates the immense importance of Britain to the ancient Near Eastern civilisations, and just how familiar with the island they were.

The Greeks had no less interest in Britain than the other Mediterranean nations, and were second only to the Phoenicians in their exploration, trading, and colonising. As the Phoenicians established colonies on the Atlantic coast of Spain, the Greeks founded settlements in southern Gaul and the eastern coast of Spain. That Greek traders were familiar with Britain from as early as the 8th century is confirmed by the fact that Homer, who is dated to the 7th century BC., refers to the "Tin Islands" which he names Cassiterides. It is regarded as highly significant that Cassiterides is a Celtic word – *cass* being Celtic for "tin".[40] Hesiod too,

---

39 Rufus Festus Avienus *Orae Maritimae* 81-90

40 *Iliad* xi,25 and 34 W. Dinan noted that the word *cass* -tin – is found in numerous Old Celtic names, eg. Cassignatos, Cassimara, Bodiocasses, Viducasses etc., from which he concluded that the Celtic settlement of the British Isles occurred around the 9th century BC. (at which date he placed Homer). *Monumenta Historica Celtica* Vol.1 (London, 1911) p.2

from the same epoch, refers to the "Holy Isles" as occupying a region far to the north-west.

The first swords, it should be noted, were made of bronze, and it can be no coincidence that the Latins of Italy borrowed their word for sword, *gladius*, from the Celtic *calad*. The vast importance of Britain in the history of bronze production and manufacturing technique is a topic to be examined further presently.

It is apparent then that the Greeks were greatly influenced by the British Celts during the most formative period of their history. Much of their mythology was derived directly from the British, with the Hellenes even preserving on occasion actual British names and words. But the trade was not all one way. The insular Celts were much influenced by their Mediterranean visitors, from whom they derived many words and terms, as well as the science of letters, and many technological innovations, such as the chariot. We shall shortly see how the chieftains who actually built Stonehenge were enriched by the first flowering of the bronze-trade with the eastern Mediterranean.

The Sword in the Stone

Up until the closing years of the 19th century scholars had, in conformity with the testimony of ancient tradition, generally assumed that Britain was the major, if not the sole, source of tin known to the ancient world. In addition, it was recognised that Britain had in some way a unique role in the development of metal-working and bronze manufacture in particular.

Yet by the beginning of the 20th century a major revision of history was under way. Scholars began to downplay, even dismiss, Britain's importance in the story of ancient metallurgy. The reason for this dramatic shift in opinion is instructive. Throughout the 19th century experts in Near Eastern history, Egyptologists and Assyriologists, began to speak of a Levantine Bronze Age commencing in the 3rd millennium BC. – long before the Phoenicians had opened the sea-routes to Britain in the 8th century BC. Thus the Near Eastern cultures, it was stated, must have had access to tin and tin-bronze from another source. But this position caused problems. None of the ancient authors seemed to know of any source of tin other than Britain. Still, if great civilisations using tin bronze in the 3rd millennium existed, then another source there must have been. Desperate and somewhat embarrassed attempts were made to locate this hitherto unknown store of the precious material, but to little avail. A reasonable quantity of tin was indeed discovered in Spain, but since this was almost as far away from Egypt and Mesopotamia as Britain itself, it solved nothing. Supplies of tin in central Europe, specifically Lower Saxony and Bohemia, were also found to have been exploited in antiquity, but here again the great distance from the Levant was problematical.[41]

Failing therefore to solve the problem of tin in a satisfactory way, historians at length resorted to a final expedient: It was simply ignored. At a later stage we shall see that the source of this confusion, the supposed two thousand year head start of the Levantine civilisations, is entirely chimerical. No literate civilisations existed, in Egypt, Mesopotamia, or anywhere else for that matter, before circa 1,000 BC.

Yet even without challenging the chronology, a number of scholars have recently called into question the entire notion of Middle Eastern priority, especially in relation to the evolution of metal-working and metal-smelting techniques. Examining the development of metallurgical and glazing techniques with the eye of a specialist, the mineralogist John Dayton came to the conclusion that bronze manufacture was not a Levantine discovery at all, but a European one: "If we ignore the *idee fixe* of the superiority of the civilization of the Fertile Crescent we find that there is very little evidence for the smelting of malachite or azurite [copper ores] in this area [in early times], although it was undoubtedly used for pigment."[42] Dayton then proceeds to show how the abundant deposits of copper on Cyprus were not exploited till Late Bronze Age times, because they were "of the sulphide type and need much roasting." In other words, they can only be extracted using fairly sophisticated methods. Yet the Near Eastern civilisations, at a much earlier stage, were using complex ores from Europe, "and it may well be that these artefacts were obtained as finished products and that the secrets of smelting were not known in the Middle East."[43]

But what part of Europe could have been the source of the

---

41 John Dayton *Minerals, Metals, Glazing, and Man* (London,1978) p.72
42 Ibid. p.76
43 Ibid. p.77

technological revolution that launched the Bronze Age? The general consensus at present is that central Europe, supposedly the home of the Beaker People, was the first region to combine tin and copper to produce bronze. But Dayton is not so sure: "Although the ores of Central Europe are very similar to those of Cornwall, generally they contain less copper and more nickel and cobalt, and are not so suitable for the production of bronzes."[44] Even more to the point, in Cornwall, and only in that region, copper and tin are found together, already mixed in an ore form:

> "The mineral veins of Devon and Cornwall are often situated on the coast and the blue copper ores exposed on the face of the cliffs. The mixed copper/tin ores could have been easily worked by early man. It can be no coincidence that megalithic tombs are densely grouped around the copper/tin/lead deposits in the St Just area, while a whole group of early settlements ring Bodmin Moor."[45]

Almost certainly true bronze was discovered in this way, and in Dayton's view it is highly likely that it was thus worked for many years before anyone discovered that tin, existing separately, could be mixed with copper to produce the same material:

> "Cornwall is one of the rare areas where these mixed ores [of copper and tin] occur as outcrops on the cliffs. Such deposits, as at Cligga Head, Gurnards Head, Pendeen and at Mount's Bay, were most probably the source of natural bronzes in the Middle Bronze Age long before tin was known as a metal. Cornwall therefore has a strong claim to be the home of Mycenaean and Shaft Grave bronze, at least on the geological evidence."[46]

Astonishingly then, the discovery of bronze seems to have taken place in Britain. The Bronze Age revolution was launched here. That certainly, for Dayton, seems to be what the geological evidence tells us. The wealth of the Wessex culture, that branch of Beaker culture responsible for raising Stonehenge, speaks eloquently, for Dayton, of the importance of Britain as

---

44 Ibid. p.70
45 Ibid.
46 Ibid. p.71

a supplier of bronze, of raw material and finished artefacts, in the Early Bronze epoch:

> "Was Wessex the middleman in the trade in Cornish and Devon coppers and bronzes to Europe, at the same time that trade existed in palstaves between England and northern Portugal and Spain (Clarke,1952)? Did the discovery of bronze actually take place in Cornwall, from mixed Cornish copper/tin ores which appear in brightly coloured outcrops on the cliffs, together with native copper, arsenical coppers, and antimonial coppers? From the evidence of the megaliths much activity was going on in this area, while Stonehenge itself was at a convenient crossroads for the copper and gold of Ireland and Wales and the tin and copper of Devon and Cornwall."[47]

The importance of western Britain in the metallurgical revolution is, for Dayton, demonstrated right at the beginning of the Bronze Age, when Beaker settlements appear in the region in great density:

> "Traces of the Beaker People have been found in Devon and Cornwall, while hut circles and monuments are thickly located in the areas where copper and tin ores abound, as on Dartmoor and Carn Brea. Faience beads have been found near St Just at Carn Creis similar to those of Middle Minoan III (Hencken, 1932:74)."[48]

The evidence then seems to be confirming more and more that the ancients did not get it wrong: that Britain did indeed have a unique role to play in ancient metallurgy. Britain, it seems, was responsible not only for the world's second Industrial Revolution, in the 18th century, but also for the first, at the start of the Bronze Age.

Over the last few years a general consensus has been reached among scholars that the myth of the sword being pulled from the stone refers to the wonder and awe with which ancient man viewed the art of the smith, the semi-magical craftsman (and original alchemist) who could produce

---

47 Ibid. p.76
48 Ibid. p.69

metal from stone. The connection with the smith's art is emphasised by the fact that the mystical sword is usually depicted emerging from an anvil. Yet this sword, it is agreed, was not made of iron, but bronze: For the motif of a perfectly formed sword being extracted from a stone fits remarkably well with the technique actually used in the making of bronze swords. The weapon was cast in a mould of clay or stone, from which, after cooling, it emerged fully formed. How appropriate then that the motif of the sword in the stone should be a central theme in the national myth of the very country in which the art of taking metal from stone was first perfected. In extracting the sword from the stone, the god Lugos/Hercules/Arthur, as patron of science and the arts, would originally have been in the act of bequeathing to the people of the island the knowledge of how to extract bronze from stone. Also, it is surely not coincidental that Cornwall, the home of bronze-making, has traditionally been linked in a special way to the entire Arthurian epic.

Britain's antique reputation as a land of sorcerers and magicians is therefore fully explained if the secret art of the bronze-smith, the first Alchemist, had its home in the country.

One last point. In the legend Arthur's magical sword Excalibur (not the sword pulled from the stone), was cast into a lake after his death. This too recalls Bronze Age (and Iron Age) practice in Europe, where vast numbers of swords have been recovered from lakes, into which they were cast as a sacrificial offering to the gods.

The Phoenician Connection

During the 19th century whole volumes were devoted to identifying cultural links between the Insular Celts and Phoenicia. Although such links are now generally ignored in scholarly works, it is important to remember that they have never been discredited. Indeed the more we discover about the belief-systems of Celts and Phoenicians, the more clear the links become. That they are now ignored by mainstream academia is an overcautious reaction to an over-reckless cultural diffusionism that dominated till the beginning of the present century.

It has always been known that Phoenician religious and cult practices had much in common with those of the Celts. Thus for example it is generally accepted that the British god Belinos (Irish Beal or Balar), one of the most important of the Celtic deities, had a name virtually identical to the primary god of the Phoenicians, Baal. It is known too that the major festival of Beal/Belinos, Beltaine, or May 1st, was also a major festival of Baal; and that in both regions the event was marked by the lighting of huge bonfires on hilltops. In the present work we have also seen how the legend of the Garden of the Blessed, wherein there grew a sacred apple-tree guarded by a dragon, is a fundamental myth of Phoenicians, Greeks and Celts. In the same way, we have discovered that the cult of Apollo and his mother Latona (Phoenician Lotan, British Lot) can be traced from Phoenicia/Palestine right through to the British Isles, and it is possible, even probable, that the names Apollo, apple and Baal are all identical. The Tree of Life, we remember, was planted in the Garden by Ba'al – "The Lord" – the name is identical in Hebrew and Phoenician.

Parallels between the names of deities abound. We may note, for example, that the Phoenician war-god Hizzus, is more or less the same as the Celtic Hesos, a title used for Mars, whilst Taranis, the Celtic thunder-god, is matched by the Phoenician Taram, also meaning thunder.[49]

Other linguistic links may be equally significant. The Irish word *carn*, or *cairn*, implying a heap of stones usually raised over a grave, is apparently identical to the Semitic *kern*, meaning a tumulus of sand or a peak. The Irish and British custom whereby individual mourners each placed a stone over the grave was precisely paralleled in Israel and Phoenicia.[50]

Some of the words common to Phoenicians and Insular Celts may serve to illustrate the trading relations between the two peoples. For example, the Irish word for tin, *stan*, is apparently Phoenician in origin. The Phoenicians were noteworthy craftsmen in many fields, so it should come as no surprise to find that a number of words pertaining to manufactured goods found their way from Phoenicia to western Europe. Among these we may cite the Irish words for glass, *gloine*, and silk, *sioda*. The latter was apparently named for the city of Sidon, a surmise supported by the fact that the same word in Welsh is *sidan*.[51] It is true that the material we now call silk was

---

49 Sir William Betham *The Gael and Cymbri* (Dublin,1834) pp.225-6

50 One of the worst maledictions an Irishman could utter was *ni cuirfidh me cloch ar do charn* ("I'll not put a stone on your cairn").

51 See for example Charles Vallancey's "Prospectus of a Dictionary of the Aire Coti or Ancient Irish" *Transactions of the Royal Irish Academy* Vol.xiii (1802)

unknown in the epoch under discussion. Nevertheless, the Phoenicians were renowned, from at least the 8th century BC. onwards, for their purple-dyed cloth, which they exported throughout the Mediterranean. It could well be that "Sidon-cloth" was originally a term applied to any of the fine purple-coloured materials originating in Phoenicia, long before it came to be applied exclusively to silk.

It is here that we come upon another, unexpected, connection with the Arthurian legend, a tradition which we might expect to reflect pre-Christian Phoenician links with Britain: And this is just the case. The various accounts of the Grail Quest are insistent that the action took place at the eastern end of the Mediterranean, with more than one version naming king Solomon (who had close links with Tyre) as well as Egypt and Babylon. Even more to the point, the Grail stories are full of accounts of ships either carrying or covered in silk. According to Malory,

> "And as he slept there came a voice that bade him go to the sea … And upon the sea strand he found a ship that was covered in heavy white silk … And as soon as he was entered, the ship departed into the sea, and to his seeming it went fleeing."

Again, in another place we read,

> "'I shall let make a ship of the best wood and most durable that any man may find' So Solomon sent for carpenters, of all the land the best … So all of this did King Solomon make as the lady devised, both the ship and all the remnant. And when the ship was ready in the sea to sail, the lady let make a great bed and marvellous rich, and set herself upon the bed's head covered in silk."

It is of course impossible to discuss Phoenician influence on the west without broaching the vexed question of the alphabet. This people, famously, were the inventors of the alphabet, a fact acknowledged by the Greeks. That the Celts did borrow the alphabet from the Phoenicians and Greeks is beyond question: The doubt remains only as to when they did so. We know that by the first century BC. both Gauls and Britons were well acquainted with writing. Even without the testimony of Caesar and others this would be obvious: for we possess coins of British kings of the first century with their names clearly inscribed upon them. The earliest proven example of Celtic literacy north of the Pyrenees is a sword of the 2nd or 1st century BC. inscribed, in Greek letters, with the name of its maker, Korisios.[52] This weapon, from Switzerland, dramatically illustrates Caesar's statement that the Gauls used Greek letters in business transactions etc.

Native tradition however placed the advent of literacy amongst the Celts much before 100 BC., and that tradition has been fully confirmed by the discovery of numerous inscriptions in the Q Celtic dialect of Spain, some of which are as early as the 4th century BC. The Irish, who claimed to be of Spanish origin, and whose Q Celtic speech was most closely related to the Spanish idiom, possessed a peculiar form of alphabetic writing named Ogham, which they said had been devised by the divine Ogma, son of Danu, whom we know was Ogmios, the Celtic Hercules. But of course the Age of Hercules was the 8th century BC. Other traditions said that the Gaels had been given the alphabet, which the Irish called the *Bethluisnion* (after the first three letters) by one Fenius Farsa, whilst they still inhabited Galicia in Spain. The name Fenius, it goes without saying, has long been equated with "Phoenicia".

I do not wish at present to enter into the convoluted and tortuous debate about the antiquity of the Ogham script or the Bethluisnion alphabet. Suffice for the moment to say that the Phoenicians, who traded regularly in the British Isles from around 800 BC. onwards, could scarcely have conducted that trade without the use, on both sides, of written documents. Furthermore, the astonishing accuracy displayed in the design of Stonehenge and the other megaliths, which we date to shortly after 800 BC., certainly points to the existence in that epoch of both mathematical and literary annotation. At a later stage we shall see how the Irish preserved a written history of their nation going back many centuries into the pre-Christian age; and how certain facts contained in these records suggest very strongly that they were, in part at least, genuinely ancient. The British, who were in even more direct contact with the nations of the Near East, without doubt also possessed such a literature; but most of it was lost following the Roman conquest.

Yet still the pre-Christian Celts are popularly portrayed as illiterate barbarians. This is entirely due to the fact that none of their stone

---

52 Ann Ross *The Pagan Celts* (London,1970) pp.98-9 The Celtic use of the Greek word-ending -os instead of the Latin -us (eg. Cunobelinos) would seem to provide additional support for the Celts' long-standing familiarity with Greek letters.

monuments are inscribed, as were those of Egypt and the other Levantine civilisations. But we know from Caesar and others that the Druids exercised a peculiarly strict control on the deployment of writing, and it is virtually certain that, until a very late period, its use on stone monuments was strictly prohibited. To them, writing was knowledge, and knowledge was power; and as long as they held sway, it would always be a secret science.[53]

---

53 The writing of the Germanic peoples is named Runic, and the word *run*, in the Celtic tongues, implies "secret". (The word "secretary" itself preserves the memory of a time when writing was a mystic, secret art) Interestingly, the Runic alphabet may also be very ancient. According to one modern writer, "The thorny, elongated and angular shapes of the runes, which look as if they belong in the seventh or sixth centuries BC., and the direction of the writing of earlier runic inscriptions (either from right to left, or boustrophedon) induced the great Isaac Taylor to suggest as the prototype of the runes the Greek alphabet as used in the sixth century BC. in the Greek colonies of the Black Sea." David Diringer *The Alphabet* (London,1953) p.513

CHAPTER 5

Sky Gods and Megaliths

A World-Wide Phenomenon

So far we have examined the mythology of ancient Britain and in the process have found that the gods and goddesses of the Insular Celts were intimately connected with the megalithic structures that dotted the entire Atlantic seaboard. We have also discovered that the mythology and cult-practices of the Celts of western Europe were closely paralleled by those of the Mediterranean peoples, particularly the nations of the eastern Mediterranean, and that in these lands too megalithic structures were identified with gods and goddesses worshipped as recently as the early centuries of the Christian era. What we have not tried to do is explain the existence of these megaliths, or the meaning of the myths attached to them. For the megaliths and the myths are inseparable, and if we wish to understand the forces which prompted the construction of these strange structures, we must attempt to grasp what the myths mean.

Innumerable volumes have been written about the megaliths. Speculation as to their meaning and purpose has been endless. Each year sees the publication of a plethora of books claiming sensational new revelations. We are already familiar with the theory that they were not built by Europeans at all, but the survivors of a lost civilisation, usually Atlantis. In more recent times we have become all too acquainted with the belief that they were raised using an advanced technology now forgotten. It is held by some that the very dimensions of the megaliths, especially of course Stonehenge, contain clues to the future of the planet, whilst others hold that the great standing-stones were built along energy-lines, or "Ley lines", and were intended by the ancients to channel this vital life-force of mother earth.

Whilst virtually all speculation of this variety can be safely discounted, it is true that the conventional explanation of the megaliths, found in countless learned textbooks, is simply not satisfactory. The standing-stones *are* a great mystery, and it is eminently clear that attempts to explain the European structures, for example, as a local phenomenon which evolved solely as a result of economic conditions along the Atlantic seaboard during the late Neolithic, simply does not stand up to scrutiny. It is quite wrong, and profoundly misleading, to see megalith-building as something peculiar to Europe: And this is a blind alley pursued by alternative thinkers almost as much as the scholarly establishment. Megaliths, or megalith-like structures, are not confined to the Celtic lands: nor indeed are they confined to the Old World. They are in found in almost every corner of the globe, where they are invariably linked to that other world-wide phenomenon, pyramid-building. Indeed the earliest phase of all civilisation, in whatever corner of the globe we wish to consider, is without exception marked by the raising both of artificial hills and other great edifices of enormous polygonal blocks of stone. Recent discoveries have shown substantial pyramids and other megalithic structures in China,[1] and these can now be added to those of Egypt, Mesopotamia, Mexico, South America, western Europe (tumuli like Silbury Hill), and various mound-structures and cyclopean masonry throughout North America and Asia. At the moment, the only areas without pyramids and other megaliths are sub-Saharan Africa and Australia, but this may change as our knowledge of the archaeology of these areas improves.

If then we attempt to view pyramids and megaliths as isolated local phenomena we are immediately ignoring a vital piece of evidence. These structures must be concrete manifestations of a phenomenon or experience that affected virtually the entire human race. If this simple fact is not taken into account the conclusions we reach about them will be false.

The last pyramids to be actually used, as far as we know, were those of Mexico, and what the Spanish conquistadors witnessed at these monuments is entirely in accordance with the literary testimony from ancient Mesopotamia, where we find the ziggurats being used as high altars upon which were performed blood sacrifices. Evidence from almost every corner of the globe makes it clear that pyramids were cult edifices of a world-wide stellar religion, a religion which viewed the heavenly bodies, especially the

---

1 See eg. *Focus* (July,1998)

sun, moon and planets as gods, and which regarded the offering of blood-sacrifices to these deities as vital to the well-being of the whole community. Indeed it was seen as vital to the well-being of all creation.

The pyramids of Egypt, it is true, were not employed as high altars, though more ancient structures (now demolished) from the Early Dynastic Age, may have been used for sacrifice. The later pyramids of the 4th, 5th and 6th Dynasties were also however sacred monuments of a sky religion. The Pyramid Texts, which we find inscribed upon the inner chambers of these later pyramids, leaves us in no doubt that they were dedicated to the same stellar gods as those of Mexico and Mesopotamia.

The very universality of the ancient stellar religion has led most scholars to conclude, quite erroneously, that the worship of sun, moon and planets was somehow instinctive to humanity. The warmth and light of the sun, it is surmised, led early humans naturally to honour this life-giving body. The worship accorded to the sun would in course of time have been extended to the moon and planets.

Yet such a conclusion is entirely mistaken. For there was a time when neither sun, moon, nor planets figured in the religious ideas of mankind. We possess very substantial evidence from the artwork of the Palaeolithic (Old Stone) epoch, particularly from the Magdalenian culture, to show that religious beliefs at this time were almost entirely concerned with ancestor-worship, sympathetic magic, and the honouring of a Mother Goddess. In all the artefacts, artwork and cult-objects of the Palaeolithic there is no evidence of a stellar religion. The sky-gods appear quite suddenly after the end of the Palaeolithic, which coincides with the end of the Pleistocene, a break-off point which, significantly enough, saw the extinction of an estimated two-thirds of all land animal species.

The evidence shows that the appearance of the sky-gods immediately after the Pleistocene extinctions is not merely coincidental.

The Dragon Cult

Along with the worship of sun, moon and planets the early Neolithic (New Stone Age) peoples also honoured a dragon or serpent figure, a motif which appears at this time quite suddenly throughout the globe. In every corner of the planet, from orient to occident, from north to south, the cosmic serpent is invariably linked to a cataclysmic flood that devastated the world and wiped out most of humanity.

Like the sky-gods, the cosmic serpent or dragon is closely associated with the pyramids and megaliths, and it is evident that many of the sacrifices offered atop these sacred mountains were dedicated to this strange god. Indeed in a very real sense pyramids were altars of the cosmic serpent. The mystery of the pyramids is inextricably connected with the mystery of the dragon.

For centuries scholars have pondered the meaning of this creature, so universally important to early humanity. The modern consensus is that the serpent is a metaphor for concepts and ideas important to primitive man, such as rebirth (the serpent sloughing its skin) and sexuality. Yet such explanations ignore a great deal of what the myths say in very graphic terms. In Egypt, Mesopotamia, India, China, Mexico and elsewhere the cosmic serpent unleashes cataclysmic floods, as well as titanic convulsions of the earth, and frequently breathes fire and brimstone upon the world. Whilst it would be possible to quote literally hundreds of such legends, one well-known account from Greece should be sufficient to illustrate the point. In the following passage Hesiod describes the encounter between Zeus and the serpent-tailed titan Typhon, a monster which sought to plunge creation into primeval chaos:

> "The Titan's form, half man, half snake, was enormous. He was so large that his head often knocked against the stars and his arms could extend from sunrise to sunset. From his shoulders there reared a hundred serpent heads, all flashing fiery tongues, while flames darted from the many eyes ... And this terrible thing would have become the master of creation had not Zeus gone against him in combat ... Beneath the feet of the father of the gods Olympus shook as he moved, the earth groaned; and from the lightning of his bolt, as well as from the eyes and breath of his antagonist, fire was bursting over the dark sea. The ocean boiled; towering waves beat upon all the promontories of the coast; the ground quaked; Hades, lord of the dead, trembled; and even Zeus himself, for a time, was

Hercules battles the serpent-god Achelous.

unstrung. But when he had summoned again his strength, gripping his terrific weapon, the great hero sprang from his mountain and, hurling the bolt, set fire to all those flashing, bellowing, roaring, baying, hissing heads. The monster crashed to earth, and the earth-goddess Gaea groaned beneath her child. Flames went out from him, and these ran along the steep mountain forests, roaring, so hot that much of the earth dissolved, like iron in the flaming forge within the earth of the lame craftsman of the gods, Hephaestus. And then the mighty king of the gods, Zeus, prodigious in storming wrath, heaved the flaming victim into gaping Tartarus – whence to this day there pour forth from his titan form all those winds that blow terribly across seas and bring to mortal men distress, scatter shipping, drown sailors, and ruin the beloved works of dwellers on the land with storms and dust."[2]

The ancients were in no doubt that such cataclysmic scenes had actually occurred, and indeed many of them linked these events to a comet or cosmic body which came near to colliding with the earth. One of them, the Roman writer Pliny, specifically identified Typhon as a fiery comet that in early times wrought havoc upon the earth:

"There was a dreadful one [comet] observed by the Ethiopians and the Egyptians, to which Typhon, a king of that period, gave his own name; it had a fiery appearance, and was twisted like a spiral; its aspect was hideous, nor was it like a star, but rather like a knot of fire."[3]

In full accordance with Pliny's testimony, comets have always been regarded as harbingers of evil, and their appearance greeted with the greatest apprehension, if not outright terror. But this in itself is now seen as a mystery; since comets are regarded as harmless, if not rather beautiful, cosmic phenomena. Pliny however clearly suggests that Typhon, the serpent-demon who threatened to overturn all creation, was a "dreadful" comet, a cosmic body that brought devastation to the earth. Is Pliny's explanation the correct one? If he were the only source connecting the cosmic serpent with a comet then perhaps there would be room for doubt;

2 Hesiod *Theogony* 823-880
3 Pliny *Natural History* ii,23

yet in legends from every part of the globe the cosmic serpent is invariably linked with, or identified as a comet. And indeed the cometary nature of the dragon, a creature with a long tail which flies through the sky and breathes fire upon the earth, is obvious enough.[4]

Chaos in the Firmament

Early peoples were obsessively interested in the skies. It needs to be emphasised that all the world's mythologies, without exception, are primarily concerned with the planetary gods; and each one of them insisted that within human memory these deities had brought utter devastation to the planet. Indeed, they had brought our world to the brink of destruction. The very concept of an Armageddon, an End of the World, a Ragnarok, which is universally shared by the traditions of mankind was, according to a theory to be examined presently, based upon prior experience. Furthermore, there are clues everywhere as to the instrument of destruction. Our language is permeated with them. Thus a "disaster" is in origin a dark or evil star; whilst a "catastrophe" is a star that overturns. It is no coincidence too that the appearance of a comet was anciently, and even in more modern times, greeted with outright terror and foreboding.

We shall argue that the cataclysmic events associated with the heavenly bodies, and the obsessive need to observe them, was of primary importance in launching high civilisation throughout the world, and with the raising of the mighty monuments we now call "megaliths."

---

4 British tradition, in the form of the Arthurian legend, has much to tell us about the dragon, and here too, the monster is unequivocally identified with a comet. It was said that immediately after the erection of Stonehenge, Ambrosius the High King died, whereupon a great comet appeared in the sky. The nobles of Britain approached Merlin to ask its meaning, and were informed that the comet signified the fate of Uther and his son. Now the head of the comet, it was said, resembled a dragon, a fact which prompted Merlin to proclaim, "Thou Uther art signified by this star with the head of a dragon. By the beam pointing towards France is denoted a son of thine, who shall be great in wealth, and extensive in sway, and by that directed towards Ireland by a daughter, whose descendants shall successively govern the whole." Uther was then elected sovereign, and assumed the title Pendragon ("Dragon-head"), as well as making the dragon his heraldic symbol. *Merlin through the Ages* p.233

There is no shortage of references to the destructive actions of the heavenly gods in ancient myth. One of the most straightforward accounts of these cataclysms, one which makes their extra-terrestrial cause abundantly clear, is the Greek legend of Phaethon – a story retold poetically by Ovid in his *Metamorphoses*, and explained in no uncertain terms in Plato's *Timaeus*. We are informed that Phaethon, son of the sun-god Helios, attempted one day to fly the solar chariot across the sky, but, being unable to control the wild steeds, brought the blazing disc disastrously close to the earth, causing a universal conflagration. In this fire the whole earth burned, rivers evaporated, and the sea boiled.

"The earth caught fire, starting with the highest parts. With all its moisture dried up, it split and cracked in gaping fissures. The meadows turned ashy grey; trees, leaves and all, were consumed in a general blaze, and the withered crops provided fuel for their own destruction. But these are trifles to complain of, compared to the rest. Great cities perished, their walls burned to the ground, and whole nations with all their different communities were reduced to ashes. The woods on the mountains were blazing, Athos was on fire, Cilician Taurus and Timolus, Oeta and Ida, a mountain once famous for its springs, but now quite dry. Helicon, the Muses' haunt, was burning … Etna's flames were redoubled … Othrys and Rhodope, destined at last to lose its snows, Mimas and Dindyma and Mycale and Cithaeron, the natural abode of sacred rites. Scythia did not escape, in spite of its chilly clime, Caucasus was in flames and Ossa too, and Pindus; Olympus, a greater mountain than either of these, was ablaze, as were the airy Alps and the snow-capped Apennines.

"Then, indeed, Phaethon saw every part of the world on fire, and found the scorching heat more than he could endure …

"It was then, so men believe, that the Ethiopians acquired their dark skins; for the blood rose to the surface of their bodies. It was then that Libya became a desert, when the heat dried up her waters, then the nymphs tore their hair, and lamented their vanished springs and lakes. Boeotia looked in vain for Dirce's fountain, Argos for Amymone, Ephyre for Pyrene's waters. The rivers, though they ran in more open channels, were no safer than the springs … Euphratos, the river of Babylon, was kindled also, Orontes and swift-running Thermodon, Ganges and Phasis and Hister … The Nile was terrified and, fleeing to the ends of the earth, hid his head, which still is hidden …

"Everywhere the ground gaped open, and light descended through the cracks into Tartarus, frightening the king of the underworld, and his queen beside him. The seas contracted, and an expanse of barren sand appeared where there had lately been ocean. Mountains which had been submerged beneath deep waters rose above the surface, and increased the number of the scattered Cyclades."[5]

It is hard to see how anyone could imagine the above passage to refer to anything other than a cataclysmic upheaval of nature involving some celestial body or other. We, who understand the laws of gravity and plate tectonics, know that should another planet or large comet come close to the earth, our world would indeed burst into flame, that great fissures would open in the ground, and that violent volcanic activity would erupt everywhere. But how could Ovid, writing in the reign of the Emperor Augustus, have gained such knowledge – had he not been simply quoting from the testimony of people in the ancient past who had actually witnessed such events? But lest there be any doubt whatsoever as to how this myth should be interpreted, let's look at what, according to Plato, an Egyptian priest told Solon of Athens concerning the very same story.

"You [Greeks] are all young … you have no belief rooted in old tradition and no knowledge hoary with age. And the reason is this. There have been and will be many different calamities to destroy mankind, the greatest of them by fire and water, lesser ones by countless other means. Your own story of how Phaethon, child of the sun, harnessed his father's chariot, but was unable to guide it along his father's course and so burnt up things on earth and was himself destroyed by a thunderbolt, is a mythical version of the truth that there is at long intervals a variation in the course of the heavenly bodies and a consequent widespread destruction by fire of things on the earth."[6]

---

5 Ovid *Metamorphoses* ii,210-265
6 Plato *Timaeus* 22

But the heavenly body responsible for these events, in spite of it being named *phaethon* ("the blazing one") was not the sun. Innumerable mythologies describe the fiery comet, with its tail of debris, that was the real author. Yet because of its fiery appearance even the ancients associated it with the sun; and Phaethon himself is regarded as the son of the sun. Modern commentators have followed the lead, and all references to this fiery god are now dismissed under the universal title of "solar myths" and "solar deities". A prime example is seen in the interpretation of Lugh, whose name admittedly means "light", as a sun-god. And even here the ancients gave the lead. In the great battle between gods and giants, to be discussed presently, Lugh drives his chariot out from behind the battle-line to the front ranks; at which point Bres, king of the titans, exclaims; "It seems wonderful to me that the sun should rise in the west today and in the east every other day."

The Celestial Tower

In every corner of the globe, from Lapland to southern Africa, and from Mexico to China, there is a tradition of how a Deluge caused by erratic movements of the heavenly bodies brought to an end a paradisal age of innocence, and how mankind (or in some cases a race of giants or titans) attempted to reopen communication with heaven by erecting a tower that reached to the sky. Westerners are perhaps most familiar with the biblical version of the story, the Tower of Babel. In this, a very late and obviously amended account, it is the ambition of humans that leads them to attempt the raising of a tower to the heavens: but mankind's plans are frustrated when God confuses their speech. In the tradition of the Greeks, a much more primeval narrative, we found that the tower-building story is connected with a devastating upheaval of nature which saw the Olympians pitted against the Titans, who endeavour to reach the domain of the gods by piling mountains on top of each other. The resulting tower however is smashed when Zeus strikes it with a thunderbolt. In the Norse myth, the giants attempt to reach Asgard by piling up a huge mound of clay, in the shape of a man. This tower is destroyed by Thor, the god of thunder, who strikes it with his hammer. From Africa there is an abundance of similar

Cretan gem showing a goddess on top of the Celestial Tower.

An early 19th century engraving of an Elizabethan May Day. (From *British Folklore, Myths and Legends* by Marc Alexander)

traditions, all of them of great antiquity, which are discussed at some length by a little-known writer named Brendan Stannard, in his encyclopaedic *The Origins of Israel and Mankind*. Stannard notes that "In many versions of the separation myth, the departure of Heaven brought to an abrupt end a previously paradisal age, during which man and the gods were in close communication. Sickness, death and the necessity of labour now entered man's domain. Man found himself abandoned and destitute of the necessities of life – fire, animals, food, etc., and in some myths mankind attempted to renew the communication by building a bridge to heaven. In the Ashanti (Ghana, Ivory Coast) version, the woman who hit the sky with her pestle tried to build a pillar by stacking mortars one on top of the other. But this collapsed and caused the deaths of many people … the Wapare of East Africa narrate how mankind built a tower so that they could attack heaven. When the supreme god saw what they were up to, the earth quaked and the tower broke in two and buried its builders."[7]

Before looking at some possible explanations of the tower myth, we should recall that it is an essential element of the Lugos/Hermes/Merlin story. The Greek Hermes of course is linked to the Tower in his fundamental symbol, the *Kerykeion* (*Caduceus*), the staff or pole which gives him access to the realm of the gods. The *Kerykeion* is also, significantly enough, connected to the cult of the phallic menhirs, or *herme*, found throughout the Greek world. Furthermore, it should be remembered that the tradition of Hermes is inseparable in all its elements from that of Abraham, the founding-father of Israel, whose abortive sacrifice of Isaac (on a mountain top) takes place immediately after the fall of the Tower of Babel. In Greek tradition, Hermes is equally the source of high civilisation and blood sacrifice.

These elements are of course also (and even more completely) found in the Celtic version of the myth, whether it be told as the story of Lugos or Merlin. The latter character, the child prodigy, is destined for sacrifice by the tyrant Vortigern, whose tower is continually being destroyed by earthquakes. Merlin of course evades the sacrifice, but it is evident that the myth relates very clearly to the origins of the blood sacrifice ritual, and therefore to the origins of civilisation. In his guise of Lugos, the Celtic Hermes is equally linked to the Tower. In the Irish account, Lugh's mother

---

7 Brendan Stannard *The Origins of Israel and Mankind* (Lancashire, 1983) p.761

Ethne, we recall, is locked in a crystal tower by the evil titan Balor, whilst he plays an extremely important role in the cosmic battle of the Plain of the Tower (Magh Tuireadh), where the giants are overcome by the gods. Lugh is present too at the Tower of Breogan, or Brigantia, whence the ancestors of the Gaels depart for their new home in Ireland. In at least two Irish traditions, the tower is recalled as having been located in the midst of the ocean. Thus the *Lebor Gabala* ("Book of Invasions") describes the tower as being of gold, and being continually washed over by great waves. The British writer Nennius describes the tower as a pillar of crystal, an object encountered by the Gaels as they crossed the sea to Erin.

It is evident that the phallus cult of Hermes is derived in some way from this celestial tower or pillar. It must also be related one way or another to the concept of the Sacred Mountain, and thus to pyramid-building. Certainly phallus-worship, and along with it dragon-worship, appears in the Near East right at the first phase of literate civilisation, a period that saw the erection of the pyramids. But what then did the tower/phallus consist of? Clearly it was not a human construction, and over the last few years various theories have been put forward. Two American writers have recently suggested a gaseous protrusion, perhaps a mingling of gas and dust, from the earth. Another idea, more plausible, is that the earth's close encounter with the mighty comet recalled in the Typhon and Phaethon stories had electro-magnetically "recharged" the planet, and that the Tower was a plasma funnel of electrical energy that became visible at the Poles (inhabitants of the northern hemisphere would of course only have seen the funnel emanating from the North Pole). This certainly seems to be a reasonable supposition, as much other tradition about the Flood cataclysm speaks of unusual electrical phenomena (the thunderbolts of the gods) in the immediate aftermath.

If the Tower was electrical, and if it was also the original Staff of Hermes, this would perhaps further explain the intertwined "battling" serpents. These would have been serpent-like electrical sparks flickering up and down the plasma pillar. Such a solution would also explain the tradition that the staff/wand gave Hermes access to the heavenly abode of the gods. We recall that in most of ancient mythology the tower was intended by its builders to re-establish contact with the gods in the sky.

It is surely significant too that in the Arthurian myth king Lot (ie. Lotan/Leviathan), the cosmic serpent, is portrayed as the ruler of Orkney, whilst other evidence points to the Orkneys as the original setting of the Gorgon/Balor myth. If the plasma pillar emanated from the North Pole, an observer on the headlands of northern Scotland would have seen it as being situated in the archipelago. Since the dragon Lotan is also the same as Ladon, the serpent which entwined itself around the sacred apple tree in the Garden of the Hesperides, this would indicate that the Tree of Life, or World Tree, is another manifestation of the Tower.[8] It could be that at certain times the uppermost parts of the plasma pillar put forth great branch-like sparks, and it seems that even the words "tree" and "tower" (Old English *torr*) are etymologically linked.

Virtually all versions of the World Tree myth, it should be noted, have a dragon either entwined around it or lurking at its roots. Thus in the Scandinavian version the dragon-monster Nidhogg gnaws at the roots of Yggdrasill.

The whole concept of a world-axis, or pole (children to this day expect to see a physical pole at the North Pole), along with the various traditions linked to it, such as the May Pole, thus ultimately derive from a visible pole anciently observed in the far north. We recall at this point how in the Welsh version of the myth Lludd/Lud was instructed to find the centre, or axis, of the country (or the World Axis), in his quest to locate the battling dragons. Yet another clue comes in the testimony of the Roman poet Ovid, who describes how the catastrophe unleashed by Phaeton aroused the dragon of the north: "The Serpent which lay close to the icy pole, and had till then been sluggish with the cold, no danger to anyone, now sweltered in the heat, and was roused to unprecedented fury." (*Metamorphoses* ii, 160-170) As the most northerly land known to the early Phoenicians and Greeks, Britain would naturally have been specially connected by them to the world pole or tree; and this of course would have further enhanced the country's mystical reputation. All of which, if correct, provides yet more evidence to support our view that much of Hellenic mythology was concerned with and influenced by British tradition.

Such ideas must however, for the moment, remain somewhat

---

8 The biblical Abraham, whose relationship with Hermes and the Tower Myth has already been remarked upon, is further linked to the caduceus with its entwined dragon-serpent by his brother-in-law Lot (ie. Lotan of Phoenicia and Lot of Orkney), whose wife is turned into a pillar of salt during the cataclysmic destruction of Sodom and Gomorrah. This is the same crystal pillar emanating from the pole (the home of the Gorgon-demon Balor) that appears in Gaelic tradition.

speculative. What is clear is that the destruction of the Tower or celestial phallus was clearly associated with great upheavals of nature on the earth; and the builders of the Tower are invariably the rebellious titans whose battle with the divine powers unleashes devastation upon the earth. The battle between the gods and the titans becomes the archetypal war in heaven between the forces of good and evil. This is the Arthurian Battle of Camlann, when the rebel Modred's dark forces are overcome.

The Tower legend may thus be linked to the first phase of high civilisation, when a period of celestial calm was inaugurated by a disaster in the heavens, a disaster which in some way or other definitively put an end to terrestrial links with heaven. It was at this point, probably many generations after the initial Deluge catastrophe, that the whole custom of blood-sacrifice, along with pyramid and mound-building, makes its final appearance. The practice of blood (and human) sacrifice, we shall see, had been firmly established by the priest-kings of the age as a means of averting the complete destruction of the world..

Before moving on, it should be remarked that the great shrine of Avebury may well represent a gigantic depiction of the Tower Legend. William Stukeley's reconstruction of the monument shows what appears to be two enormous battling serpents whose heads meet at the central circle. The primeval mountain or tower is represented by the great mound of Silbury Hill, which stands directly between the two great serpentine avenues.

Wars of the Gods and the Titans

The Tower which appeared after the Deluge remained visible to all mankind for many centuries, centuries which saw continued upheavals of nature on the earth. In biblical tradition this was the epoch of the patriarchs, whose wanderings throughout the Near East were beset by continual heavenly-sent calamities. Most famously, Abraham and his tribe escaped by the skin of their teeth the cataclysm (of "fire and brimstone") that smashed the twin cities of Sodom and Gomorrah, whilst a few centuries later Moses was enabled to lead his people to freedom from bondage in Egypt after the country was struck by ten devastating plagues.

This epoch of upheaval is recorded throughout the world, where human sacrifice was enacted to avert the wrath of the fearsome denizens of the firmament. On occasion, the comet-god which had brought the Deluge would again draw dangerously close to our world, with frightening consequences for its inhabitants. Traditions of the Celts speak of repeated incursions of the sea, of entire landmasses consigned to the depths of the ocean, of the earth shaking violently, and of huge walls of water sweeping over the countryside. Irish tradition states that on one occasion a mighty wave inundated the entire country, killing all but three people.

British tradition too makes it perfectly clear that in the time of the children of Don, the gods of the Mabinogi, as well as in the epoch of Arthur, Britain was continually threatened by the destructive savagery of nature. Taliesin, the legendary poet-seer who sat at the court of king Arthur, mentions the devastating power of the unleashed sea on numerous occasions, and specifically relates these events to earthquake activity:

"Ho, that sound, is it the earth quaking?
Is it the sea overflowing from its usual banks to reach the feet of men?"

Much of Taliesin's work illustrates how the terrors of ancient times were incorporated into the colourful body of medieval Romance:

"When Amaethon came from the land of Gwyddion, from Segon with the powerful gate, the storm raged for four nights at the height of the fine season. Men fell, even the woods no longer sheltered against the wind of the deep. Math and Hyvedd, the masters of the magic wand, had unleashed the elements. Then Gwyddyon and Amaethon held counsel. They made a shield so strong that the sea could not engulf the best of the troops."[9]

Other medieval Welsh poets gave an important place to the same theme: for example, in a piece attributed to Gwddno, we find:

"Seithenhin, arise, go from here and see the green battle-line of the waves,

---

9 *Book of Taliesin* poem xv

The sea has covered the land of Gwyddno again.
Cursed be the girl, guardian of the spring, who sighed before freeing
the fearful sea.
Cursed be the girl, guardian of the spring, who struggled before
freeing the ravaging sea."[10]

Small wonder that the fearsome, fiery-red Celtic goddess of battle was
called Mor-rigan, "Queen of the Sea".

The above examples are but a small sample of their type found in Welsh
literature. All the characters mentioned here, it should be remarked, are
clearly placed alongside Arthur and his companions. The related traditions
of Cornwall are equally explicit in placing Tristan, another Arthurian hero,
in a time of great natural catastrophes. This latter character, we are
informed, was a son of the king of Lyonesse, the semi-legendary region
drowned forever by a vast wave which swept in from the ocean. From this
cataclysm, it was said, only a hero named Trevelyan (supposed founder of
the famous Cornish family) survived.

In all traditions, this age of calamity was finally brought to an end when
the gods, representing the forces of light, waged all out war against the
titans or giants, the perpetrators of these calamities. Typically, the leader of
the giants is the comet-god or dragon-monster, who is portrayed as of
hideous countenance, like the Gorgon, and dealing death and destruction
on the earth. In Greek legend, all the titans who assaulted Olympus had
serpentine lower bodies. In the Irish version of this final battle, the giants,
named Fomorii (from "under the sea"), are led by Balor, the ferocious Irish
Gorgon whose gaze alone could kill whole armies. The Fomorians, we are
told, had long oppressed the children of Danu, who, tiring of their rule,
refused any further tribute. (There is possibly here a memory of the awful
tribute of human sacrifice paid regularly to the Cosmic Serpent). In a rage,
the titan army gathered together, resolving to put Ireland under the sea
forever. Battle is typically joined at the Cosmic Pillar, or World Tree, which
the dragon-monsters of the titans have raised in order to reach the celestial
regions. There is then an apocalyptic encounter, during which great chasms
are ripped in the earth, mountains melt in rivers of lava, thunderbolts of
immense power are hurled across the heavens, and vast waves sweep over

---

10 *Black Book* poem xxxviii

the landmasses. In the Greek account Zeus is said to have forbade Helios, the sun, to shine during the battle. But in the end the gods are triumphant. The tower is smashed, or disappears, and the Dragon king of the giants is slain and decapitated. In most myths, the decapitation is performed by a Hercules-figure, who employs a shining celestial sword. From this point onwards, the Serpent king is harmless, and tribute to him and his followers can now be abandoned. The Hercules-god who kills the Dragon is regarded as a world-saviour, and his glorious victory becomes the chief annual commemoration of the peoples. Great monuments were erected to mark the event, and ritual re-enactments of the celestial battles were performed. The time of year at which the victory took place, August, was named after the hero responsible; Lugnasad, the "triumph of Lug".

We have already quoted at some length one incident in this ancient theomachy (the bout between Typhon and Zeus); whilst the story of Phaethon provides a very similar account of a related and almost identical incident. How then are these myths interpreted by modern authorities? Two of the most respected of these are the American Joseph Campbell and the Englishman Robert Graves. According to Graves,

> "The historical incident underlying the Giants' Revolt ... seems to be a concerted attempt by Macedonian mountaineers to storm Hellenic frontier fortresses, and their repulse by the Hellenes' subject-allies."[11]

Thus Graves sees history in these events. Presumably, though his opinion is here not recorded, he would have interpreted the Celtic, Norse, Vedic, Chinese, Mexican, and Babylonian theomachies (wars among the gods) in much the same way, as local tribal conflicts. The interpretation of Joseph Campbell is not much different; though he adds a patriarchal/matriarchal element to the dispute:

> "The reader will have recognized ... the pattern of the Greek war of the Titans and the gods, the darker brood of the all-mother, produced of her own female power, and the brighter, fairer, secondary sons, produced from her submission to fecundation by

---

11 R. Graves *The Greek Myths* Vol.1 p.133

the male. It is an effect of the conquest of a local matriarchal order by invading patriarchal nomads, and their reshaping of the local lore of the productive earth to their own ends."[12]

The average reader, having looked at any of the ancient descriptions of these conflicts (and it needs to be emphasised again that this story is found from Mexico to China and back), will find it incredible that the most respected mythologists of the 20th century can interpret, or misinterpret, in such a way. Yet Graves and Campbell are not entirely to blame. Having been assured by the astronomers, geologists, physicists, and a host of other specialists, that the ancient theomachies could not possibly mean what they said they meant, modern commentators were forced to search around for some alternative meaning: and euhemerist interpretations, long the stock-in-trade of those trying to "explain away" ancient myths, were once more called upon to do the job. But it must strike the honest reader as strange in the extreme that euhemerism – the attempt to make gods into ordinary men – the favourite tool of the medieval scholasts, should still be so widely used and accepted in the present century. Nevertheless, such is the authority and prestige of this school that it is the opposing view, the view which does not euhemerise, which does not attempt to "re-interpret" the myths, that is still deemed to be "lunatic fringe". In view of which we must ask ourselves; Have we left the Middle Ages yet?

It should be remarked here that a more recent and even more amusing variant of this euhemerism would see in the titanic battles of the gods an ancient nuclear war between alien invaders. Yet this interpretation, absurd though it may be, at least holds onto the "giant" dimensions of these events (they are, after all, conflicts between giants) whereas the more respectable euhemerism of Graves and Campbell misses even that.

12 Joseph Campbell *Occidental Mythology* (Penguin, 1964) pp.79-80

Catastrophism

The view which sees metaphor or human history in ancient reports of catastrophes has held sway, almost unchallenged, for the past century; but the victory of this theory was by no means inevitable.

With the rebirth of classical learning during the Renaissance, European scholars began, for the first time, to cast a critical eye upon the Bible. Efforts were made to discover what truth might lie behind the stories of miraculous events described in the Old Testament, as well as to integrate Hebrew history and tradition with that of Greece and Rome. William Whiston, the renowned astronomer and student of Isaac Newton, was one of many scholars of this time to suggest that the Deluge of Noah had been caused, not by perpetual rain, as the Book of Genesis implies, but by devastating tidal effects resulting from a close encounter between the earth and a giant comet.[13]

By the middle of the 18th century attempts at a scientific classification of geological strata were well under way. The savants of the time soon came to realise that earlier geological ages had seen the earth inhabited by vast numbers of creatures no longer in existence. The new science of palaeontology was concerned not just with the discovery and classification of these species, but with trying to discover why they became extinct. Georges Cuvier, the greatest of the early palaeontologists, was convinced that the extinct genera had been wiped out by cataclysmic events. This concept, which came to be known as "catastrophism", was shared by almost all earth scientists until the last quarter of the 19th century. Contrasting the superficially tranquil appearance of the earth's surface with the evidence for cataclysmic destruction beneath, Cuvier mused on how the observer,

> "... is not led to suspect that Nature ... had her intestine wars, and that the surface of the globe has been broken up by revolution and catastrophes. But his ideas change as soon as he digs into the soil which now presents so peaceful an aspect."[14]

---

13 W. Whiston *New Theory of the Earth* (1696)

14 G. Cuvier *Essay on the Theory of the Earth* (5th ed. 1827) p.240 (English trans. of "Discours sur les revolutions de la surface du globe, et sur les changements qu'elles ont produits dans la regne animal")

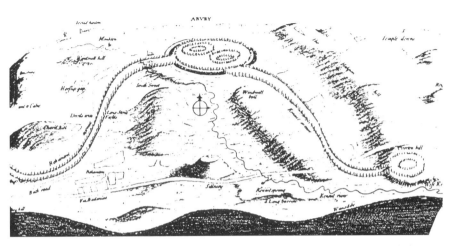

Origin of the Welsh dragon and George's dragon of England. William Stukeley's plan of Avebury, illustrating his theory that it was the temple of a dragon cult. Note also the mound / pyramid of Silbury Hill in the foreground.

Chinese dragon, showing clear parallels with Avebury dragon configuration.

The Serpent Mound of Ohio, part of a great North American dragon-worshipping and mound-building culture.

145

In his numerous publications Cuvier made it very plain that he regarded these upheavals of nature as world-wide events. Whilst he never explicitly endorsed the then widely-held view that such cataclysms had to be the result of collisions with other cosmic bodies, neither did he rule them out. Yet this catastrophist explanation of myth, as well as of mass extinction, was overturned in the latter years of the 19th century, when the "uniformitarian" concepts of Darwin's friend Charles Lyell gained the upper hand. So complete was the victory that by the early years of the 20th century textbooks were being written which decreed that the cataclysms described in ancient mythology were entirely fabulous, and that the catastrophist ideas of great thinkers such as Whiston and Cuvier belonged to the "lunatic fringe", alongside the works of the Flat Earth society.

Yet just when it seemed that catastrophism was as extinct as the mammoth, the whole controversy was reignited by one of the most maverick scientists of the 20th century. In his *Worlds in Collision* (1950) Immanuel Velikovsky used mankind's ancient traditions to demonstrate his thesis that immense catastrophes of nature had occurred in the recent past. Around 1,450 BC., Velikovsky claimed, a great comet had given the earth a near miss, devastating our planet with giant tidal waves, showers of meteorites, and massive tectonic convulsions. It was this comet, said Velikovsky, that gave rise to the legend of the dragon.

Velikovsky's ideas provoked a storm of controversy almost as violent as the events he described in his first book, and repeated attempts were made to have his work suppressed. Yet by the 1980s, much of what he said in *Worlds in Collision*, and which had seemed so outrageous at the time, was beginning to be quietly taken on board by the academic establishment. Thus for example it became clear, following the researches of Luis Alvarez, that the dinosaurs had been wiped out by some form of comet or asteroid impact, and in 1984 two of the most respected of British astronomers, Victor Clube and Bill Napier, published a book entitled *The Cosmic Serpent: A Catastrophist View of Earth History*, which more or less endorsed much of what Velikovsky had said in *Worlds in Collision*.

One of the most important criticisms levelled at Velikovsky during the 1950s concerned dates and dating-systems. How could he claim an earth-shattering event occurred around 1,450 BC., if the great civilisations of the time made no mention of it? Egyptologists, for example, claimed that they knew the very coronation date of the pharaoh who sat on the throne of

Egypt in 1,450 BC. In addition, monuments such as the pyramids, which they confidently dated to the third millennium BC., would surely have been levelled to the ground by events of the magnitude described by Velikovsky. Yet clearly they were not.

Even before the publication of *Worlds in Collision* Velikovsky became convinced that there was something dramatically wrong with ancient chronology, and he commenced work on a series of books entitled *Ages in Chaos*, whose purpose was to demonstrate the need for a drastic reduction in the length of pre-Christian history. Velikovsky died in 1979, before he could complete *Ages in Chaos*, but the work he began has continued to the present day. My own researches, conducted in co-operation with Professor Gunnar Heinsohn of Bremen University and Dr Heribert Illig of Munich, has led me to conclude that the reduction in ancient chronology proposed by Velikovsky was inadequate. Right to the end he adhered to the conventional idea that Near Eastern civilisations commenced in the 3rd millennium BC., two thousand years earlier than those of America and China. Believing that the ziggurats of Mesopotamia and the pyramids of Egypt predated the tumuli of the Americas and China by 2,000 years, Velikovsky was unable to fully comprehend the significance of the phenomenon.

But Egypt and Mesopotamia had no 2,000 year head start. All early civilisations commenced simultaneously in various parts of the globe around 1,000 BC. – and these civilisations, with their priest-kings and blood sacrifices, came into being as a result of the cataclysms so recently witnessed by humanity. The traumatised survivors of the catastrophe of 1,450 BC. sought, by means of ritualised violence, to control events over which they had, in reality, no control whatsoever. The gods who lived in the sky, it seemed, delighted in death and destruction. What if they were voluntarily offered victims? Perhaps they might leave the world in peace! High places, altars, (Latin *altus*) usually on mountain-tops, were sought out, and upon these victims were offered to the dragon. When people once again settled in the low-lying regions, artificial mountains, or pyramids, upon which the sacrifices could be performed, began to be erected.

Thus, by quirk of fate, was literate civilisation born. The erection of the sacred hills needed organisation. It needed building skills. It needed measuring skills. It needed record-keeping skills.

For seven centuries or so the comet, the dragon-monster, hung over the earth like a Sword of Damocles, threatening, with its apparently erratic, elliptical solar orbit, to repeat the carnage it had wrought upon the earth in the middle of the second millennium BC. However, around 800 BC., or shortly before, the comet came on a collision course with another member of the Solar System (the planet Mars, according to Velikovsky) and was removed as a threat. The clash between this body and the comet was recalled in the universal myth of the dragon-slayer. In this titanic "battle" the comet, or cosmic serpent, lost its tail; it was in effect "decapitated", and mythology everywhere recalled how the dragon-slaying hero cut the head off the great dragon (as in the Balor/Bran/Medusa tale).

The peoples of the earth rejoiced. They thanked the gods for deliverance. The Age of Sacrifice (as Hindu tradition rightly names it) was over. The dragon-monster of chaos had been slain, and the great heroes of the time are recalled as having put an end to human sacrifice.[15] In this way Perseus and Hercules were dragon-slaying heroes who rescued many victims destined for sacrifice to the beast. All over the earth great structures were raised in commemoration. These "megaliths" were fashioned from enormous tight-fitting blocks of stone, and were designed specifically to be earthquake-proof. The tectonic convulsions which had so recently gripped the planet had not yet fully subsided, though mankind was now fully confident that they eventually would.

The truth then is that the pyramids and megaliths do hold a great secret in their massive structures, a secret infinitely more dramatic and certainly more terrible than anything imagined by the purveyors of most "alternative" pyramid theories. These were the structures "raised", said Homer, "by the hands of giants for god-like kings of old." As they stand, they are mute witnesses to a time when chaos reigned in the heavens, when the members of the Solar System could not necessarily be relied upon to maintain their accustomed paths through the firmament. These great monuments, from the infancy of civilisation, speak to us of mankind's escape, in the not too distant past, from a very real Armageddon.

---

15 Over two centuries ago William Stukeley argued in great detail that the megaliths of Britain were temples of a dragon-cult. Stukeley pointed to the serpentine shapes carved on many of the megaliths, and also to the serpentine shape of the standing-stone avenues at Avebury. Many of the stones at Avebury are now demolished, so the serpent shape is not as obvious to the modern viewer, yet a glance at Stukeley's sketch of Avebury leaves little doubt that he was on the right track.

The Fiery God of the Megaliths

Over the past thirty years scholars have been repeatedly surprised, indeed astonished, by the accuracy with which the megalith-builders aligned their monuments with the movements of the heavenly bodies. But the skill displayed by architects of supposedly the third millennium BC. has perplexed academics. Small wonder the field has been open to every crackpot idea in the book.

Yet if the scientific and mathematical knowledge of the megalith-builders were not puzzling enough, the technology of the Atomic Age has opened our eyes to new and wholly unexpected mysteries. In this regard one of the most astonishing discoveries in recent years has been the abnormally high levels of radioactivity, as well as electromagnetic anomalies, found within many of the stone circles.[16] The disclosure of this fact prompted a whole myriad of speculation and outlandish theorising. Most popular has been the idea that the circles were the sites of visitations by intelligent extra-terrestrials. Another popular explanation of course is that our ancestors had access to a sixth sense which helped them locate centres of "energy".

But there is a more probable answer to the problem. As we have noted, the Irish name for a stone circle was "beltany", a word that denoted "Beal's fire". One of the most devastating aspects of the cosmic disasters postulated by Velikovsky was the meteor showers, debris from the great comet's tail that poured like hail upon the earth. Meteorites themselves were regarded as holy, and many were enshrined in temples. The spots where they landed were also sacred; the gods had touched these places with their heavenly fire. Throughout the ancient world indeed meteorites were regarded with the utmost reverence, and there are accounts from virtually every culture of sacred stones that fell from the sky which were afterwards venerated as symbols of royal and divine authority. The Kaaba in Mecca is one famous example of a shrine erected round a meteorite. The most sacred relic of Troy, the palladium, was likewise a rock that fell from the sky. The Egyptians called meteorite iron *bia*, or "metal from heaven", and tools of this material were employed in the performance of the most sacred religious rituals. The cult of the phoenix, the magical bird which immolated itself in fire, was intimately connected with meteorites. The

---

16 See eg. P. Devereux and I. Thomson *The Ley Hunter's Companion* (London,1970) p.70

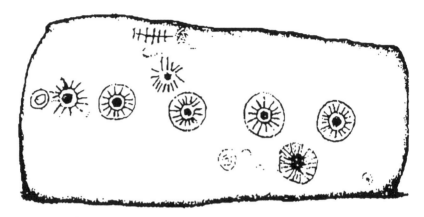

Kerbstone from New Grange, showing seven solar or stellar symbols, probably representing the seven gods – ie the five planets visible to the naked eye, plus the sun and moon.

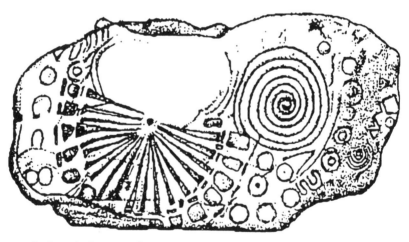

The "Sundial" Stone of New Grange. Note the spiral-shape, found on all megaliths and probably representing the spiralling tail of the comet Typhon.

Egyptians named the phoenix the benu-bird, a name identical to the word used for the pyramid-capstones, *benben*. The original benben, it was said, fell from the sky. The benben came to symbolise the primeval hill (or tower) that originally appeared above the waters of chaos. That a rock which fell from the sky was also linked to a flood-motif, as well as to the whole cult of pyramid-building, tells us much about the origins of this universal custom.

Pyramids, or sacred tumuli, were also linked in Celtic tradition to this same sky-obsessed religion. So too were sacred rocks which fell from the sky. Almost certainly in this category was the Irish *Lia Fail*, the Stone of Destiny, on top of which were crowned the High Kings of Ireland until it was taken to Scotland in the early Middle Ages.[17]

The ancients, it should be noted, could not have recognised a meteorite rock to look at. The rocks round which they erected their temples must have been observed falling.

Some of the megaliths were thus erected at meteorite impact sites. Yet the ancients were also in awe of another type of heavenly fire, thunderbolts. Velikovsky postulated interplanetary thunderbolts as an explanation of the myths which pictured the planetary deities wielding them.[18] Certainly there is no question that the dragon-slaying deity, whom we identify as the chief god of the megaliths, was armed with a thunderbolt. Taranis, the god of the heavenly wheel, was a thunder-god, as were his Greek counterparts Zeus and Hercules. In his seminal work *Die Veraltete Vorzeit* ("The Ageing of Prehistory"), Heribert Illig of Munich has argued for linking megalith-, particularly menhir-building, with thunder-gods, and has suggested that some of the more colossal menhirs may even have been designed to channel blasts of this divine fire to earth. He also suggests a link between such menhirs and the Tree of Life symbol, upon which sacrificial victims were put to death.[19]

It would appear then that the profusion of circular temple-building

---

17 The Stone of Scone, returned to Scotland in 1996, is almost certainly not the original, which all contemporary accounts describe as meteorite-like. A meteorite inscribed in Gaelic writing discovered in a gorge close to Scone in the early 19th century stands a far better chance of being the real thing.

18 Velikovsky *Worlds in Collision* (1950)

19 Heribert Illig Die Veraltete Vorzeit: Eine neue Chronologie der Prehistorie. Von Altamira, Alt-Europa, Atlantis uber Malta, Menhire, Mykene bis Stelen, Stonehenge, Zypren (Frankfurt,1988) p.115

during the megalithic epoch may have been largely due to the enormous number of meteorites then impacting on the earth, as well as the profusion of electromagnetic phenomena occurring at the time.

Earthquakes and *Klimasturz* in Early Celtic Times

It is not my purpose in the present volume to examine geological, climatological, or palaeontological evidence. Yet the disturbances of nature recorded by various ancient traditions, and dated by virtually all of them to the 9th and 8th centuries BC., have left their mark clearly in the archaeological and geological records, and in order to forestal any attempt to suggest that such evidence does not exist, I feel it would be appropriate, at this stage, to present a small sample of it. I emphasise that it is a small sample, and covers only the period I have considered most relevant to the present study.

During what has come to be known as the Urnfield and Hallstatt epochs (normally identified as Late Bronze/Early Iron), the people of central Europe frequently dwelt in villages constructed in the middle of lakes. R. Nordhagen and H. Gams were among the first to survey these lake dwellings in a scientific manner. To their great surprise, these men found that the lake dwellings of the Alps and southern Germany were not abandoned gradually, but were overwhelmed, in the 8th and 7th centuries BC., by massive inundations of water. These disastrous events were accompanied by powerful tectonic upheavals. Lake shorelines were tilted from the horizontal, in a manner that could only have occurred through the action of tremendously powerful earthquakes. Such, for example, was the case in the Ammersee and the Wurmsee in the foothills of the Bavarian Alps, and other lakes on the fringes of the Alps.[20] It was noted that Lake Constance had risen thirty feet at the time, whilst its bed was tilted dramatically. The same effects were observed in regions far from the Alps, especially in Scandinavia.[21] These disruptions were also dated to the 8th

20 R. Nordhagen and H. Gams "Postglaziale Klimaanderungen und Erdkrustbewegungen Mitteleuropa" cited from Velikovsky's *Earth in Upheaval* (1956)
21 See Velikovsky *Earth in Upheaval* "Klimasturz" and "Lake Dwellings"

and 7th centuries BC. A number of European lakes, such as the Ess-see and Federsee, were emptied of all their water as a result of these events. The Isartal (valley of the Isar) in the Bavarian Alps, was "violently torn out" in "very recent times".[22] Around the Inntal in the Tyrol the "many changes of river beds are indicative of ground movements on a grand scale."[23] Apparently all the lakes of the Swiss Alps, as well as the Bavarian Alps, the Tyrol, and the Jura, were subjected to the same forces.

It hardly needs to be stressed that the overspilling of lakes and disruption of rivers thus disclosed by archaeology accords precisely with the great natural events recounted in the Celtic traditions.

Nordhagen and Gams presented extensive evidence demonstrating that these disasters were accompanied by sudden climatic changes. Analysis of flora and fauna showed that there had been a marked deterioration of the European climate sometime in the 8th century. This evidence, together with the findings of other scholars, was placed before scientists gathered for the International Geological Congress in Stockholm in 1910. It was demonstrated there that major climatic fluctuations had taken place throughout the globe over the past few thousand years.

Since the 1910 Congress much work has been done in this field, and it is now accepted that a great climatic "plunge" or Klimasturz happened throughout Europe, Asia and North America at the end of the Subboreal period, ie. in the 8th century BC. The most extensive work was carried out by Scandinavian scientists. One of these, Rutger Semander, noted that "The deterioration of the climate must have been catastrophic in character."[24] G. Kossina, another prominent scientist of the period, agreed that the change had been brought about with suddenness.[25] Scientists from many fields noted that changes in the flora were especially marked. Areas that had supported temperate deciduous forests of oak and beech were almost overnight denuded of their cover. In some areas these were replaced by pine, in others by peat. The latter was the case in Britain and Ireland, where peculiar conditions resulted in the rapid formation of extensive peat bogs. It is still possible, in Ireland, to view the stumps of ancient oak

---

22 H. Gams and R. Nordhagen loc. cit.
23 Ibid.
24 R. Semander "Klimaverschlechterung, Postglaziale" cited from *Earth in Upheaval*
25 G. Kossina in Mannus, Zeitschrift fur Vorgeschichte cited from *Earth in Upheaval*

The bog-oaks, which died out following the great 'Climate Plunge' of c.700 BC., usually rest on a layer of clay and gravel. Above them, in the peat, are found artifacts of Ireland's Bronze and Iron Ages.

forests, which died in the 8th and 7th centuries BC., underlying the country's enormous peat bogs. On the continent too Nordhagen and Gams discovered, from analysis of pollen, a "radical change of life conditions, not a slow building of fens."[26]

This of course merely scratches the surface of a vast body of evidence relevant to our subject. Throughout the world, scientists have noted similar effects in strata dated to the 8th and 7th centuries BC. In some places (as in Ireland and Scotland) beaches were raised, on occasion by many metres. In other places, land was submerged.[27] Volcanic activity too was very much in evidence at the time, whilst all over the world the catastrophic effects of water inundations have been observed.

We thus find that the evidence uncovered by science in no way disagrees with the traditional material examined in the previous sections. In the present work it has been argued that the majority of the European megaliths were erected in the wake of a great natural catastrophe, or series of catastrophes, occurring around 830 BC. It has also been suggested that it was this catastrophe which led to the changes in the world's climate observed by the scientists, producing in Europe a cooler and more humid environment. The changed climate led to the rapid appearance of substantial peat-bogs in many areas of Europe. From this it should be evident that most, if not all, of the peat-bogs covering the uplands of Britain and Ireland formed as a result of this last great climate-plunge, or *klimasturz*. Yet in the British Isles the formation of these bogs is not attributed to the *klimasturz* that devastated central Europe in the early 8th century BC. On the contrary, it is held, an earlier *klimasturz* killed off Britain's upland oaks. But there is a good reason for this attempt to postulate two climate-plunges.

Hilly regions throughout the British Isles have revealed more than oaks beneath the peat. In various places stone circles and other megaliths have been discovered when peat has been removed for fuel. Such, for example, was the case at Machrie Mar in Arran, Scotland, where a previously concealed stone circle was revealed after the upper layers had been cut

---

26 Gams and Nordhagen loc. cit.

27 In many areas of England and Wales, for example, there are numerous examples of submerged forests. These are dated as "probably Post-Glacial or Recent". H.B. Woodward *The Geology of England and Wales* (1887) p.523

away.[28] The stones of this circle, and other structures covered by peat growth, rested upon the hard earth underneath, and there is no question that any of these could have been built upon an already-existing bog.

From this it is evident that some of the megaliths, perhaps most of them, were erected during, or immediately before, the last great climate disturbance. But since the megaliths of Britain are believed to have been raised during the second and third millennia BC., it was surmised that the last major climatic disturbance in Britain had not been contemporary with that of central Europe, which destroyed Late Bronze Urnfield and Hallstatt settlements. Yet the *klimasturz* of mainland Europe must also have affected the British Isles. It was accompanied, we remember, by massive tectonic upheavals. How then is the apparent absence of the 8th century *klimasturz* in Britain explained? In fact, it is not. The question is simply ignored.[29]

28 Aubrey Burl *Prehistoric Stone Circles* (Shire Publications,1979) p.10 Burl in fact makes it quite plain that large numbers of megaliths were erected on land that subsequently became covered in peat. This for example was the case at Callanish, on the island of Lewis, where the removal of the peat in the 19th century revealed the true extent of the monument, whilst at the other end of the scale a tiny stone circle was excavated from the peat at Beaghmore, County Tyrone, in the 1970s.

29 Nevertheless, a very brief examination of the 7th century BC climate plunge is found in H. Godwin's *The History of the British Flora* (London, 1956). Godwin however fails to connect the British climate disturbance with the much wider event described by the German and Scandinavian scientists, and fails completely to understand its connection with the vast seismic activity identified by those scholars

CHAPTER 6

The Age of Heroes

The Eighth Century BC.

There was a point in the histories of all ancient peoples when the purely mythical epoch, the age of the gods, came to an end. After this, history proper, as we would understand it, began. But it began only very gradually, and there was a prolonged period in which the gods interacted with men, when, as the Bible describes it, the sons of God consorted with the daughters of men. The fruit of these unions were neither gods nor men, but demigods; beings of lesser stature than the gods themselves, but infinitely superior to ordinary mortals. These were the heroes; and their epoch is commonly termed the Heroic Age.

The hero-demigods of old Ireland, Cuchulainn, Fionn and their companions, as well as those of Britain, Arthur and his knights, belong to this final generation of divine beings. Such characters, we shall see, like Hercules of Greece, were essentially planetary deities, yet by this stage they had become thoroughly anthropomorphised, and, although still capable of titanic feats, took on the dimensions at least of ordinary mortals. How much of their nature was divine; and how much human? This is a question that has long exercised the minds of men;

> "Were Conchobar and his Ulster champions, Fionn and his Fianna, Arthur and his Knights once living men round whom the attributes of gods have gathered or were they ancient deities renamed and stripped of some of their divinity to make them more akin to their human worshippers? History or mythology? A mingling, perhaps, of both. Cuchulainn may have been the name of a real Gaelic warrior,

however suspiciously he may resemble the sun god [Lugos] who is said to have been his father ... It is the same problem that confronts us in dealing with the heroic legends of Greece and Rome. Were Achilles, Agamemnon, Odysseus, Paris, Aeneas gods, demigods, or men? Let us call them all alike – whether they are Greek or Trojan heroes, Red Branch Champions or followers of the Gaelic Fionn or the British Arthur – demigods. Even so, they stand definitely apart from the older gods who were greater than they were."[1]

As we have said, it is normally assumed that different ancient cultures experienced their Heroic Age at different times and in different epochs. This is due to the fact that the interpretation of myth hitherto holding sway (whether for example that of James Frazer, Robert Graves or Joseph Campbell) bears little or no relationship to our interpretation. Whereas we suggest that myths largely represent a human reaction to cataclysmic events of nature that occurred at a specific time in the past, these other writers would see the perennial, day to day concerns which still affect us all (the seasons, birth, death, reproduction etc) as the major source. Yet such interpretations, we repeat, can only be adhered to by ignoring most of what the myths tell us in very graphic terms.

If then cosmic catastrophes in the heavens are the primary source of myth, and if these events came to an end in the eighth century BC., this would suggest that the Heroic Age, the age that brought the strictly mythological epoch to an end, occurred everywhere in the eighth century BC.: And that after this time, in lands that were fully literate, the age of history, properly speaking, began.

Is this the case?

The facts speak for themselves. Evidence from many lands suggests that the eighth century BC. was a crucial period for mankind. Many nations traced the beginnings of their history, and also of their calendar, to that period, whilst some held that no accurate history preceding the 8th/7th century existed. This was the epoch that saw the emergence of historical consciousness. Before that, both in the orient and the occident, there is only myth and legend. In the words of one eminent historian;

---

1 Geddes and Grosset *Celtic Mythology* (1999) pp.130-1

"It is a strange fact, and one that appears never to have been given the attention it deserves, that the strictly 'historical' period … stretches back exactly to the sixth [we would say seventh] century before the Christian era, as though there were at that point a barrier in time impossible to surmount by the methods of investigation at the disposal of ordinary research. Indeed, from this time onwards there is everywhere a well-established chronology, whereas for all that occurs prior to it only very vague approximations are as a rule obtained, and the dates suggested for the same events often vary by several centuries."[2]

Everywhere there is the suggestion that immediately prior to this period unusual events of nature terminated the Age of Bronze and launched the Age of Iron. A few examples should illustrate the point.

It was near the middle of the 8th century, according to modern archaeology, that the Etruscans established themselves in north and central Italy.[3] Herodotus informs us that the Etruscans had originated in Lydia, in Asia Minor, and had left their home in the wake of a disastrous famine.[4] The great city of Rome, situated at the southern end of Etruria, was founded in the 8th century,[5] apparently by refugees arriving from the sacked city of Troy. Migration precipitated by natural disasters led to warfare, but Troy was apparently destroyed not by armies, but by a powerful earthquake. This is suggested by Virgil, where he has a goddess remember the city's destruction thus;

"There, you see masses of masonry scattered, stones wrenched from stones, and smoke and dust billow upwards together, there Neptune himself is at work shattering the walls and the foundations dislodged by his mighty trident, and tearing the whole city from its site."[6]

Neptune was the Roman name for Poseidon, whom the Greeks called "Earthshaker" and who was symbolised by a horse. When Troy was finally

---

2 Rene Guenon *The Crisis of the Modern World* (trans. London,1942) p.14

3 D. Randall-MacIver "Etruscan Tombs" *Antiquity* ix No.33 (March,1935) p.50

4 Herodotus i,93

5 Traditionally in 735 BC.

6 Virgil *Aeneid* 610-15

excavated it was discovered, much to everyone's surprise, that the greatest stage of the town, Troy VI, had been destroyed by a massive earthquake.

If Troy was wrecked by an earthquake in the 8th century, then perhaps we also have an answer to the question of why the river Scamander changed its course and threatened to drown the Greek hero Achilles.[7] Indeed the story of Achilles' battle with the Scamander is very reminiscent of the accounts of "erupting" rivers given in the Irish traditions.

Immanuel Velikovsky pointed out that the battles between the gods recounted by Homer in the *Iliad* referred quite simply to catastrophic events in the skies at the time. Throughout the story we hear of clashes between Ares (Mars) and his arch-enemy Athena (the great comet), and these, Velikovsky insisted, were part of the upheavals in the skies that led to disasters on earth.

But of course the Greek Heroic Age, or, as it is now sometimes designated, the Mycenaean epoch, is normally placed in the 15th, 14th and 13th centuries BC. How do we reconcile this with an 8th century date? It is impossible at this stage to go into a detailed discussion of Greek chronology, or to explain how and why it was erroneously reconstructed. Suffice for the moment to state that those nations of the Near East, such as Greece, Egypt, and Babylonia, which are said to possess histories long predating the eighth century, in reality possess no such thing, and these phantom "histories" are based on a series of monumental errors committed by the archaeologists of the 19th century. Some of the evidence relating to Egypt's chronology will be examined in the final chapter; here we shall take an extremely brief look at some of the abundant evidence showing the necessity for a dramatic reduction in the date of the Greek Mycenaean/Heroic Age . We need, for example, only look at the various circumstances surrounding the Trojan War. This event is "traditionally" dated to 1184 BC., on the strength of an absurdly high estimate of 40 years for a generation. Yet we are told that Aeneas the Trojan hero put in at Carthage on his way westwards to find a new home in Italy. Carthage, however, was not, by general consent, established until the middle of the 8th century. King Midas, an 8th century monarch of Phrygia, was a contemporary of the Trojan Campaign, and the Phoenicians, who mastered the seas in the 9th and 8th centuries, were powerful allies of the Trojans.

---

7 Homer *Iliad* xxi

Traditions surrounding the Olympic Games tell the same story. The Greeks dated the beginning of history proper, *historikon*, from the foundation of the Olympiads. Prior to that was *mythikon*, the age of myths, and it is generally agreed that the Games were founded in the eighth century, in the year 776 BC. to be precise. Yet Homer tells us that heroes who fought at Troy took part in the Games. Again, it was said that the Olympiads had been established by Hercules, well before the commencement of the Trojan Campaign. As we shall see towards the end of the present chapter, various ancient peoples, including the Romans and the Irish, also had their "olympiads", and these were invariably linked to a great event involving the god Mars. Thus it was said that shortly after the founding of Rome, Romulus established the Equiria, a gymnastics festival, in honour of Mars.[8] In the same way, the Irish celebrated a gymnastics festival, the Aonach Tailteann, or Tailton Games, in honour of the god Lugh/Lugos, whilst some have argued that an analogous event also took place in Britain in the vicinity of Stonehenge. The Irish event, celebrated every August, included horse and foot races, wrestling and other types of combat, and there is strong evidence that it was held in honour of Hermes, the god of wisdom, and Mars, the war god.[9]

Now Hercules, according to a number of ancient sources, was the god Mars, and evidence would seem to suggest that the almost universal custom of having martial games in honour of Mars commemorates some form of cosmic event in the 8th century BC. As we have seen, Hercules was the dragon-slayer *par excellence*. He it was who battled the serpent-tailed Triton, and slew the serpent-headed Hydra. Velikovsky's hypothesis was that sometime early in the 8th century BC. Mars had crossed the path of the serpent-tailed comet, diverting it away from the earth, and saving our planet from destruction. Here the name Hercules is significant, for it apparently means "Glory of Hera". Hera of course was Mother Earth.

It is evident then that the martial games honouring Mars were intended

---

8 MacGeoghegan *The History of Ireland* (New York,1845) p.13

9 *Lugnasad*, the Old Irish name for August, implies "triumph of Lug", and this triumph, we have seen, was the triumph gained by Lugh and Ogma, as well as the other gods, against the titan Fomorians at the battle of Magh Tuireadh, the "Plain of the Tower". In the Celtic myth of gods versus giants it is Lugos (Hermes) who is mainly responsible for the victory, whilst in the Greek myth the real hero of the gods was Hercules. But Hercules is himself an alter-ego of Mars. The name Tailton, as we saw in the previous chapter, is also linked to Hercules.

to celebrate this god's decapitation or destruction of the Cosmic Serpent.

Hercules performed Twelve Labours, and it is clear that these represented the signs of the zodiac, or the months of the year. In performing his labours, it seems that Hercules/Mars was establishing a new calendar: and in fact, as we have seen, the ancients looked on Hercules as a god of learning. Velikovsky explained the calendar changes of the 8th century as a direct result of near-collisions between the earth and other cosmic bodies at that time.

The Chronicles of Britain and Ireland

During the early middle ages a whole mass of literature, both in Britain and Ireland, but more especially in Ireland, claimed to tell the history of the kings, champions and wise men of these islands many centuries into the pre-Christian past. There is no doubt that the Irish, in paticular, possessed a vast literature dating back to the very first years of the Christian era and perhaps even before. Many of the medieval texts preserved phrases and words which were obscure and obsolete even then, which the medieval transcribers felt obliged to explain to their own readers. A large number of books, said to be written in Druid times, are named as the source of the information appearing in the medieval chronicles; and there is in fact very good evidence to suggest that the Druids did possess a substantial written literature. The Spaniard Ethicus of Istria, for example (4th century AD.), was said to have travelled to Ireland, where he spent some time "examining their volumes", whilst we are told that Saint Patrick condemned and burned 180 volumes of the Druid lore.

The histories of pre-Christian Ireland, and to a lesser extent Britain, provided by the medieval chroniclers, are said to have been either derived from or directly copied from these Druid texts; and it is evident that the great amount of information relating to pagan times, with for example very accurate descriptions of the Celtic gods and heroes, as well as knowledge of pre-Christian festivals and the Ogam script, would suggest that the monks did indeed copy huge amounts directly from texts of pagan date. But is this sufficient reason to give credence to the pre-Christian histories also provided by the medieval writers, which, in the case of Ireland, trace the story of the Gaelic High Kings (the "Milesians" or children of Mil Espaine) back roughly thirty-five generations into the pre-Christian past? Unfortunately, it seems that we must exercise the greatest caution in this regard.

It is beyond question that during the early centuries of the Christian era there was an attempt, both in Britain and Ireland, to turn the native gods, held in high esteem by the great mass of the people, first into Christian saints, and, at a later stage, into ordinary kings and leaders. In the words of one authority,

> "It was the policy of the first Christianisers of Ireland to describe the loved heroes of their still half-heathen flocks as having handed in their submission to the new creed. The tales about Cochobar and Cuchulainn were amended to prove that those very pagan personages had been miraculously brought to accept the gospel at last ... Daring attempts were made to change the Tuatha De Danann from pagan gods into Christian saints ... Brigit, the goddess of fire, poetry and the hearth, is famous today as St Bridget or Bride."[10]

Precisely the same process is observed in Britain, where St Alban, for example, promoted as the first Christian martyr of Britain, is fairly obviously Albion, the eponymous hero-deity of the land. At a later stage, however, in both islands, it was deemed that the acceptance of the new saints was, "not sufficiently general to do away with other means of counteracting the still living influence of the pantheon of Gaelic [and British] gods."[11] The solution was drastic. A fresh school of euhemerists,

> " ... arose to prove that the gods were never even saints but merely wordly men who had once lived and ruled in Erin. Learned monks worked hard to construct a history of Ireland from the Flood downwards. An amazing genealogy, compiled by Eugene O'Curry from the various pedigrees the monks elaborated and inserted into the Books of Ballymote, Lecan and Leinster, shows how not merely the Tuatha De Danann but also the Fir Bholgs, the Fomorii, the

10 Geddes and Grossert loc. cit. p.185
11 Ibid.

Sons of Mil Espaine and the races of Partholon and Nemedh were descended from Noah. Japhet, the patriarch's son, was the father of Magog from whom came two lines, the first being the sons of Mil Espaine, while the second branched out into all the other races."[12]

We see precisely the same process clearly at work in Geoffrey's *History of the Kings of Britain*, where well-known deities like Corineus (Cernunnos), Lud, Lear, Belinus, and Brennus, as well as Arthur, are made into early kings and provided with reign lengths and exact chronologies. In Ireland, a whole history of the island, comprised mainly (or perhaps entirely) of euhemerised gods, and taking us back to the very dawn of creation, was provided by the medieval monks.

"Having once worked the gods first into universal history and then into the history of Ireland [and Britain], it was an easy matter to supply them with dates of birth and death, local habitations and places of burial. We are told with precision exactly how long Nuada, the Daghda, Lugh and the others reigned at Tara. The barrows of the Boyne provided them with comfortable tombs. Their enemies, the Fomorii, became real invaders who were beaten in real battles. Thus it was thought to make plain prose of their gods."[13]

It is clear then that if we wish to use any of the material contained in the pre-Christian "histories", we must proceed with the greatest caution. The euhemerisers, we saw, provided precise dates in the early Christian era for Cuchulainn and his associates, and for Fionn MacCumhaill and his. Yet these characters, we have demonstated, were gods and demigods of the Heroic Age, an age we have fairly precisely located in the early first millennium BC., in the eighth century, roughly. Nevertheless, there exists some evidence to suggest that elements of the chronicles purporting to deal with the pre-Christian epoch are genuine.

A number of factors are here worthy of note. The claim of a Spanish origin for the Gaels, the insistence that their settlement in Ireland took place amidst mighty upheavals of nature, and the claim that the earliest of the High Kings were cultural innovators and men of great wisdom.

---

12 Ibid. p.186
13 Ibid.

The Irish traditions were very consistent in their claims that when the children of Milesius arrived the land was beset by "eruptions" (Irish *tomaidhm*). These "eruptions", evidently powerful earthquakes, changed the courses of rivers, made lakes both appear and disappear overnight, and caused irruptions of the sea, in the form of great tidal waves. Such events, if they occur during the actual settlement, are accredited to the magical powers of the Tuatha De Danann, who, notwithstanding the attempts of Christian chroniclers to make them into mortal men, nevertheless retained some of their supernatural powers. Often however the eruptions are not interpreted mythically, but recorded as simple facts. Consider for example a typical entry in "The Annals of the Four Masters", recounting events in the second year of the reign of Eremon, Ireland's supposed first Gaelic High King:

"The Age of the World, 3503. The second year of the reign of Eremhon over Ireland. Amergin Gluingeal, son of Milidh, fell in the battle of Biletineadh this year by Eremhon. The eruption of the nine Brosnachs, ie. rivers of Eile; of the nine Righes, ie. rivers of Leinster; and of the three Uinsionns of Hy-Oiliolla."[14]

Similarly, in Keating we find:

"The fourteenth year after the death of Eibhear, Eiremhon died at Airgeadros at Raith Beitheach, beside the Feoir, and there he was buried. The same year the river called the Eithne burst over land in Ui Neill; and the river called the Freaghobhal burst over land between Dal nAruide and Dal Riada."[15]

Modern scholarship is of course at a loss to explain such statements. The majority of commentators simply ignore them. When they are mentioned it is normally briefly, and the suggestion is made that they represent somewhat exaggerated accounts of ancient river floods. However, the rivers "erupted", they did not merely overflow. Nor do flooding rivers explain the sudden appearance and disappearance of lakes recounted in the same passages; nor indeed the mass irruptions of the sea.

---

14 *Annals of the Kingdom of Ireland* (trans. O'Donovan, Dublin,1856)
15 Keating *History of Ireland* Vol.1 sec.22

Support for the view that these medieval Irish traditions are derived from the deepest antiquity is provided by the fact that Gallic myths and legends, as recorded by Roman writers, speak of more or less the same things. It is in fact evident that Continental Celtic mythology laid great stress upon nature's destructive forces. As in the Irish accounts, these are generally identified as catastrophes of earthquake and flood, and they precipitated migrations. In a famous passage of Ammianus Marcellinus, where he quotes Timagenes, we read:

"According to ancient druidic teachings, the population of Gaul is only partly indigenous, and expanded at various times to include foreigners from across the sea, and people from beyond the Rhine who had to leave their homes either because of the hardships of war, a constant problem in those countries, or because of the invasion of the fiery element that roars on their coasts."[16]

What, we may ask, was the "fiery element" that roared on the sea? Did the Druids here refer to tidal waves or fiery disturbances in the skies? Notably, disturbances in nature are here linked to tribal migration, an element in Celtic tradition that we encounter with great frequency.

The Cimbri were one of the most renowned tribes of ancient Europe, with an identity partly Celtic and partly Germanic. They too had a legend, alluded to by Strabo, of forced migration caused by the action of the sea:

"How are we to suppose that the Cimbri were driven from their original homeland by a high tide in the ocean when we now see them today living in those same places? ... Is it not absurd to suppose that a whole people could be driven from their homes by resentment against a natural and continual phenomenon which recurs twice a day? In any case, this extraordinary tide appears wholly fictitious. since variations in the level of ocean tides are quite regular and seasonal."[17]

Indeed the ocean tides are quite regular and seasonal, and it is just this fact that gives credence to the Cimbrian legend: for the Cimbri must have

---

16 Ammianus Marcellinus xv,9
17 Strabo vii,2

been well aware of the normal behaviour of the tides, and they could scarcely have invented such a ridiculous story had the events recounted by them not been extraordinary. Continuing in his sceptical tone, Strabo exclaims:

"Neither do I believe ... that the Cimbri brandish their weapons at the mounting waves to drive them back, nor, as Ephorus says of the Celts or Gauls, that they train themselves to fear nothing by calmly watching the sea destroy their homes, which they later rebuild, and that floods have claimed more victims among them than war."[18]

A strong hint that these destructive waves from the sea were far from being normal tide-action or storms, is provided by Aristotle, who specifically links them with earthquakes. Speaking of human courage, he muses, "When one goes to the extent of fearing neither earthquake nor rising waves, as the Celts claim to do ..."[19]

Like their Irish and continental counterparts, the bards of Wales emphasised the terrible fury of the sea in an age long past: And here too, tribal migration is one of its results. Thus in the *Triads of Britain* we read:

"The third invasion of [of Britain] was that of the men of Galedin who sailed in ships without masts or rigging to the isle of Gweith [Isle of Wight] when their country was flooded."[20]

The men of Galedin were almost certainly the Gauls – Galatae – and this invasion must refer to the mass migration of Celtic-speaking Gauls to Britain. Of great interest is the fact that the various Gallic immigrations into Britain are recalled in medieval literature as having been led by Hercules, as indeed is the immigration of the Gaels into Ireland from Spain.

Whilst these other Celtic sources do provide some corroboration for the Irish chronicles, it must be again stressed that most of what they say can probably have no basis in history. The memory of mighty irruptions of the sea and the overspilling of lakes would have been too traumatic to be erased

---

18 Ibid.
19 Aristotle *Nichomachean Ethics* viii,7
20 *Triad* 109

from the national consciousness: Yet the detailed life-stories of generations of High Kings can only be seen as largely if not entirely spurious. Having said that, there are tantalising hints that some of the events recounted may be partly historical. For many of the early High Kings, who are supposed to have reigned during the disasters, are regarded as Sage Kings; and in this regard their characters parallel the early kings and lawgivers of other cultures and civilisations far removed from Ireland. And secondly, the cataclysmic eruptions, say the chronicles, die away in intensity and frequency as the centuries pass. This is a detail of great importance.

Ireland, it is said, saw its worst natural disaster during the reign of Tighernmus, a character reviled by Christian commentators as a practioner of human sacrifice, who is supposed to have reigned a couple of centuries after the intial settlement of the Gaels. Nevertheless, from this point onwards, the "eruptions" begin to be reported less and less. Indeed, only a few generations afterwards, we hear the last of them. This was during the funeral of the High King Melghe Molbhthach. "When his grave was digging," we are told, "Loch Melghe burst over the land in Cairbre, so that it was named from him."[21] If the chronology provided in the annals is correct (which of course we do not for one minute suggest is the case), this would have occurred sometime in the fourth century BC.

One of the major points stressed by Immanuel Velikovsky was that earthquakes, caused originally by the disruptive gravitational pull of other heavenly bodies, would have continued well after the offending planet or comet had departed from the immediate vicinity of the earth;

> "On the basis of the material offered in the foregoing pages, the assumption is made here that earthquakes result from torsion of the crust following a change in the position of the equator and the displacement of matter inside the globe caused by the direct attraction of a cosmic body when in close contact. Pull, torsion, and displacement were responsible for mountain-building too.
>
> "If this conception of the causes of earthquakes is correct, then there must have been fewer earthquakes during the course of time since the last cosmic earthquake. The regions of the Apennine Peninsula, the eastern Mediterranean, and Mesopotamia, for which we have reliable records, can be compared in this respect to the same

---

21 "The Four Masters loc. cit.

regions today.

"Earthquakes in Asia Minor, Greece, and Rome are described or mentioned in many classic authors. For the purpose of comparison with earth-tremor activity of the present day, it is enough to point to fifty-seven earthquakes reported in Rome in a single year during the Punic wars (-217)."[22]

But Italy and the Near East are perhaps not the only areas that kept records of earthquakes; the same phenomenon seems to be recorded in the Irish annals. The "eruptions" grow less and less frequent after the time of Tighernmus, until, about three centuries later, we hear the last of them. These final Irish earth tremors (if there is any truth whatsoever in the chronicles) must have occurred around the fourth century BC. Italy is a more seismically active part of the world than Ireland, so it should come as no surprise to find that Rome was still being afflicted by such a large number of tremors as late as 217 BC.

Two other circumstances, we have said, would suggest that some credence at least must be given to the pre-Christian Irish records. The Gaels are said by them to have come from Spain; a claim which shall be examined in the final chapter; and the early High Kings are regarded as men of wisdom and cultural innovators; a factor which links them to other ancient kings of the eighth and seventh centuries BC.

The Sage-Kings

As befits an age of such awe-inspiring events, the eighth century BC. was everywhere the Age of Heroes. Men who lived at the time had watched the gods in action. They had seen the arrows of Hercules and Apollo (meteorites) showered upon the earth. They had viewed the awesome thunderbolts of Jupiter hurled across the skies. They had watched in terror as Poseidon, the Shaker of Earth, had set the ground under their feet in motion and propelled vast walls of water over the headlands. Above all, they witnessed the decapitation in the skies of the terrible Serpent of Chaos, the monster losing the giant tail it had dragged across the heavens.

22 Velikovsky *Worlds in Collision* p.267

This event was the great watershed that defined all future developments. The cult of the serpent, which had demanded hecatombs of human beings, could now be abandoned: And sure enough, the heroes of the time employed themselves in ending this barbaric practice (Centuries later, in Ireland, Saint Patrick was credited with the same feat).

We can only guess at how these events affected the people of the time. Certainly the entire planet experienced what could only be described as a cultural revolution. This revolution touched every aspect of human life, manifesting itself in the construction of the immense temples and pyramidical structures, as well as an outpouring of philosophical and religious works. It became an age of sages, seers and prophets, men who had been inspired by the awesome events they were witness to. In Israel, this was the time of Moses, an enemy of the serpent-god, who established a completely new religious system for his people. In Persia, the epoch saw the appearance of Zoroaster; in India it was the time of the great avatar Krishna (another serpent-slayer), whilst in China the Taoist sages were active. Greece too had its sages and seers. Theseus, for example, the legendary king of Athens, was credited with formulating various wise laws.[23] Hercules of course was believed to have initiated great social and religious changes. The Romans looked to Romulus as a great legislator and reformer.

In the same way, all the primeval kings and god-kings of Britain and Ireland, as well as being the builders of the monuments, were regarded as culture-bearers and religious innovators. These were Homer's "god-like kings", for whom the giants raised the mighty temples. Some of the megalithic Passage Graves in the Boyne valley were linked by tradition to these High Kings. Thus Carn T. at Loughcrew was identified by its first excavators in the 19th century as the tomb of one of the wisest, Ollamh Fodhla, as it conformed in detail to the description of his burial-place in ancient legend.

In Ireland, the fifth High King, Irial Faidh, was remembered for the innumerable beneficial laws he enacted, whilst his son Ethrial, who succeeded him, was long recalled as a great poet, some of whose compositions, like those of his contemporary the British Taliesin, were still recited in the Christian age. He was also said to have composed a history of his people up to that time. The eighth High King of Ireland, known as

23 See eg. Plutarch *Theseus* 24 and 25

Tighearnmhas, was remembered for his technological innovations:

"It [was] ... Tighearnmhas who first found a mine of gold in Ireland; and Uchadan was the name of the artificer who used to refine the gold for him; and it was in Fotharta east of Lithfe he used to smelt it. It was in the time of Tighearnmhas that clothes were first dyed purple, blue and green in Ireland. It was also in his time that embroidery, fringes and filigree were first put on mantles in Ireland."[24]

Greatest of all the Irish Sage Kings however was Ollamh Fodhla, who was reputed to have lived a few generations after Tighearnmhas. His name means simply "Sage of Erin", and many of the most enduring laws and customs of the Irish were dated to his reign.

British tradition, as preserved for example in Geoffrey of Monmouth's *History*, also speaks of Sage Kings who reigned immediately after the settlement of the land by Brutus, the eponymous ancestor of the people. We can of course take with a pinch of salt many of the claims made by Geoffrey and others of his ilk (such as the supposed Trojan ancestry of the Britons), though the evidence would suggest that their writings, like those of the Irish, contain at least a nucleus of genuinely ancient material. This is proved, as we have seen, by the very clear references to catastrophic disturbances of nature in many of the accounts. The Sage King who raised Stonehenge is not named by Geoffrey, for the simple reason that the monument was already strongly connected to Merlin, who was nevertheless placed many centuries after Brutus' initial settlement. That Stonehenge was raised in honour of the god Arthur/Lugos is beyond question, yet it may be that some of the material relating to Arthur properly belongs to the king who built it. Could it be that his name is yet preserved? Certainly the chances are that a ruler so powerful would be remembered in folk tradition. His monument alone, like the pyramid of Cheops, would perchance guarantee his immortality.

I believe it reasonably possible that the king who erected the great Round Temple of Britain was named Vlatos, recalled in medieval British tradition under the name Bladud, who was, as we have already indicated, almost certainly identical to the Hyperborean sage Abaris, reputedly the

---

24 Keating *History of Ireland* Bk.1 Sec.xxv

preceptor of Pythagoras. In the British tradition Bladud has all the appearance of a god, flying high above the great temple of Apollo at New Troy. Yet the deification of real people is a common enough phenomenon, and we need only recall how the Egyptians turned Imhotep, the architect of the Step Pyramid at Sakkara, into the god Imouthes/Asclepius.

Against this, it has to be admitted that the name Abaris could be little more than a variant of Abal (Celtic "apple"), a local title for Apollo. Certainly the links between the Hyperboreans and Apollo's cult would support this interpretation. Nevertheless, early Celtic warrior-kings regularly adopted the names of their tutelary deities (witness the warrior Brennos who invaded Greece in the 3rd century BC.), so Abaris could possibly (though it is unlikely) be the name of a real priest-king devotee of Apollo/Belinos, whose name perhaps translates as "Apollo's man".

Alternatively, it may be that the Welsh name for Stonehenge, *Gwaith Emrys*, may contain a reference to its builder. Emrys, one of the titles of Merlin, has usually been dismissed as a Welsh transliteration of the Latin Ambrosius; yet evidence uncovered in the present work suggests otherwise. As with so much else in British tradition, what is popularly traced no further than the Romans or even the early Christians has in fact a much more ancient pedigree. Emrys is really a Welsh rendering of the Vulgate Arthurian Bors, Boras, who, as we have already demonstrated, is even now linked to the area just west of Stonehenge. The true antiquity of the link between this name and the monuments of Salisbury Plain is also, we have seen, demonstrated by the fact that Hecataeus of Abdera regarded Boreas and his descendants as the keepers of the sacred precinct of the Hyperboreans – a precinct identified even by sceptical scholars with Stonehenge and Avebury.

The name Emrys/Boras may also be linked to that of the Irish hero-deity Eber/Emer, one of the legendary Galician colonizers of Ireland. Certainly the most important innovators amongst the various megalith-building groups were the folk of the Atlantic (Irish-Spanish) culture, who imported many of the Mediterranean techniques into the British Isles. Could it be that these ancient megalith-builders are here recalled?

The primeval traditions of Britain and, even more especially, Ireland need to be re-examined in the light of our new understanding, and we may reasonably hope that they will provide the framework for reconstructing the history of these islands in the pre-Christian centuries.

Thus the period that saw the end of the cosmic upheavals, which we hold to be the 8th century BC., was an epoch of revolutionary progress in all fields. The Druid priesthood of the Celtic realms mobilised their efforts chiefly towards the creation of a new religious orthodoxy, in which esotericism was of primary importance. They codified their teachings and passed them on to selected persons. Theirs however was not a knowledge to be spread democratically throughout the population. They went to great lengths to ensure that their wisdom would remain secret. Little did they realise how successful they would be! So successful indeed that their own descendants have lost sight of their achievements, and attributed their greatest feats, the megalithic monuments, to another priesthood and another time.

The Celtic Olympiads

A central concept of Velikovsky's was that all the great festivals of early mankind commemorated or celebrated the cosmic events so recently observed in the heavens. This applied not only to the overtly religious rituals associated with the temple-pyramids, but to virtually every custom and tradition of popular culture. In particular, he emphasised that athletic festivals, with their ritualised combats, were in all probability re-enactments of the cosmic combats in the skies. Thus it was the 8th century BC., that epoch of cosmic instability, which saw the establishment of the Olympiads in Greece and the Equiria in Rome. The Greek Olympiads, we have seen, were linked to Hercules, the dragon-slaying hero deity, while the Roman Equiria were linked to Mars, the god of war. A number of ancient sources make it clear that Hercules and Mars were originally one and the same god,[25] and it seems virtually certain that the violent sporting events of the classical world, including even the later gladiatorial contests, can all trace their inspiration to the bloody sacrificial rituals of the Bronze Age.

Yet as our knowledge of ancient cultures far removed from Europe improves, it becomes clear that such ritualised sporting events were a

---

25 This is claimed by Macrobius (*Saturnalia* iii,12,5-6) on the authority of Varro, whilst in Eratosthenes we read; "Tertia est stella Martis quam alii Hercules dixerunt." (Mars is the third star, which others say is Hercules).

feature of all civilisations. Thus the deadly ball-games of Mesoamerica, played out in the vicinity of the pyramid-complexes, were explicitly viewed as re-enactments of cosmic battles amongst the planets.[26]

Sacred sporting events were also a feature of Celtic culture. According to the Irish legends, Lugos (Lugh Lamhfada) established an annual festival of athletic and martial events at Tailton in Meath, the *Aonach Tailteann*, or Tailton Games. The events included horse and foot races, wrestling and other types of combat, and were, in MacGeoghegan's testimony, comparable to those "instituted at Rome … by Romulus in honour of Mars."[27] The competitions were no myth; "These olympiads" says MacGeoghegan, "always continued among the Milesians [Irish] until the arrival of the English."[28] We learn from the same source that the games were held for exactly thirty days – fifteen days before and fifteen days after the first of August (*Mi Lughnasa*), and that they commemorated the victory gained by Lugh and Ogma over the Fomorian giants at the Plain of the Tower.

The Tailton Games can therefore definitely be linked to cosmic upheavals of nature in the first half of the first millennium BC., the very upheavals that accompanied the migration of the Gaels to Ireland early in the 8th century BC. Thus these Celtic olympiads were not only comparable to those of Greece and Rome, but were contemporary with them. Furthermore, they appear to have been, like the Grecian olympiads, established in honour of the combats of Hercules. According to Robert Graves, "the Tal syllable is often present in the primitive names of Hercules. In Crete he was called Talus, the man of bronze, whom Medea killed … The Irish Tailteann Games are probably called after an agricultural Hercules the first syllable of whose name was Tal."[29] We have of course already identified Stonehenge as a temple of Artos/Hercules – the most important temple of that god in the British Isles, indeed in the whole Celtic world. Now we ask ourselves, is it possible that Britain too had her own olympiads, her own martial and athletic festival (no doubt, as befits the character of Lugos, combined with a festival of poetry and bardic skill)

26 See eg Benny Peiser "Cosmic Catastrophes and the Ballgame of the Sky Gods in Mesoamerican Mythology" *SIS Chronology and Catastrophism Review* Vol.XVII (1995)
27 MacGeoghegan *The History of Ireland* (New York, 1845) p.33
28 Ibid. p.13
29 R. Graves *The White Goddess* p.136

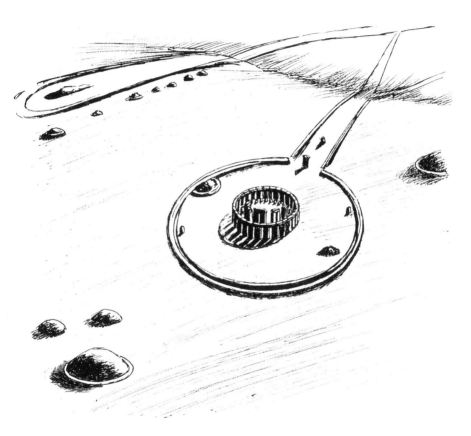

Stonehenge and its vicinity at the height of the Wessex epoch, showing the Cursus in the background (after an illustration by W. B. Robinson, in "Illustrated London New", 1922).

taking place in the vicinity of Stonehenge?

To begin with, if such a festival did exist, and of that there is every likelihood, it was almost certainly held in close proximity to Stonehenge. The central position of the monument is here crucial. Among the Irish, the national festival was held in Meath (Irish *Mid*), a name denoting "middle", and it is evident that the central area of the kingdom was regarded as having an important symbolic or magical significance. (In this regard we should recall how the mythical battle at the Tower was believed as having occurred at the mid-point of the earth, the World Axis, at the Pole). Stonehenge likewise occupies the mid-point of southern Britain, a fact which cannot be accidental. Scarcely a better meeting place or middle place could be conceived of.

Certainly the idea that Stonehenge and its immediate vicinity was used for athletic contests is not a new one. As early as the 17th century William Stukeley had identified the Cursus, a lengthy oblong feature surrounded by a low dike, as a hippodrome for chariot races and other athletic contests. Hence the name Cursus, a name that has stuck for the simple reason that no one has been able to suggest a more likely use for it.

We have already seen how the *Pythian Odes* of Pindar refer to Perseus' journey to the "wondrous road of the trysting place of the Hyperboreans." Gerald Hawkins believed this "trysting place" (Greek *Agona*) to be another classical reference to Stonehenge or Avebury, or both. Noting that *agona* "can mean a gathering place for sports, trials, battles or other activities," Hawkins asks "Was this Hyperborean *agona* a racecourse or parade ground like the Cursus, an enclosure like Woodhenge or the Sanctuary, a great open circle like Avebury, an eminence like Silbury Hill, a cathedral-court-observatory like Stonehenge – or all of them?" "What road," Hawkins continues "could be more wondrous than that which led to the complex, magical trysting place of the great monuments of Salisbury Plain?"[30]

If the Gorgon slain by Perseus was the same as Balor and Bran, the dragon-headed protector of Britain, then the sporting events held at this Hyperborean *agona* would have celebrated the very same event as that celebrated by the Tailton Games in Ireland, which marked the death and decapitation of the dragon-headed Balor.

I would suggest that the Cursus was indeed a racetrack, and that the Stonehenge complex was the venue for a pan-British athletic and poetic

---

30 G. Hawkins *Stonehenge Decoded* (London, 1965) p.86

festival held either every year, or every four years, in honour of Hercules/Arthur. The founder of the games would of course, as in Ireland, have been Lugos/Hermes/Merlin, the great benefactor of mankind who also constructed the monument. From this perspective we can see how the entire tradition of Arthur and his jousting knights would have been rooted in the athletic and poetic festival of Stonehenge. We tend to think of the chivalric principle as being a peculiarly Christian concept; and there is no doubt that the idea as it occurs in the medieval Arthurian stories is heavily coloured by Christian thinking. Yet many, or most, of the values of chivalry (courage, heroic fighting ability, love of poetry etc.) were already present and occupied a vastly important place in Celtic culture, and it would have been the easiest thing in the world for the medieval troubadours to turn the jousting pagan heroes of ancient Britain into the Christian heroes of the Middle Ages that we have come to know.

CHAPTER 7

New Horizons

The "Megalithic" Peoples

Textbooks state that the earliest megalith-builders of Europe were a "Neolithic" people of unknown ethnic identity, who were in time replaced or absorbed by various "Bronze Age" races (also megalith-builders) identified by their pottery styles and burial-customs. Altogether these Neolithic and Bronze Age people are said to have dominated western Europe for almost three millennia before being overcome and absorbed by the Iron Age Celts around 500 BC.

The builders of the first megaliths are identified as the Long Barrow people, from the shape of their graves, whilst the first metal-using people, who are believed to have initiated the Bronze Age around 1,600 BC., are named the Beaker people, on account of the distinctive shape of their pottery. The Beaker people are believed to have originated in northern Europe, and to have overrun and absorbed the earlier Neolithic settlers, just as their descendants were in turn overrun by the Celts. It was a regional variant of the Early Bronze culture, named Wessex, which was responsible for the second and third phases of Stonehenge.

There is thus a widely held (though much criticised) assumption that new cultures in early Europe represent new races or ethnic groups.

The language or languages spoken by the various Neolithic and Bronze Age peoples are said to be unknown, though it is generally assumed that they were "pre-Celtic". Nevertheless, scholars admit that much of what they know about megalithic culture is echoed in the belief-systems of the later Celts, and that there was a strong cultural continuity from Neolithic to Iron Age and beyond. The present study has added substantially to that picture of continuity, reinforcing our thesis that the megaliths were the earliest Druid temples.

Whilst we cannot be certain that all the "Neolithic" and "Bronze Age" megalith-builders in Britain spoke a from of Celtic, it is highly likely that they did, and that changes in burial-practice, pottery-styles etc. had less to do with invasion or immigration than with changes in technology and religious practice. It is interesting to note in this regard that the so-called Beaker people are found occupying exactly the same areas and villages as their Neolithic predecessors.[1] This is not to say that invasion and immigration did not occur. Obviously both did. But there is as yet absolutely no evidence to suggest that any of these groups in Britain were pre-Celtic, or spoke a non-Celtic language. Nothing has yet been discovered to suggest a pre-Celtic substratum in the ancient populations of the British Isles. If such a substratum existed, we might expect it to have left its mark in a body of pre-Celtic place-names. Yet there is little or no evidence for such place-names.[2]

Everything we have found suggests that since the late Neolithic, Bronze and Iron Ages were largely contemporaneous, it is both fruitless and erroneous to try to identify these with different waves of immigration. There were changes in pottery styles etc., but the evidence would suggest that they developed at a much quicker rate than is now admitted, and that furthermore in many cases different styles, supposedly from epochs separated by many centuries, coexisted for long periods of time. It is now admitted, for example, that Beaker Folk were "contemporaries both of indigenous late neolithic groups and their early bronze age descendants,"[3] whilst "The extent to which [Neolithic] natives and [Beaker] newcomers worked together on these great [megalith-building] projects is problematic,

---

1 R.R. Hughes and D.R. Brothwell 'The Earliest Populations of Man in Europe, Western Asia and Northern Africa' in *The Cambridge Ancient History* Vol.1 part 1 (3rd ed.) p.170

2 The Celtic immigration "was sufficiently early for pre-Celtic speech to have left no recognizable trace upon the British names of people or places which, from the time of Caesar onwards, Roman authors committed to writing. It is natural to expect that place-names still in use to-day might preserve such traces; but even in the case of river-names, the most conservative of all, no examples can be quoted with certainty. Professor Ekwall sums up a discussion of the whole subject by saying: 'I cannot point to any definite name that strikes me as probably pre-Celtic.' " R.G. Collingwood and J.N.L. Myres *Roman Britain and the English Settlements* (Oxford,1937) p.19

3 Colin Burgess "The Bronze Age" in Colin Renfrew ed. *British Prehistory* (1974) p.172

but they were clearly present together at many sites."[4] The writer here quoted also remarks on "The fallacy of the traditional bronze age pottery sequence – beakers with inhumation, followed by food vessels with inhumation in the early bronze age, enlarged food vessels and collared urns with cremations in the middle bronze age, and late collared, cordoned and encrusted urns in the late bronze age." This sequence, although now known to be largely fictitious, has proved "very resistant to attack."[5]

So there we have it, from the pen of one of the most respected British archaeologists. The late Neolithic was in fact contemporary with the Beaker/Early Bronze; yet the Early Bronze is itself indistinguishable from the Late Bronze Age (and presumably also the early Iron Age).

We are therefore on fairly secure ground when we declare that the first megaliths, and probably the majority of them, were erected in the 9th and 8th centuries BC. by Celtic-speaking peoples, from various parts of Europe, who arrived in the wake of the final series of cosmic upheavals and climatic disturbances. That these settlers were mainly peasant farmers who employed stone tools for most of their needs says absolutely nothing about their language or ethnic grouping.

Yet in case it should still be doubted that both Celtic and Germanic-speaking peoples were not far removed from their Stone Age roots, it should be pointed out that the word for "knife" in these languages – including Gaelic *scian* and Old English *seax*, is closely related to the old Indo-European word for "stone" (Latin *saxum*). In the words of C.L. Barber "Originally, it seems, a stone and a cutting implement were the same thing."[6] Admittedly, Barber is here referring to a time before the general diffusion of Indo-European speakers, though he favours a European location as the home of these languages, and does not date this dispersal before 1,500 BC. In addition, he also makes it clear that a primitive form of metallurgy, centred round the working of copper, was in use among the Indo-Europeans prior to their dispersal.[7]

This of course is precisely the situation we find at the beginning of the megalith epoch.

---

4 Ibid. p.174

5 Ibid. p.176

6 C.L. Barber *The Story of Language* (Pan Books,1972) p.93

7 Ibid. "They [the early Indo-Europeans] were probably in the transitional stage when stone is still the predominant material for tools and weapons, but metal is beginning to be used."

The Iberian Connection

We have seen how Ireland's most venerated traditions stated that the ancestors of the Gaels (known as the children of Milidh, or "Milesians") were of Spanish origin. The arrival of the Milesians in Ireland was said to have occurred around 35 generations (roughly 700-800 years) before the birth of Christ, and their journey to the emerald isle took place amidst great upheavals of nature.

Modern scholarship, of course, has generally dismissed this claim, judging it highly improbable that the Celtic population of Ireland could have come from distant Iberia, rather than the adjacent lands of Britain and Gaul. Nevertheless, the fact that the Irish named a genuinely Celtic land (Galicia in northern Spain, where moreover the peculiar Q Celtic dialect of the Gaels is also attested) as their place of origin, and the fact that a similar tradition exists in Spain, has always suggested the possibility that the story may have some basis in fact. In the previous chapter we have looked at evidence of an entirely different nature which would also lend support to the accuracy of these Irish accounts. Yet there exists even more proof, this time from the realm of archaeology, which will be seen to further corroborate this venerated tradition.

Over the past fifty years archaeologists have discovered very real links between primeval Ireland and Spain. These links, it is now known, were established in the late Neolithic epoch, at the dawn of the megalith-building age, and endured into the early Iron Age. Scholars were surprised to discover that the Irish Passage Graves, most famously the majestic structures of the Boyne Valley, were apparently identical in design to a whole class of Spanish monuments. The parallels were detailed and precise; and included designs (especially a variety of spiral motifs and lozenges) carved upon rocks, and decorated stone basins discovered in the "burial chambers" of the most important monuments. So compelling is the evidence that the Spanish origin of much insular megalithic culture is now part of accepted wisdom:

"If the passage graves can be plausibly interpreted as the temple-tombs of a relatively sophisticated professional priesthood, or religious elite of some kind, which practised collective burial, and the long barrows and cairns as the monuments of a different but related branch which emerged and flourished specifically in northern Europe and Britain, there can be little doubt that this priesthood began the major part of its career in Iberia where the passage graves almost certainly originated."[8]

The Irish claimed that their ancestors were from Galicia in northern Spain, specifically the region of Briganza (modern Corunna), which means in effect that they were Celtiberians, the hybrid race of Spain, partly of Celtic and partly of Iberian origin. Studies of ethnic features have shown the Irish passage-grave builders to be identical to those of Spain.

> "... the Iberian and northern skulls are sometimes described as a Eurafrican branch of the Mediterranean race and might support the idea that the caste emerged in Iberia by means of the hybridization there of more than one stock. It is indeed tempting to link the appearance of a characteristically European Atlantic form of religious monument with the appearance of a characteristically Atlantic European texon of people associated with it and to see the resulting stable religious caste as spreading steadily northwards, taking institutions, religion and rules of recruitment and intermarriage with them."[9]

Scholars failed to connect the archaeological evidence with the legend because of course the Iberian-style megaliths had already been dated to the third millennium BC. by the time their Spanish origin was confirmed. The legends placed the advent of the Milesians only about 800 years before the Christian era, which of course is close to the beginning of the Iron Age.

But with our new understanding of the past yet another mystery resolves itself. The ancestors of the Gaels did indeed sail from northern Spain right at the beginning of the megalith-building age – around 800 BC. Although this epoch was "Neolithic" in the sense that stone tools were widely employed by everyone, it was also "Chalcolithic" (Copper Age) and very close to the beginning of the Bronze Age proper, which, as we shall see, only commenced in the middle of the 8th century.

---

8 Euan MacKie *The Megalith Builders* (Oxford,1977) pp.184-5
9 Ibid. p.185

Stone, Bronze and Iron

It was of course the discovery of stone implements in association with many of the megaliths that first prompted scholars to date them to the Neolithic (New Stone) Age. The fact that artefacts and tools made of various metals, including bronze and iron, were also frequently discovered in and around the megaliths came to be seen as proving little other than the fact that the monuments continued to be used into the Bronze and Iron Ages. It was the stone implements that were seen as crucial, indicating the *terminus post quem* (starting point) of megalithic culture.

Yet the idea that there was a Stone Age, followed neatly by a Bronze Age, which was in turn followed by an Iron Age is a gross and misleading simplification. As noted earlier, Stone, Bronze and Iron Ages overlap, and all three materials were used concurrently for many centuries. Indeed there is evidence to suggest that stone implements were widely used by the peasantry throughout Europe well into the Christian era.[10]

During his famous excavations of Mycenaean sites in Greece, Heinrich Schliemann uncovered vast quantities of stone tools, including knives and arrowheads of flint and obsidian, fashioned in typically neolithic style, together with tools and weapons of metal, in obviously Late Bronze Age contexts. Describing his findings at Tiryns, Schliemann remarks, "As in Troy and Mycenae, so in Tiryns, stone implements were in use at the same time as tools of bronze."[11] But obviously aware of the potentially controversial nature of what he had just said, he hastily adds, "I wish to mention on this occasion, that, according to Professor Heinrich Brugsch, battle-axes with stone hammers were among the spoil which Thutmes III

---

10 Stone tools are frequently found in late Iron Age settlements. See eg. Brian Lacey's report on the excavation of a rath in Antrim (1991) In parts of the Near East, such as Egypt, stone implements were used even into the 19th century AD. Noting this, Gaston Maspero commented upon the difficulty of assigning Egyptian flint implements to any particular epoch; "Until quite recently ... the flint implements which had been found in various places [in Egypt] could not be ascribed to them [the earliest Egyptians] with any degree of certainty, for the Egyptians continued to use stone long after metal was known to them. They made stone arrowheads, hammers, and knives, not only in the time of the Pharaohs, but under the Romans, and during the whole period of the Middle Ages, and the manufacture of them has not yet entirely died out." *A History of Egypt, Chaldea, Syria, Babylonia, and Assyria* Vol.1 (1906) pp.61-2

11 H. Schliemann *Tiryns* (London,1886) p.173

brought back from the highly-civilized states of Western Asia, together with weapons and armour of bronze, and gold and silver works of art."[12]

But alongside the stone and bronze implements Schliemann also uncovered numerous artefacts of iron, and there is much evidence to suggest that iron was widely employed throughout the Near East at this time.[13] Homer, whose epic *Iliad* deals with the period studied by Schliemann speaks frequently of iron, which has a very clearly defined place in this otherwise Bronze Age culture.

As noted earlier, both the Mycenaean epoch of Greece and the 18th Dynasty of Egypt properly belong in the 8th and 7th centuries BC., and represent the beginnings of the Iron Age. But the Bronze Age too, we have said, only begins in the 8th century (at which time the Phoenicians opened up the sea-routes to Britain). This means, essentially, that the Bronze and Iron Ages begin more or less simultaneously. This, I shall argue, is correct, though for two or three centuries iron played a secondary role to bronze, for reasons that will become apparent.

It is an accepted principle that any culture which can produce bronze already possesses the technology to produce iron. This is due to the fact that charcoal-burning furnaces are needed to melt copper (at 1,083OC.). But once the technology of charcoal-burning is understood, it is relatively easy to achieve the temperature necessary to smelt iron (1,535OC.) And this is exactly what we find. Iron-working, including the smelting of iron from ore, is found right at the beginning of the Bronze Age in all of the Near Eastern cultures. Yet there is no doubt that during the Bronze Age iron plays a role subservient to that of bronze. Thus in the *Iliad* Homer describes a classic Bronze Age civilisation, where bronze is the metal used for weapons, including swords, knives, spearheads and arrowheads. Iron however does occur, and is described in such a way as to indicate familiarity. Yet it is never used to make weapons. It is the metal of tools. Why should this be so?

A rudimentary understanding of the properties of metals reveals bronze to be a harder, though more brittle material than pure (or wrought) iron. Thus bronze is capable of taking a much sharper edge than iron – which explains why bronze was used for many centuries for weapons and razors.

---

12 Ibid.

13 Iron was in fact used as early as the pyramid-building epoch. See eg H. Garland and C. Bannister *Ancient Egyptian Metallurgy* (London,1927)

Flint Arrow-head (Nimrud). (after Rawlinson)

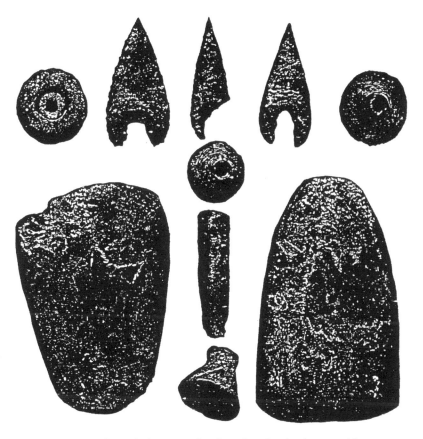

Stone tools, including arrowheads and axeheads, discovered by
Schliemann in Bronze Age burials at Mycenae. Artifacts of iron were
discovered in the same interrments.

On the other hand wrought iron is not as brittle as bronze. A plough made of iron would not snap upon hitting a rock, as one of bronze certainly would. Thus in the *Iliad* iron is used for agricultural tools, with ploughs specially mentioned.

It was only with the development of steel manufacture (through the process of case hardening) that iron began gradually to replace bronze as the preferred metal for weapons.

The Greeks recalled the advent of iron swords very clearly in a story recounted by Pausanias, which told how a traveller from Sparta was astonished to see a craftsman in Tegea forging a sword of iron.[14] This event, we are told, occurred during the reign of the Spartan king Anaxandrides, which must therefore place it in the early 6th century. If by the Iron Age we mean the point at which iron replaced bronze as the metal for weaponry, this is when the Iron Age began.

To summarise then, the age of metals, properly speaking begins around 1,000 BC. with the Copper Age (wrongly named Early Bronze). This epoch was contemporary with the flowering of the Neolithic, and was characterised by the use of finely-wrought stone tools, with a tiny amount of metal, usually native copper, and usually cold hammered, for a few specialised purposes. Sometime in the 9th century, probably in the latter years, true bronze was discovered, almost certainly in Britain, where we have seen ore of mixed copper and tin occurs naturally.[15] From that point on, smelting techniques were developed and improved, and iron, which had been known earlier from meteorites, began to be worked. Yet iron remained subsidiary to bronze until case hardening techniques were developed, sometime in the 6th century.

All during this period, and long afterwards, stone tools of typical

---

14 Pausanias iii,3,7 and iii,11,8

15 Recent attempts to claim that tin reserves in Anatolia fuelled the Bronze Age long before the Phoenicians discovered Britain display both poor thinking and basic dishonesty, and can only be prompted by a desperate attempt to explain the supposed existence of a Bronze Age a thousand years before the Phoenician voyages. The economics prove the fallacy. If reasonable supplies of tin existed in Anatolia, the incredible cost of journeys to Britain could never have been recovered. People would simply have bought the cheaper Anatolian tin. Herodotus (5th century BC.) casually remarks that in his time the tin employed in the Hellenic world came from the Cassiterides – ie. the British Isles. (iii,115) The tiny amounts of tin discovered by geologists in Turkey during the 1990s were almost certainly unknown to the ancients.

Neolithic style continued to be employed by the ordinary peasant farmers of Europe and the Near East. All metals were incredibly expensive, due to the obvious difficulties of transporting ore and finished products, as well as the labour-intensive nature of production techniques. For many centuries peasant farmers simply could not afford metal tools. Yet everyday tasks around the farmstead required cutting instruments of various kinds. These were supplied by the local stone-tool manufacturers whose workshops are still very much in evidence throughout the countryside.

The mighty temple-complexes of Stonehenge and Avebury almost certainly owed their existences to the wealth generated in the south-west by the newly-established metallurgical industries of the 8th century BC. Archaeologists were astonished at the wealth exhibited in the tombs of the Wessex people, that branch of the so-called Early Bronze Age responsible for the final phase of Stonehenge. The "unique regional concentration of rich graves in Wessex" provides a contrast to the "general poverty" of other British Early Bronze graves.[16] It is known that "The power and wealth of these chieftains was based on their dynamism and their commercial success, in particular their skill as middlemen in channelling trade from Ireland, Europe and the Mediterranean through their territory."[17]

Thus the wealth and power of Stonehenge's builders was based on trade – their trading links with the eastern Mediterranean are beyond question. Yet the writer of the above words did not dare take the next logical step and connect that Mediterranean traffic with the well-attested tin-trade of nearby Cornwall. Such a step would have been tantamount to admitting that the first flowering of the Bronze Age was directly connected with the first exploitation of Britain's copper and tin resources, and that, as the ancient writers always insisted, Britain was of primary importance as a source of tin. We have seen that the very motif of a sword emerging from a stone, the central theme of Britain's national myth, is a direct clue to the country's significance in the Bronze Age revolution. However, as everyone knows, Britain's tin was not exploited till the Phoenicians opened the Atlantic routes around 800 BC.

---

16 Euan MacKie *The Megalith Builders* (Oxford,1977) p.96
17 Colin Burgess "The Bronze Age" in Colin Renfrew ed. *British Prehistory* (1974) p.184

A Megalithic Priesthood

Whilst it has always been accepted that the megaliths of western Europe, particularly the greater structures like Stonehenge and the passage graves of the Boyne valley, must have been constructed by an organised and sophisticated people, the true extent of their sophistication only became apparent when in the 1960s a number of professional astronomers and mathematicians, beginning with Gerald S. Hawkins, began to survey the monuments with the intention of establishing astronomical alignments. The most astonishing discoveries had to wait till the 1970s, when the work was famously taken up by Professor Alexander Thom, who quickly realised that most, if not all, the monuments had significant astronomical orientations, and that the architects displayed fairly advanced mathematical knowledge, as well as the use of a standardised measure, which Thom called the megalithic yard.

Though many academics could not accept Thom's conclusions, his general thesis has now been taken on board, and it is widely agreed that a skilled group of astronomer priests, whose prestige was enormous, held sway over much of western Europe at the time. In the words of Euan MacKie;

"The discovery that elaborate geometrical knowledge – previously thought to have been unknown before the time of the ancient Greeks perhaps 2,000 years later – and advanced skills in planning and field measurement underlie the design of the stone circles is surely one of the great breakthroughs in British archaeology this century. It has revealed a totally unexpected aspect of what appears at first sight to be a barren and unpromising group of prehistoric structures. One conclusion could be that, since the megalithic yard and the geometry are found throughout Britain (and in Brittany as well), there was a class of wise men in existence at that time whose members designed temples and sanctuaries for their own purposes. This evidence could also suggest that such a class was a highly trained national one rather than formed of scattered bands of primitive shamans and medicine men. If this conclusion were favoured, the question would immediately arise where such a class could have been trained, and one answer would surely have to be –

somewhere among one of the main centres of the Neolithic population where the finest of these monuments are located."[18]

Yet as MacKie himself concedes, Thom's conclusions have not gone unchallenged. The idea that a highly sophisticated priestly class could have existed in 3rd millennium Neolithic Europe is just too much for many people to swallow. But the description of this priestly order painted by MacKie and Thom could very well be applied to the Druids. Indeed, if one did not know better, one would imagine they were trying to describe the Druids.

Of course, if the majority of the megaliths were actually erected between the 9th and 7th centuries BC., then both the priesthood and the sophisticated knowledge and organisation displayed by them become much more comprehensible. So too does the evidently Celtic nature of the religion and religious practices of the megalith-builders. In this context it is worth noting that the four "station" stones surrounding the outer sarsen circle at Stonehenge provide, among other things, an alignment for sunset on May Day, the Celtic festival of Beltane. In the words of Aubrey Burl;

"Because a square would have been as suitable as a rectangle for defining these two alignments [midsummer sunrise and extreme moonset] it is arguable that the designers built a rectangle so that its ESE-WNW diagonal would point to sunset at the beginning of May, an occasion that the iron-age Celts still celebrated two thousand years later on their great fire-festival of Beltane."[19]

We recall that the Irish name for a standing-stone circle is "beltany".

Near Eastern Chronology

It is impossible to place Stonehenge and the European megaliths in the 8th and 7th centuries BC. and leave the pyramids of Egypt, as well as the

---

18 Ibid. p.185
19 Aubrey Burl *Prehistoric Stone Circles* p.37

tholos tombs of Greece and the ziggurats of Mesopotamia in the 2nd and 3rd millennia.

Elsewhere I have dealt in some detail with the origins of Egyptian civilisation, which is shown to commence around 1,000 BC. a full 2,000 years after the date found in the textbooks.[20] In another place I have shown how Egypt's pyramid-building age commenced around 820 BC. – precisely in accordance with the earliest surviving megaliths in Europe and elsewhere.[21]

Whilst this is not the place to examine Near Eastern chronology in any detail, I wish to present a small sample of the truly overwhelming evidence demanding a dramatic reduction in the length of pharaohnic chronology.

To begin with, it should be stated that the earliest chronology of Egypt we possess, that of the Greek writer Herodotus, places the pyramid-building pharaohs, Cheops, Chephren and Mycerinus, immediately before the Ethiopian pharaoh Shabaka (Sabakos), with only one king, Anysis, intervening. Since the Ethiopians are known to have conquered Egypt sometime near the middle of the 8th century BC., Herodotus' chronology has always presented something of a puzzle. Other writers (later than Herodotus) seemed to place the pyramid-building kings many thousands of years before the Christian era; Herodotus placed them just a few centuries before.

One solution has been to suggest that the order of Herodotus' Egyptian history is corrupt, and that the pyramid-builders were misplaced by a later editor. Yet an honest appraisal of the evidence, much of which is now simply ignored in the textbooks, would suggest that Herodotus got it right, and that Egyptian chronology needs to be shortened dramatically.

We might note, to begin with, the actual architecture. Quite apart from the stunning achievement of the builders of Cheops' and Chephren's great monuments, which apparently display an intimate knowledge of Pythagorean geometry, there is the simple fact, repeatedly ignored, that the Egyptians of this time employed the arch.[22] Yet the arch, it is held, and so it is stated in textbook after textbook, was not known before the 7th century BC. Thus we are required to believe that the Egyptians of the 3rd millennium (along incidentally with the Akkadians and Sumerians of

---

20 In my *Genesis of Israel and Egypt* (1997)
21 In my *Pyramid Age* (1999)
22 F. Petrie *Egyptian Architecture* (London,1938) pp.71-2

Mesopotamia) discovered the use of the arch, which was then forgotten for almost two thousand years, only to be reinvented by the peoples of the Near East in the 7th century BC.

This strange phenomenon of discovery in the 3rd millennium, followed by a loss and then a rediscovery in the first millennium is something that can be observed in many areas of Near Eastern history.

Take as another example the use of iron. The Egyptians of the Pyramid Age were quite familiar with iron (another fact ignored in textbooks), which was used for both ceremonial purposes and for ordinary tools. The iron used in religious ritual was generally of meteoric origin, as revealed by its high nickel content, but the material used in tools had little or no nickel, and was thus smelted from ore.[23] So plentiful were iron artefacts at this time that one writer was moved to suggest that in Egypt the Iron Age "may yet be proved to have even preceded the Bronze Age."[24] Yet iron too, after having been widely used in the Pyramid Age was virtually forgotten for almost 2,000 years, only to be rediscovered again in the 7th century.

It is precisely the same story when we come to look at glassmaking and glazing techniques.. In his seminal work *Minerals, Metals, Glazing and Man* (1978) the mineralogist John Dayton traces the development of glazing techniques throughout the Near East, and concludes that a whole class of glazing technologies employed during the Pyramid Age could not have been known about in the 3rd millennium BC. Once again, glazes used by the pyramid-builders were forgotten for almost two millennia, only to re-emerge in the first millennium.

As an answer to the problem Dayton, although not an historian, suggested a radical shortening of Egyptian chronology.

In terms of relationships with other nations we find a similar phenomenon at work. The Egyptians of the Pyramid Age were well acquainted with the Phoenicians, and indeed trade with the cities of Tyre and Byblos was of great importance to the pharaohs of the time. So familiar were the peoples of this region to the Egyptians that their name for a seagoing boat was *kbnwt* ("Byblos boat").[25] This can only mean that the Phoenicians of the Pyramid Age werc already established as a great seafaring nation. Yet once again, this anticipates by 2,000 years the very

---

23 H. Garland and C. Bannister *Ancient Egyptian Metallurgy* (London,1927)
24 Ibid. p.5
25 Margaret S. Drower in *The Cambridge Ancient History* Vol.1 part 2 (3rd edition) p.384

real expansion of Phoenician commercial enterprise in the 9th and 8th centuries BC.

This then is but a small sample of the truly enormous body of evidence which tells us very clearly that a radical rewriting of ancient history, not just in Europe, but in Egypt and the entire Near East, is in order, and that all early cultures which are aligned to the chronology of the Near East, need to have their histories shortened by almost two millennia.

Dates and Dating-Systems

Modern scholarship first placed Stonehenge and the other megaliths in the remote pre-Celtic past because of the discovery of stone implements in association with them. It seemed perfectly reasonable to postulate a Stone Age preceding the various metal-using epochs. Yet it was forgotten that stone and metal can be used together; and so a grotesquely extended chronology was accepted on the strength of what might be termed the forensic evidence, which nevertheless contradicted the evidence of tradition.

Yet even as 20th century scholarship began to find an increasing number of reasons to reassign the megaliths to the Druids (eg. advanced mathematical knowledge), a new system of dating, hailed as the ultimate in forensic science, entered the debate.

The discovery by Libby in 1949 that living organisms absorb radioactive carbon, or Carbon 14, from the atmosphere, was quickly recognised as an invaluable new tool in the repertoire of the archaeologist. As soon as a living organism dies it ceases to absorb Carbon 14, and from then on the proportion of radioactive carbon in the body of the organism begins to decline. Since this decline or "decay" occurs at a fixed rate, it is held that we can determine with great accuracy the age of any artefact containing once-living organic material. Archaeologists were quick to avail themselves of the revolutionary new technique, and samples from prehistoric sites throughout Europe were soon being subjected to analysis. Whilst the results obtained were not always consistent, and indeed some were wildly inconsistent, enough information was gathered to convince scholars that the accepted dates for megalithic civilisation were broadly correct. Any doubt about the great age of these structures was finally put to rest, and their non-association with the Druids fully confirmed. One after another, material from the megaliths yielded dates in the second, third, and even fourth millennia BC.

So great is the prestige of "hard" science in our culture that few people have dared to even question these results. Nevertheless, in many other fields scientific conclusions are regularly questioned, and frequently overturned. This is particularly the case with regard to medical and dietary science, as well as forensic science applied to criminal investigation.

As a matter of fact, the radiocarbon system of dating is well-known by those in the field to have a number of major drawbacks.[26] For one thing, samples can be contaminated, and it is virtually impossible to know that they have been. Contamination comes in many forms, and can either increase or decrease the readings, making the sample under investigation appear either much younger or much older than it is. The most simple, yet possibly most pervasive form of contamination is that of water. Water literally washes the radioactivity out of a sample, making it look older. There is absolutely no way of knowing whether a control sample has been exposed to water. Now the rain-drenched climate of Britain ensures that virtually everything found in the earth has been washed repeatedly and thoroughly. A recent murder case, highlighted in a *Horizon* documentary screened by the BBC., addressed this very problem.[27] An Englishman who, in a fit of remorse, had confessed to murdering and dismembering his wife brought police to the spot where he had buried her head. Sure enough, the detectives uncovered the partial skull of a woman, complete with some still surviving fleshy tissue. They were astonished however when scientists from the British Museum, who radiocarbon dated the remains, declared that the body was 1,500 years old. Other forensic scientists however, who reconstructed the woman's features, declared that in their opinion the body was indeed that of the vanished wife. The documentary concluded by offering the opinion that bodies found in boggy conditions take on the date of the sodden earth wherein they are interred. In short, the water had

---

26 See for example *New Scientist* (September, 1989) p.26, where it is noted that the margin of error quoted by some laboratories in their dating techniques may be two or three times greater than admitted. Whilst some laboratories, it is claimed, are consistently correct, others have been shown to produce dates that are up to 250 years out. Unforeseen errors, it is said, can arise in the chemical pre-treatment of small amounts of material, and dates can be way out on samples only 200 years old.
27 BBC 2 *Horizon*, 4th March 1999

leeched much of the carbon isotope from the remains, making it appear vastly older than it was. A major plank in the radiocarbon edifice, the constancy of rates of day, is therefore demolished.

Given this remarkable fact, which in any case has always been well understood by the scholarly community, we may well wonder how esteemed academics can then dare to use radiocarbon readings of samples of wood, leather and bone recovered from the ground in an attempt to date Britain's prehistoric cultures? Yet such readings are still regularly published, without comment.

With wood there is an added complication. A tree can live for hundreds of years, but at any given time only absorbs radioactive carbon into its outermost layer. Thus it is necessary to know the age of the tree when it was cut down, as well as the part of the tree from which the timber was derived, before we can even begin to talk about an accurate reading. Yet once again, timber is indiscriminately dated by scientists and the results published without comment.

A third problem is the tendency of scientists to dismiss anomalous results that do not conform to preconceived ideas. Thus a substantial number of results obtained from megalithic samples have produced startlingly recent figures; yet these have not been published, or have at best been reduced to footnotes, because, ironically enough, the researchers have deemed them to be "contaminated". In the words of one eminent scholar;

> "Some archaeologists refused to accept radiocarbon dates. The attitude probably, in the early days of the new technique, was summed up by Professor Jo Brew, Director of the Peabody Museum at Harvard, 'If a C14 date supports our theories, we put it in the main text. If it does not entirely contradict them, we put it in the footnote. And if it is completely 'out of date', we just drop it.'"[28]

---

28 David Wilson *The New Archaeology* (New York, 1974) p. 97 An example of this pernicious practice is seen in the fate of samples from the tomb of pharaoh Tutankhamun subjected by the British Museum to the radio-carbon method. The samples, consisting of fibres of a reed mat and a palm kernel, produced dates of 844 BC and 899 BC respectively. These were broadly in line with the date for Tutankhamun predicted by Velikovsky, but were roughly 500 years too recent for textbook chronology. In spite of assurances given to Velikovsky, the dates were never formally published. See Velikovsky's *Peoples of the Sea* (1977) p.xvi

Perhaps the greatest problem with regard to radiocarbon dating is the question of environment. All researchers in the field assume that environmental conditions have more or less always been as they now are; at least as far back as humanity's first appearance on the planet. Yet if what we have said in the present paper is correct, if the earth has been subjected to repeated and devastating interaction with extraterrestrial bodies such as comets, then we must assume that atmospheric conditions were not always the same. During these episodes our planet's atmosphere would have suffered major disruption, and this would undoubtedly have had an effect upon the radiocarbon levels. Given a period of cosmic disturbances, with attendant massive vulcanism as well as conflagrations, much 'old' carbon (ie. carbon with a depleted proportion of carbon 14) would be released into the atmosphere – to then be absorbed by living organisms. In such circumstances plants and animals would have a much lower percentage of radioactive carbon in their systems than present day organisms.

This is a well-documented problem, and is termed the "Seuss effect" after the scientist who first identified it. Its impact is not theoretical, but proven. In this way it was demonstrated, for example, how the massive use of fossil fuels in the 20th century (with their attendant release of great amounts of "old" carbon led to some startlingly anomalous results,

> "We are told that plants in a rich old carbon environment were radiocarbon dated several thousand years older than they actually were, and a tree by an airport was actually dated to be 10,000 years old."[29]

Thus another major plank of the radiocarbon edifice, the constancy of initial conditions (as well as rates of decay), collapses.

I emphasise that the list of problems mentioned above merely scratches the surface. The whole question of how we date the ancient past will need to be reconsidered in a fundamental way. Other "scientific" systems, such as dendrochronology, have entered the fray over the past couple of decades, only to confuse the picture even further. Ultimately, they are all used very

---

29 Charles Ginenthal "The Extinction of the Mammoth" *The Velikovskian* (special edition) Vol.III 2 and 3 (1999) p.184

much as statistics (unfortunately) are: to prove whatever the researcher wishes to prove.[30]

In the final analysis, the idea that human beings evolved high civilisations up to three thousand years before the dawn of the Christian era goes back to Near Eastern chronology and history. The Egyptians, Babylonians, and, to a lesser extent, the Hebrews, claimed to trace their histories back to the third and even fourth millennia. Well before the dawn of the science of archaeology these dates were accepted by the scholastic intelligentsia of Europe; and so venerated and entrenched were they that science could not uproot them. They are still there, these dates based on venerated tradition, in the textbooks of the world's libraries.

---

30 Gwen Schultz, a prominent scientist, has stated her belief that "The possibility that all methods [of dating] used today are wrong must be acknowledged." *Ice Age Lost* (New York, 1974) p.28

Epilogue

The question of who built Stonehenge and the other megaliths, as well as the relationship of these monuments to the Arthurian legend is not simply one of interest only to antiquarians, anthropologists and historians. Much more is at stake. If even a small portion of what has been proposed in the present volume is correct then we are involved in a fundamental reassessment of everything we know about human and natural history. Indeed a reassessment of almost every field of human knowledge is called for. It is difficult to express or comprehend the magnitude of the revolution that may well be worked upon our consciousness and upon our view of ourselves in relation to the universe around us.

Since the latter years of the 19th century scientists and academics of every variety have presented to the populace a view of the past that radically contradicted ancient tradition. The ancients, they said, were wrong when they said that the world had been, within the memory of mankind, beset by catastrophic upheavals of nature. On the contrary, the scientists proclaimed, the world has maintained a more or less pleasant state of equilibrium for tens or even hundreds of millions of years. Any climatic changes occurring within that span, such as the Ice Ages, were the result of very slow and very gradual changes in the terrestrial environment. These changes took thousands of years to effect.

Yet we now find that this scenario is fictitious. It appears that only eight centuries before the dawn of the present era the earth suffered the last in a series of encounters with an erratic cosmic body, an encounter that had catastrophic consequences for our planet. The earth's tectonic plates went into violent convulsions and vast earthquakes were unleashed. The climate in the northern hemisphere changed dramatically, with temperatures falling by up to three degrees Celsius. Tidal waves repeatedly swept over low-lying regions. In the midst of this chaos human populations were uprooted. Elsewhere I have shown how this calamity enabled the children of Israel to escape their bondage in Egypt, propelling them en masse through the Sinai Desert to their Promised Land.

In like manner the tribes of Europe fled their devastated homelands in search of new pastures. It was then (around 800 BC.) that the first waves of Celtic-speaking peoples crossed the English Channel from Gaul. To archaeologists, these are the Beaker People. But simultaneous with the migrations from Gaul and northern Europe another group of Celtic-speaking peoples, this time from Iberia, crossed the Bay of Biscay and established settlements in western Britain, Ireland and Scotland. These Celtiberians, who had already established contact with the civilised peoples of the eastern Mediterranean, introduced the monumental Passage Grave, a version of the Mycenaean tholos tomb, into the British Isles.

Tradition in Britain and Ireland makes it abundantly clear that these migrations were undertaken amidst terrifying disturbances of nature, disturbances everywhere linked to the Cosmic Serpent, the comet-deity, the dragon of chaos and world-destruction. Nevertheless, it is clear that by this stage another cosmic body, later identified as the saviour-god Hercules, had in some way removed the Cosmic Serpent as a threat to the earth. No longer was it necessary to perform the savage ritual deemed necessary to appease the blood-lust of the serpent; human sacrifice. The peoples of the earth celebrated this liberation by erecting great "megalithic" temples, which were aligned with precision to the movements of the sun, moon and planets, who were their gods. It was then that Stonehenge was raised, probably in the first half of the 8th century, say around 775 BC., an event almost certainly contemporary, or very nearly so, with the erection of the great pyramids at Giza in Egypt.

Stonehenge, along with most of the other stone circles, was thus raised in honour of a sky-god, a god of fire and light, who was the slayer of the dragon. This was the original High King of Heaven, the son of Jupiter, who would forever be the archetypal hero, the eternal friend and protector of mankind. This was the god who restored order to the cosmos, who instituted the calendar as it now exists, with its twelve months. To bring about these twelve periods of the moon was a labour that could be performed only by a son of the gods. Yet in his titanic struggle to overcome the serpent his gigantic club frequently smashed against mother earth, unleashing fearsome earthquakes. He ripped Italy from Sicily, and pushed apart the mighty rock pillars at the entrance to the Mediterranean, which henceforth bore his name.

But the hero who performed these deeds was not one of the original Olympian pantheon; he was a new star in the sky, who appeared when the human race was already quite old. Thus Hercules/Arthur does not appear as one of the first gods. He is, in fact, only half-divine; his benevolence to and love for mankind firmly identifying him with humanity. More than any of the other gods he is anthropomorphised. He walks among men, taking part in their trials and struggles. He gathers a group of twelve human heroes around him, who nevertheless sit at the circular table of the stars. He is by far the most loved of the gods. He is, amongst the quarrelling and amoral family of Jupiter, the one sure sign of a greater goodness. In time, it was said that he entered the underworld and came back, and that he ascended bodily after his death to be among the other gods. This was his final victory. Over death itself.

Small wonder he was so much loved by afflicted humans in their vale of tears.

Eight centuries later a prophet from Judea, well aware of Hercules and his story, took upon himself the mantle of the son of Jupiter, and was joyfully proclaimed the Son of God by the peoples of the Roman Empire.

REVISED CHRONOLOGIES

BC.	BRITAIN	IRELAND	GREECE
	LATE NEOLITHIC AGE	NEOLITHIC AGE	NEOLITHIC AGE
	CATASTROPHIC DESTRUCTION	**CATASTROPHIC DESTRUCTION**	**CATASTROPHIC DESTRUCTION**
	Arrival of first Celtic-speaking immigrants ("Beaker People")	Arrival of first Celtic-speaking immigrants ("Passage Grave" culture)	EARLY BRONZE AGE ("EARLY HELLADIC")
			"Pelops" establishes Olympic Games
			Mycenae fortified with "Cyclopean" walls
			Greeks establish close links with Minoan Cretans
			Atreus
			Heroic Age myths formulated.
			Fall of Troy
			Greeks establish settlements in Asia Minor.
800	Bronze-smelting perfected in Cornwall ("Sword in the Stone")	"Eremon" first High King	
		Erection of Passage Graves in Boyne Valley	
	EARLY BRONZE AGE	EARLY BRONZE AGE	
	Trade with Phoenicia and Greece begins	Ethrial, earliest of the Sage Kings	
	Stonehenge III ("Round Table")		
700	Wessex Culture ("Arthurian")	Heroic Age Cuchulainn and Fionn MacCumhaill legends formulated	Greeks settle in southern Italy and Sicily
	MIDDLE BRONZE AGE	MIDDLE BRONZE AGE	Dorian Invasion of Peloponnese
	LATE BRONZE/IRON AGE ("Hallstatt Culture")	Ollamh Fodhla, greatest of the Sage Kings	LATE BRONZE/IRON AGE
	End of period of earthquakes and climate disturbances	LATE BRONZE/IRON AGE	Age of the Tyrants
		End of period of regular earthquakes and climatic disturbances	
600		High King Sirna. Last of the "eruptions" recorded in his time	Thales
			Pythagoras

Index